Faith&
Ferment

Faith & Ferment

AN INTERDISCIPLINARY STUDY OF CHRISTIAN BELIEFS AND PRACTICES

Joan D. Chittister, OSB
& Martin E. Marty

Editor
ROBERT S. BILHEIMER

Augsburg Publishing House · Minneapolis
The Liturgical Press · Collegeville

FAITH AND FERMENT

Contributors

ROBERT S. BILHEIMER is executive director of the Institute for Ecumenical and Cultural Research and a minister in the United Presbyterian Church in the U.S.A.

JOAN D. CHITTISTER, O.S.B., Ph.D., is prioress of the Benedictine Sisters of Erie, Pennsylvania, (Roman Catholic) and professional consultant to religious organizations.

MARTIN E. MARTY, Ph.D., is professor of the history of modern Christianity at the University of Chicago, and associate editor of *The Christian Century*. Dr. Marty is a member of the Association of Evangelical Lutheran Churches.

BETTY WAHL POWERS is a novelist and member of the Roman Catholic Church, and a resident of Collegeville, Minnesota.

WILLMAR L. THORKELSON is a journalist associated with Religious News Service and the Sun Papers in Minnesota. He is a member of the American Lutheran Church.

HERBERT W. CHILSTROM, Ed.D., is bishop of the Minnesota Synod of the Lutheran Church in America.

J. TIMOTHY POWER is a priest of the Roman Catholic Church, and pastor of Pax Christi Catholic Community, Eden Prairie, Minnesota.

RICHARD J. MOUW, Ph.D., is professor of philosophy at Calvin College, Grand Rapids, Michigan, and a member of the Christian Reformed Church.

JEROME P. THEISEN, O.S.B., S.T.D., is abbot of St. John's Abbey, Collegeville, Minnesota, and a priest of the Roman Catholic Church.

DON E. SALIERS, Ph.D., is professor of theology and liturgics, Candler School of Theology, Emory University, Atlanta, Georgia, and a minister of the United Methodist Church.

Contents

General Introduction to the Faith and Ferment Study
by *Robert S. Bilheimer* 9

Part 1: Presentation of the Data
by *Joan D. Chittister* 19

Will the Lord Find Faith?:
Introduction to Part 1 21
1 Your People Shall Be My People:
    Changing Relationships 25
2 Crucible and Measure:
    Suffering and Crisis 42
3 Valley of Darkness, Valley of Hope:
    Death and Dying 49
4 When the Lot Is Cast into the Lap:
    Control of Life/Moral Motivation 60
5 Contact with the Living God:
    Personal Spiritual Development 70
6 Out of the Depths I Cry to You, O Lord:
    Sin, Guilt, and Compassion 83
7 In Holocausts and Burnt Offerings
You Take No Delight, O God:
    Social Justice 98
8 Put Not Your Trust in Chariots:
    Foreign Policy and War 110
9 The Garden of Eden Revisited:
    Ecology 122
10 Here I Am, Lord; Send Me:
    Occupation 130
11 Between the Times of Christ and the Kingdom:
    The Church 137
12 And They All Heard in Their Own Tongues:
    Overall Trends 155

Part 2: Historical and Theological Analysis
    by Martin E. Marty 163

    Introduction to Part 2 165
    13 Social Behavior 189
    14 Development 202
    15 Faithfulness and Continuity 234
    16 Tolerance for Ambiguity 244
    17 Two Church Clusters 258

Part 3: Essays in Response to the Data 265

    1 *Betty Wahl Powers* 267
    2 *Willmar L. Thorkelson* 273
    3 *Herbert W. Chilstrom* 278
    4 *J. Timothy Power* 284
    5 *Richard J. Mouw* 290
    6 *Jerome P. Theisen* 296
    7 *Don E. Saliers* 303

Appendices 309

    1 Denominational Differences on Critical Issues 310
    2 Concerning the Sample
        by Robert Fulton and Greg Owen 334
    3 Methodology of the Anthropological Probe
        by Luther P. Gerlach and Betty Radcliffe 338
    4 Personnel of the Study 346

Index 348

General Introduction
to the
Faith and Ferment Study
ROBERT S. BILHEIMER

The study which this book sets forth was announced as being "ecumenical." That implied an objective drawn from the ecumenical movement itself. This 20th-century development, now visible—although not equally—in all branches of the Christian churches around the world, has acknowledged a general objective. Explicitly or implicitly, the ecumenical movement in the churches seeks *wholeness* in personal and church life. This sense of wholeness refers to all those who follow Christ in all the churches. It refers to "all in each place," whether the "place" be the world or a locality. Moreover, in its ecumenical sense, wholeness refers to the constant Christian search, beyond fragmented responses to God, for completeness in faith and in witness. Rife with debate as to the specific shape that "the wholeness of the church" should take, the ecumenical enterprise generally accepts that high concept as a main objective.

This objective informed the purpose and the methods of our present inquiry. The study included all the churches within our field of vision.

Robert S. Bilheimer is executive director of the Institute for Ecumenical and Cultural Research and a minister in the United Presbyterian Church in the U.S.A.

It also included many aspects of personal and church life, and it approached them from different viewpoints. It would be presumptuous to claim that this or any such study can probe the full implications of "the wholeness of the church" at any one time. We do not make that claim, but rather that the study has been animated by the ecumenical vision.

The ecumenical movement in general has grown during more than a half century of intense worldwide change, and this has helped to form a specific purpose of the movement and its agencies. The impact of change upon the churches has put a premium on thinking ahead, on anticipating the needs and issues to be faced five or ten years hence, and of taking thought in preparation. Much of this, of course, is done by churches individually. Ecumenical agencies, however, have put "wholeness" and the research/think-tank function together, on the grounds that Christians and churches need each other and face many problems together. This study has been conducted and is offered with this specific ecumenical purpose in mind: to provide data and analyses which will help Christians and churches to think ahead, together and singly, concerning their future life and witness.

The Faith and Ferment Study in General Outline

After two years of exploration, including a pilot study, the Board of Directors of the Institute for Ecumenical and Cultural Research in Collegeville, Minnesota, decided in 1977 to proceed with an inquiry, entitled Faith and Ferment, as to how Christian faith affects the life of church members in Minnesota, in order to gain information concerning the internal conditions of the churches and their relation to society.

It is no small matter, however, to discover the current condition of churches. As the attempt was planned, three problems arose, and the manner of their resolution indicates the general character of the research program.

First, a manageable terrain was required. The Upper Midwest is sociologically distinctive, but this five-state area seemed too large for the research capacities of the Institute. Instead, the Institute chose its state of residence. Minnesota is broad in sociological scope, and both its general and its church cultures have had coherence.

Second, churches are difficult subjects for such research. They are personal spiritual communities as well as institutions; they are marked by special beliefs that differ from one another; they possess their own histories, cultures, and loyalties. To discern the present condition of any group of churches requires different views of them, lest their complexity be flattened out by a single focus. Accordingly, the Faith and Ferment study employed disciplines and expertise in four areas: sociology, anthropology, psychology, and theology. These were put together in an overall design for the conduct of the study, which we shall presently describe.

Third, information as to the spiritual and ethical potential of churches is at best elusive. One may measure membership and financial capacities, but spiritual qualities are less readily charted. In final analysis, the best solution to this problem seemed to require data gathering as widely and carefully as possible, at the same time setting forth modest expectations as to the result. On the one side, the possibility of useful information was apparent; on the other, the subjectivity of social science studies, of which Martin Marty was to write helpfully later, was clear. The prospectus of the Faith and Ferment study said:

Both interdisciplinary and ecumenical means are employed so as to give reasonable assurance that the results are representative, typical and not badly skewed or merely idiosyncratic. It is fully recognized that hard, scientific precision is not possible in view of the subject matter of Faith and Ferment and in view of the disciplines employed. In final analysis, the aim is to produce *hypotheses of weight* concerning the dimensions, the problems and the promise of the present situation.

The Design of the Study

The design of the inquiry, developed by two groups, called for a demarcation of its domain, for three methodologies, and for a plan of collaboration among the research disciplines involved.

The Domain

To a degree, the domain of the study was provided by its subjects, namely, church members. Particularly in the parts of the study which employed anthropological and psychological disciplines, church members were encouraged to state their own concerns to the interviewers. As the ensuing volume will show, this resulted in a body of information which would not otherwise have come to the fore. In other parts, the domain of the study was carefully defined. Questions were derived from or related to the following three constructs.

The first was composed of 12 categories, each of which included from seven to 27 questions. These categories were as follows:

1. Changing Relationships
2. Suffering and Crisis
3. Death
4-5. Control of Life/
     Moral Motivation
6. Personal Spiritual Development

7. Sin, Guilt, Compassion
8. Social Justice
9. Foreign Policy and War
10. Ecology
11. Occupation
12. Church

The second construct affected the above categories. This called for questions about basics of Christian faith: God, Christ, Holy Spirit/Church, and humanity (personal or social or international, and combinations where appropriate). Each of the 12 categories in the first construct contained questions which derived from the four categories of the second construct.

The third was of a different order. It called for questions which pertained to the historical understanding of Christian faith, to the way in which that is now conceptualized, and to the empirical correlation of these in a person's life. Questions drawn in this way were also included in the 12 categories above.

Methodologies

Three methodologies were employed.

The design of the study called for a sociological probe. The instrument was the questionnaire, composed in the above way, and including 243 items for response. A total of 1017 were returned. These included questionnaires from persons in all churches in Minnesota. From the numerically small Eastern Orthodox churches and a number of small Protestant churches an insufficient number of responses to be statistically significant was received, and these, regrettably, are not included in this report. The sampling procedure and response rate are reported in Appendix 2, which is taken from the report of Professor Robert Fulton and Dr. Greg Owen. "The data presented," they write, "provide a reliable base upon which to achieve the stated aim of Faith and Ferment, namely, 'to provide hypotheses of weight concerning the dimensions, the problems and promise of the present situation.'"

Secondly, the study included an anthropological probe. Mindful of the value of traditional small scale community research, the anthropologists in Faith and Ferment turned to other models. The "trouble case" method and the "social drama" model were important, and combined under the concept of a "social debates" model (see Appendix 3). Techniques included the observation of events, interviews of individuals singly and in groups, following new sources suggested by people being interviewed, study of written material, and the formulation of hypotheses based on these techniques and tested by further similar observation and interview methods.

The third aspect of the Faith and Ferment design was personal interviews. One hundred and one were conducted, each lasting from two to five hours. A portion of the interviews were drawn from those who returned questionnaires and were chosen by the fact that they were statistical deviates or "outliers," meaning that they deviated markedly from the regression line of one questionnaire score upon the other. Other interviewees were drawn from those interviewed by the anthropology team and from others who expressed interest. The interviewer was trained and experienced in the conduct of interviews and frequently discussed the processes with appropriate consultants. The objective was to probe as deeply as possible into the person's experience with the basic issues included in the domain of the Faith and Ferment study. The interviews were taped and transcribed, and extensive notes were made and codified concerning different subjects.

Interdisciplinary Collaboration

The designers of Faith and Ferment did not want the various aspects of the study to be simply additive, with results from the questionnaire, inquiry by the field research team, and personal interviews standing merely alongside one another. Interdisciplinary collaboration was achieved in two principal ways. The first—as noted—was the general, although not detailed, use of the questionnaire by the field research team and by the interviewer. Thus responses from the anthropological study and from the interviews would—and do—reflect and enlarge upon responses to the questionnaire.

The most substantial degree of interdisciplinary collaboration, however, was achieved through the work of Sr. Joan Chittister, as a religious and a social scientist (communication theory with an emphasis in social psychology). As Project Coordinator, she had opportunity to be immersed in the three probes during the course of their conduct.

Subsequently, she was asked to prepare the unified presentation of the major findings which appears in this volume. "Major findings" is used advisedly, because the Faith and Ferment study has turned up far more data than can be assimilated in one volume, as may be gathered from the documentation which lies behind this present volume.

The Documentation

This documentation falls into four parts, as follows:

1. A report in double-spaced typescript of 322 pages submitted by Robert Fulton and Greg Owen. This reports the replies from 1017 respondents to each question in table form, with a prose description following each table, and the replies, in table form, according to the six demographic categories of the study (see below, concerning print-outs). This report is available upon application, at the cost of photocopy duplication at the time application is made.

2. Computer printouts for each of the 243 questions containing, in addition to an abbreviated form of the question, the absolute frequency; relative, adjusted, and cumulative frequencies in percentages; the mean, mode, standard error and standard deviation, etc., of each question, according to the following demographic categories:

a. General frequencies   e. Age
b. Denominational membership   f. Rural-urban
c. Clergy-laity   g. Education
d. Men-women   h. Income

There are two sets of computer printouts for each of the above demographic categories: one contains the six-column Likert Scale frequencies (*strongly agree, agree, agree slightly, disagree slightly, disagree, strongly disagree*); the other contains a four-column Likert Scale of the frequencies, with the *strongly agree* and *agree* columns combined and the *disagree* and *strongly disagree* columns combined.

Those using these printouts will note that the Fulton-Owen presentation uses a single figure for all *agree* (and *disagree*) and that the Chittister presentation uses a different method. This method combines the *strongly agree* and *agree* (and *strongly disagree* and *disagree*) to form one figure to indicate settled convictions. On the grounds that the *agree slightly* and *disagree slightly* represent "leanings" but not settled convictions, gray areas rather than clear-cut ones, they are segregated. Where these figures are significant and used in Chittister's manuscript, they are indicated as such.

These printouts are in the archives of St. John's University, Collegeville, Minnesota, and may be consulted there. Computer discs are available at cost upon application, and computer printouts may be obtained upon application at cost at the time of application and subject to the scheduling processes at the University of Minnesota.

3. A report in double-spaced typescript of 314 pages of the anthropological probe, by Luther P. Gerlach and Betty Radcliffe. This report is in Alcuin Library at St. John's University in Collegeville, Minnesota. The report is available upon application, at the cost of photocopy duplication at the time application is made.

4. A typescript document, single-spaced, of 63 pages, prepared by Sr. Stephanie Campbell, O.S.B., presents abstracts of each of these interviews. Each abstract is divided into five sections. This document, "Abstracts of 101 Interviews conducted by Margaret Brudos as part of the Faith and Ferment Study of the Institute for Ecumenical and Cultural Research, Collegeville, Minnesota, 1982" is available upon application at the cost of photocopy duplication at the time application is made. Transcripts of the tapes of 101 personal interviews are in the Archives of St. John's University, as are copious notes made by the interviewer, Ms. Brudos, classified according to various interests.

For the following, application should be made to the Institute for Ecumenical and Cultural Research, Collegeville, Minnesota 56321.

1. Photocopy of the Fulton-Owen Report
2. Photocopy of the Gerlach-Radcliffe Report
3. Photocopy of the Campbell "Abstracts"
4. Copies of Faith and Ferment computer printouts or use of computer discs

For use of the documentation for Faith and Ferment in Alcuin Library, St. John's University, Collegeville, Minnesota, application may be made to the Library Staff.

Sr. Chittister used all of the above documentation in the preparation of her presentation. The documentation will undoubtedly support many specialized studies, and all those connected with Faith and Ferment hope that many will be undertaken.

As part of the plan for reporting, the Chittister manuscript was submitted to the other participants in the research prior to publication. It received no corrections as to the accuracy with which the manuscript reflected the respective portions of the research. To avoid normal human error as much as possible, the figures in the manuscripts were checked twice against the printouts, by different people. We express thanks to Carroll Arnold of Pennsylvania State University for careful reading of and resultant comment on the manuscript.

The Design of This Book

The design of this book harks back to the opening paragraph of this Introduction: the primary objective of the study is to be helpful to the churches and their people. To this end, the book first presents the data in 11 chapters corresponding to the main categories of the study. Following this is Martin E. Marty's historical and theological analysis of the data, offered to assist the reader's own efforts to locate the data in both historical and theological perspectives. The final portion of the book consists of reactions from Betty Wahl Powers, and Willmar Thorkelson as lay people; Herbert W. Chilstrom and J. Timothy Powers as pastors; and Richard J. Mouw, Jerome P. Theisen, and Don E. Saliers as theologians. The above authors were not belabored with the full documentation of the study or each other's work, but wrote on the basis of Joan Chittister's manuscript.

We thank the following:

- the 1017 people who returned questionnaires and the pastors whose efforts made this response possible; the large but undetermined number who, individually and in groups, orally and by written material, collaborated in the anthropological probe; and the 101 who agreed to be interviewed;

- those who provided generous contributions to fund the study in the amount of its $197,000 budget, namely, Jack C. Crocker, Charles M. Grace, Hella Mears Hueg, Jim W. Miller, Northwest Area Foundation, H. C. Piper Jr., Gerald Rauenhorst, and Rose Totino;

- those whose names appear in Appendix 4, who planned, guided, and conducted the study; and their associates, who in secretarial, bookkeeping, editorial and other ways, contributed to the study;

- and in particular Sr. Dolores Schuh, C.H.M., Administrative Secretary of the Institute for Ecumenical and Cultural Research, whose administrative and editorial gifts contributed substantially to the completion of the study.

The undersigned is the Executive Director of the Institute for Ecumenical and Cultural Research, the Board of Directors of which joins in the above expression of thanks; he also thanks a generous, critical, and supportive Board.

ROBERT S. BILHEIMER
Editor and Project Director

PART ONE

Presentation
of the Data
JOAN D. CHITTISTER

Will the Lord Find Faith?

Introduction to Part 1

Every year seminaries across the country graduate ordained ministers for many Christian denominations. Every Sunday people go to church. Every week children go to catechism classes. Every day people are buried with Christian funeral rites. Over and over again the churches baptize; pastors give sermons; people make decisions; nations make claims; peoples make demands; church groups talk about conversion; ministers preach salvation. But the question is whether or not there is a connection in it all. What does being Christian have to do with living life? How really different are the different churches? What do people expect from the institutional church, and what are they getting there? What do Christian people really believe about the great questions of the time—military supremacy, homosexuality, the equality of women, the role of law—and, on the other hand, how do they now respond to eternal questions—the divinity of Jesus, the character of the Bible, the purpose of life, the nature of the church?

Those are the things this book is about. It is based on the answers

Joan D. Chittister, O.S.B., Ph.D., is prioress of the Benedictine Sisters of Erie, Pennsylvania (Roman Catholic), and professional consultant to religious organizations.

of some 2000 church members and ministers who reside in a single state, from all denominations in all parts of Minnesota, rural and metropolitan. These people talked for hours about why they believe what they believe; they responded in writing; they allowed researchers into their homes and churches and parish groups. The result is a close-up view of the ideas and attitudes of these Americans who belong to churches at this moment in history.

To know what is in the catechisms and theology texts of a given faith is certainly one way to determine the depth or orientation of a religious tradition; but that is not the only way; it may not even be the most substantive way.

There are at least two reasons for this. In the first place, what the books teach and what the people believe may be two different things. Second, the various facets of the Christian community may accept a common concept but read its implications quite differently. For instance, Christians may accept without question that Christ came for the upbuilding of the kingdom of God but differ markedly in their perceptions about where and how that upbuilding ought to be done— by charity or by justice, by prayer or by action, by withdrawal or by involvement. Only an investigation of living belief can reveal what Christianity is in the minds of the people who profess it.

A major purpose of this research, then, was to discover the nature of the moral and spiritual concepts now alive among church members in Minnesota, in order that the results would be not only informative but stimulating to the Christian community throughout this country who share a common culture and a common Christian formation.

Determining the lived tradition of a community is one thing. Discovering how those concepts affect social structures or are embedded in individual reactions is completely another. *What* groups do because they believe something to be true or essential is important to the whole social fabric. *How* basic beliefs touch personal self-worth or security has a great deal to say about the positive or negative effects of religion on life patterns. For those who believe that the kingdom is now and is to be built here, the church may well become a social action center, whether conservative or liberal, as well as a place of Sunday service. Those whose God is a stern and rigid parent may be rigid in their own expectations of others and more comfortable with rules and rewards than with risk.

A second aim of this study, therefore, was to identify the social-psychological effects, ramifications, or complexities which flow from the religious beliefs of the Christian community, understanding that only by analyzing attitudes and behaviors, as well as beliefs, can a full picture of the current Christian culture be drawn.

The introduction stresses the need to prepare for the future. The study was not designed to make recommendations along that line, but to be used as a resource for those in the churches who plan. Consequently, this study was designed to provide data that would allow church people and leaders to identify emerging trends and emphases that may be capturing the focus and energy of the Christian population, even in the face of older practices and concerns. Furthermore, the study sought information as to whether the beliefs held by a sample of persons in communities of believers are authentic developments in the Christian traditions. Are Christians within the various denominations more or less close in basic beliefs now than they have been? Are they in continuity with their own beginnings?

We also wanted information from which church people could draw implications for the churches themselves. Is the church addressing issues that people consider important to their attempts to be Christian today? Does what is being preached from the pulpit have anything to do with people's needs or concerns? Is seminary preparation enabling new pastors to deal with the life questions of the congregation that the new minister hopes to serve? Is the church a positive influence in the coming of the kingdom or only part of the problem?

To get this information we asked such questions as:

• What is the function of church?

• How much control does anyone have over life developments, even if they do think that the essence of Christian life is moral responsibility?

• What constitutes justice, and when is it an imperative?

• What does death do to the Christian spirit? How does being Christian affect our attitude toward death?

• What constitutes "spirituality": going to church, praying, ministering to others?

• Does faith have anything to do with suffering and crises? Do suffering and crises have anything to do with faith?

• Are sexism and racism social or moral issues?

• What is the Christian obligation toward national policies?

• What, if anything, does ecology or energy use or conservation have to do with being Christian? Should churches have anything to do with subjects like ecology?

• Is sin real, or is it only a diminishment of psychological growth? Are guilt and guilt feelings the same thing? Are backsliders forgiveable?

• When people do "right," why do they do it? to escape punishment? to have people respect them? to get to heaven? to build community? to keep the law? to maintain a sense of personal principle even though they know others will disapprove and punish?

• How necessary are prayer and worship to Christian identity?

We did not explore the concerns or convictions of people who do not make the church a facet of their lives. Someone should. That information could both enrich and illuminate these findings, but that would be information of another kind. Our focus has been on people in the pews—to hear their philosophies, their opinions, and their explanations of how they think the church relates to life.

This is a book about believers and what they believe now, what they're uncertain about, what they're struggling with, on what issues they're likely to agree or differ. It is a book for clergy and laity alike. Most of all it is a book for those who are willing to explore their own life direction, goaded by the question of the evangelist Luke who challenged, "But when the Son of Man comes, will he find any faith on the earth?" (Luke 18:8).

I

Your People Shall Be My People
Changing Relationships

In another age the subject of this chapter would never have been Changing Relationships. In past eras relationships simply were not supposed to change. Above all else, perhaps, Christianity was a network of clear relationships. Role definitions were part and parcel of morality; community expectations were certain and largely without ambiguity. Fidelity, control, responsibility, and commitment were key. Parents were to be honored; children were a blessing; obedience was an obligation; authority was paramount. Wives were to be subject to their husbands and recognize childbearing as a way for them to work out their eternal salvation. The father was master of the family, ruler of the church, and a sign of God's dominion and providence over all humankind. Wives could not be "put away"; marriage was forever. Chastity in every facet of life was required as a manifestation of personal control, of separation from sin, of "the indwelling of the Holy Spirit and the glorification of God." In some human beings—white and male—God was most glorified and most clearly imaged. They were the obvious masters of the world, subject to God but born to rule. And the foundation of all these relationships or the plumb line that ordered them all, was the deep and abiding consciousness that God was to

25

be loved and praised, that it was the relationship to God that would, ultimately, be upheld or disturbed by the association of one person to another.

If the data from Minnesota churches are any indicator of general norms, *then* today each of these ideas is under stress among members of Christian churches no less than in the society around them. Not only do the data confirm trends that have been present in American life for several decades, they identify a rising consensus about relatively new social concerns.

Relationships in the Family

Worship

In an era of drive-in restaurants, television evangelism, two-car garages, bowling leagues, teenage dances, and night school for older adults, the church members who participated in this study claim that family worship at home is a regular and even frequent part of their lives. Over two-thirds (67%) pray at meals "most always." Almost half (48%) say they worship at home as a group every single day by reading Scripture or some spiritual book, with the rosary, or in family night prayer. Twenty-five percent reported that they never pray as a family or, if they do, make it a practice only on holidays. In interviews people who talked about family prayer described in detail how they themselves had been trained as children and how the habit was with them still. One woman described "hearing God" in prayer and having her husband pray for her as the two greatest supports of her life. For most Catholics, Evangelical Covenant members, Lutherans, and Baptists in the sample (51%-68%), family worship is reportedly a daily exercise. For members of the UCC and Episcopalians (30%), on the other hand, daily family prayer is a much less pronounced feature of their spiritual development. But for most church members of all denominations it has some value at some times. A relationship with God, it seems, is still part and parcel of most family relationships. Interestingly, the data indicate that families either pray together daily or they pray together seldom. Weekly (8%) or monthly (4%) prayer sessions in the home barely exist, a fact that reinforces the explanation that prayer is a habit to be developed, not a ritual that is practiced intermittently.

Parenting

The relationship between parents and children has taken on a character that is on face reflective of an American philosophy of life but nevertheless not without religious meaning. "Control and the strong discipline of children" are values for only a third (36%) of these survey respondents, data which must mean that the biblical virtue of obedience, as it was once preached and practiced, is in flux. Training for self-discipline, on the other hand, is considered (68%) a major function of parental authority. Thus the field research team observed Christian groups who have become active in public school policymaking in order to protect curriculums which "get children to think on their own, and to think through how they make hard decisions." In fact, most of these respondents (74%) believe that parents should allow children to share decisions about rules with them. This emphasis on the child as decision maker and self-directed person models a response to authority that may have reshaped the institutions of this generation. People who have been brought early to autonomy and independence may relate to authority figures outside the family in new ways too. Apparently the church as well as the government will continue to find itself with members whose concepts of freedom, conscience, and law lie far outside the patterns of authority set by previous generations.

This study indicates also that the issue of sex education of children, an essential dimension in human relationships, has moved beyond the confines of family. Very few of the respondents (6%) believe that sex education in the public school is "always wrong and ought to be eliminated." The numbers may mask the state of the issue, however. The field research discovered sex education in the public schools to be an issue which, though important, actually served most to signal a cluster of topics of religious interest. The observers reported that some religious groups see the schools as exceeding or contradicting what parents, churches, and the Bible teach.

These church members argue that the emphasis in the schools on cultural pluralism is eroding the absolutes of Christian and American family life by encouraging children to question their own family standards and to accept the premise that no custom or behavior is ordained, that anything is possible. Sex education is not the only educational concern of some Christian parents. History courses bring into question the superior value of American life. Science courses are said to be based on the premise that science can do everything, that God does not exist, and that God does not matter. And sex education courses are considered immoral, a spokeswoman of one of the church groups said, because "they encourage sexual behavior partly because they do not say that chastity is right." For some, sex education in schools raises a question about multiple dimensions of the Christian world view.

Nevertheless, 30% of the participants think that courses in sex education in public schools should either be at the option of the parents or are a "regrettable" but probably necessary trend. More, a full half of the participants feel that courses in sex education should actually be required in the academic arena. Clearly, the notion that public school classes on sex erode or contradict the family values promoted by Christian churches is less of a worry to most Christians—especially to church members in city settings—than it has been in the past. Where the issue is present, however, it may signal deep and basic differences in the Christian community about a spectrum of values and relationships far and beyond the matter of sexual development.

Marriage Vows

It is certainly not a discovery to point out that the indissolubility of marriage, once an accepted part of American life, has faded in practice. Divorce court statistics have been rising steadily over the years. In the last decade many studies have documented the fact that more and more marriages not only deteriorate over time but are dissolved with increasing regularity and after relatively brief unions. What may be important, however, is that Christians who go to church regularly (80%) consider themselves close to God (80%), and say that their faith is steady (98%), also consider divorce either "a reasonable solution," "a necessary provision," or "a matter of personal decision and a recognized human right" (30%). Very few (15%) consider divorce "always wrong or sinful." Divorce, it seems, no longer carries the force of moral or religious judgment. The majority (55%) think of it simply as "required" to alleviate insurmountable human problems. This view of divorce as the lesser of two evils rather than a manifestation of sheer wantonness or irresponsibility is confirmed by data concerning two of the other items studied: the group's attitude toward extramarital sex and their regard for the families of previous marriages. In each area the awareness of commitments and obligations remains extremely high.

As far as these Christians are concerned, the marriage contract may not be irrevocable, but it is definitely inviolable. "Open marriage" is acceptable to only three percent of this population. For 85% extra-marital sex is "always wrong or sinful." Once marriage is entered into, the bond is total and faithfulness is of the essence. On the other hand, the dissolution of a marriage is no sign that it can be ignored or forgotten. On the contrary, 59% of these respondents think that even after divorce a person's Christian responsibility extends not only to the divorced spouse and children but also to grandparents and other relatives of the past marriage. Though the contract or union may have been broken, the relationships that were generated there are considered to be, in at least some ways, perpetual and as much objects of Christian commitment after divorce as before it.

These distinctions between marriage and family are subtle and, some might even say, specious, but apparently they exist and may go far toward the development of a new sense of Christian responsibility or contemporary model of extended family—in which case, too little may be being said about either by anyone in the churches.

Family Planning

In the Christian tradition arguments against birth control rest largely on the belief that the primary purpose of marriage is both procreation and the control of lust. These arguments emphasize the procreative aspects of sex in marriage rather than other positive aspects of sex. Whatever the emphasis, those positions have clearly lost hold on the Christian imagination, at least at this time. Over three-fourths (77%) of the population of this study firmly disagree with the idea that artificial methods of birth control and family planning are immoral, and an additional 9% disagree with that notion at least "slightly." In fact, from 84%-98% of every denomination other than Roman Catholic consider birth control moral. Of Catholics, though one-third (33%) are firm in their rejection of artificial methods of birth control, another 40%, like the Protestant community around them, simply do not consider it a moral evil.

Of more interest, because the issue is both current and a center of public controversy, is the fact that to these randomly chosen participants abortion is almost as acceptable as artificial methods of birth control. But some important aspects of the data need to be examined. In the first place, almost one-third (30%) of all respondents take the position that abortion is always wrong or sinful, without justification or acceptance. People who felt this way told the field research team that one of the reasons they oppose sex education in the schools is that abortion is presented in these classes as "an obvious and easy and perfectly normal remedy for unwanted pregnancies," with no mention whatsoever of the morality of these decisions. They see it as a natural link to euthanasia, because it brings into question the dignity and sanctity of all life. They consider it an attack on the Christian family. They see abortion as a prime example of a secular humanism that implicitly views the "human" to be master of life and not subject to God. If people can decide who lives or dies, they are not recognizing either the biblical principle that life is sacred or the commandment, "Thou shalt not kill." Evidently, for these Christians the matter is closed. A closer examination of the responses, however, shows that although the remaining almost three-quarters (70%) of the population accept abortion, only 15% believe that it should be entirely a matter of personal choice. Almost half (45%) would permit abortion only in extreme cases. Whatever their definitions of "extreme," this 45% does not look upon abortion casually. Nor is it a matter of clear consensus even among the majority who accept abortion as sometimes moral. But it is, at least in Minnesota, admissible in the church community, even to more than one-third (35%) of the Roman Catholic population, to more than three-fourths of the Lutherans (77%), Baptists (78%), and Covenant Church members (78%).

If the data pointed up in this chapter can be generalized to any significant degree, the concepts of marriage and family and children and the meaning of one for the other are in a state of flux, even among confessing Christians. What is more, the field study data suggest that it is precisely this flux in God-person-family relationships that alarms conservative Christian activists who believe that churches themselves have ignored the biblical laws of life and family.

But fluid relations within the family may indicate that the family is more a channel of social changes rather than the source. For outside the home, too, there are major shifts occurring in the way these American Christians regard both their place in society and their roles in life.

Relationships in Society

Racism

In theory at least, the members of Christian churches who responded to this study accept the idea of equality. This commitment to equality is based firmly on Scripture and is apparently decisive. Almost unanimously (94%) the respondents reported that the biblical assertion, In Christ "there does not exist among you Jew or Greek" (Gal. 3:28; cf. Rom. 10:12) implies that there should be no racial or color discrimination in any Christian church. They denounced with even stronger vigor (97%) the notion that God created blacks inferior to whites, yet were somewhat less sure as a group (88%) that it would be God's will that American Indians should have the same advantages as all the other groups in society, a factor which might indicate that Christian obligation is clearer to these respondents in theory than it is in specific cases. Nevertheless, a fundamental commitment to the Christian dimension of human equality and dignity seems clear. The role of the church in bringing the human family to fullness of life, however, is far less certain for these people than the idea that equality of persons is a facet of Christian faith.

For example, most of the respondents (64%) agree strongly and another 25% at least "slightly" to the statement that "it is part of the mission of the churches in Minnesota to help improve the position of American Indians, blacks, and Latin Americans in our communities." Despite their reactions to the meaning of biblical passages on racism, however, fewer of the participants (64%) can agree as heartily that the church itself should take action to eliminate the artificial distinctions of race, color, or status. Most (67%) say that their parishes or congregations do in reality leave racial justice matters to others, for the most part, and have developed little in the way of "strong and active programs" in race relations.

Obviously the questions, "What is Christian?" and, "What is church?" are real. Is the role of the church action? Is the church effective without action? Half the members of the study felt that the black power movement had helped them to understand that all children of God possess human dignity. On the other hand, it was surely the teaching of the church that prepared them to accept all persons as children of God in the first place. These two realities raise the basic human question as to whether equality must be given or taken if it is to be real. If

Christian people are Christian, why did there have to be a black power movement at all? Is the church dealing with the specific applications of the theology of equality if so many are ambivalent about who is and who isn't equal? And on the other hand, without the teachings of the church would the black power movement, or any movement for human liberation, succeed at all?

Whatever the answer to the philosophical subtleties of human relations, it is relatively clear that, for these participants at least, the equality of the races is now beyond question; the church is expected to be an agent in the pursuit of that equality; it is a Christian quality to oppose discrimination; and the academic argument of natural inferiority is moot.

But in significant ways, strains of prejudice and fear and struggle linger, even in Minnesota, where minority populations are small. Interview subjects often talked in continuing stereotypes.

One said he had only met blacks in the army and found them "aggressive." "I think that is because they have been oppressed a lot," he explained, "and they are just reacting to that." But he does expect blacks to be more forward than others.

Another admitted the stress he feels, knowing that most Americans are from immigrant backgrounds, but finding himself still not able to be totally accepting of the Asians in his own parish. "I'm wondering what Jesus would do," he adds, knowing that the answer to that question has something to do with the virtue of his own reaction.

Many of the interviewees argued for the equality of peoples but rejected affirmative action programs.

When I look at [the race question] I have to step back first and foremost, and understand what it means to go out and completely damn all the Chinese people, or the Germans, or Italians, or whatever, as opposed to somebody who starts looking for qualifications in people. I myself am not a bigoted person. I was at one time, many years ago. . . . But I don't think that force should have been applied to the hiring of minority people into jobs and positions where they had zero qualifications. . . . I don't see what good that does the individual, because if they are not able to perform that job, don't kid yourself, they know it, and they can see the other people that are [qualified].

Another admitted: "I'm a racist. And that's anti-Christian, I suppose, but I don't think it is," and laid out in broad strokes the elements of both separatism and syncretism, of wanting to keep unlike people out while knowing there is no clear justification for not taking them in. He makes it clear that it is the economics of Christianity—what it costs one people to make room for another—that is his real struggle. He explained:

I feel that a lot of these people, maybe through no fault of their own, are on welfare. Say blacks. I think Indians, through some fault of their own, are like they are. We're never going to solve their problem, let's face it. You're white; I'm white. To exist in this country, in a white society, you're going to have to assimilate to that society, somehow, somewhat. That Indian, putting him on a reservation, is counterproductive. You can pump all the federal funds you want in there, build them all the buildings you want, and they'll do the same thing when it gets cold: they'll pull the walls apart and burn them in the middle of the floor, because they have not been taught to work in a white man's society. And I think that's the same with the colored, the Cubans they just brought in, or whatever. They've got those Cubans sitting down there in those detention camps, really, and it's stupid. Why bring those people in, when you know they're probably never going to make it here. They're all going to go anyhow. The majority of those Cubans, if they were criminals, or whatever they say they were, and some of them were slow, mentally. That's sad; they should have help, but why send them to Madison, Wisconsin, and try to do it there? What are you going to do? All you're doing is increasing the welfare loads. They are going to be professional welfare people. How many jobs are you going to give them? Of the Mexican American problem in California and the Southeast, how many wetbacks are sitting here working and taking jobs?

Still others said they "loved blacks" but "would never march for social justice," or that they support equal opportunity for blacks but have never done anything concrete about it, that present racial issues are "the sins of the past that are being visited on the present time."

In these data, then, are signs that the "natural superiority" arguments of the last century, as well as the thought that there is such a thing as "the white man's burden," have eroded, even if not entirely disappeared. A new dimension of the Christian revelation of the relationships has broken through in our own time. It seems as if the biblical call to union with one another in Christ has been heard. There is a common understanding of the meaning of the texts for our time. At the same time, the data also indicate that the delicate interplay of social-economic forces, church, and the continuing discipline of Christian conversion is yet to be resolved, even for the church members of this society. Apparently reading biblical texts in church and applying them in the marketplace are two different exercises. Whether either one without the other is the mark of a Christian society merits thought.

Sexism

But if there are both tensions and growth apparent in black-white relations, there is even more swell and surge in the Christian churches of Minnesota over the role and nature of women and the response of the church to this issue. After centuries in which the assumed inferiority and limited definitions of woman were accepted, it is not surprising that contemporary changes in male-female relationships cause strain. What is surprising is that the data reflect so much gain in attitudes and opportunities for women in so short a time.

Aristotle, Aquinas, Luther, and Rousseau all argued that women had both a lesser purpose (sexual) and a weaker disposition (physical and emotional) than men; that men were spiritually superior and intellectually ascendent; that since God was Father, men were closer to the image of God and therefore more God-like. On the basis of those assumptions—most of them unchallenged and untested in any scientific way until recently—women have been kept from education, public service, responsibility, and independence in society, and from fullness of ministry in their churches as well. Only in the last few decades have both theology and science begun to confront and challenge those premises. Expectations have been raised for half of humankind. No institution is untouched: business, family, or church. Male-female relationships determine who will make the world's decisions, who will reap and distribute its benefits, even who will have closest and most powerful access to God. The question is a major one for the future of society, and the responses of these church-going citizens reflect the inherent tension—and the breakthroughs, as well.

In the first place, almost all the respondents (94%) accept the understanding that women and men are both created in the image of God and are therefore equal in God's sight. The sentence comes easily off the lips of people for whom Sunday school or catechism classes have been a solid part of spiritual and intellectual formation. The concepts cannot be taken for granted, though, and can cause real consternation. If both women and men are created in the image of God, then are male ministers and male deacons or elders more an image of God than a woman would be? And if so, why? And in what way? The problem is apparently real for the people in this study. For, though they have no trouble (94%) realizing that the text, "there does not exist among you Jew or Greek" (Gal. 3:28; cf. Rom. 10:12) implies that there should be no racial or color discrimination in any Christian church, no more than two-thirds (64%) can also agree that "there does not exist among you . . . male or female" (Gal. 3:28; cf. Rom. 10:12) refers not only to the kingdom of Christ but has a bearing also on the relationship of men and women in the churches of the world today. What is more, of that two-thirds (64%), some respondents (13%) can agree only slightly with the statement, which must mean that they have reservations about how equal "equal" is when it is applied to circumstances in churches as well as to the kingdom hereafter, or to human designs as well as the mind of God. These reservations are directly confirmed in the attitudes of this sampling of Christians toward the role of women in church ministry. When asked straight out whether or not women should have equal opportunities and rights with men in all aspects of church life and ministry, over half (53%) were firmly convinced that this had to be the case, but another portion (15%) could agree only slightly. The interview material helped to clarify the various positions. A minister answered:

I believe in equality for women (in the church) . . . . It's the Holy Spirit who calls. If the Holy Spirit calls a person to go into the ministry, and that person happens to be a woman, this is just the same as the Holy Spirit calling a man. I believe that he [the Holy Spirit] controls the church, and that he is in charge of the church, and he sends out his call to minister.

Women who discussed the possibility of ordination spoke about their own need to have priests to whom they could relate more freely. One said:

I would be comfortable if the pastoral team at our church had both a man and a female minister. I think it would be fun. One idea that crosses my mind about [our pastor] is that he is so near our age. He is a year older. And I think that because he is a man my age, it makes me uncomfortable sometimes talking to him. So, [I would like to have a woman minister] just for that reason.

Others recognized that though they favor the idea of women ministers, it would take an adjustment even for them. A woman explained:

[I met a woman priest whom I just love.] But it was hard to adjust to, probably because all the people with authority in the church and my whole upbringing with God as "father" and all the authority figures have always been male. But I think that is conditioning. It would be hard for me, but I would get used to it.

Almost the same proportion of these Minnesota Christians (60%) endorse or support the women's movement. Very few (10%) oppose it outright or are generally unsympathetic toward it (22%). But, despite this two-to-one division in favor of women's rights, only half (51%) of the respondents think their own parishes or congregations provide roles that women with a new feminist consciousness would be pleased with if they attempted to be part of that particular community.

What is more, though half of these respondents feel that the church must make a special effort to insure the equality of women and men in the churches (50%), the group as a whole is less committed to the idea that churches should also make a special effort to secure equal rights for women in society at large (39%). Women themselves found this difficult to deal with. One put it this way:

So much of the feminism that I have run into lately is really not equality; it is superiority. I don't buy that. I would be heavy into human liberation. I think men ought to be free of some of the ridiculous roles that they have.

Overall, including firm opinion and favorable leaning, respondents are almost equally divided, too, over whether or not the movement for women's equality has enabled them to achieve a better understanding of Christian marriage. It seems more are able to deal with the idea that the role of women in churches must change than with the thought that other aspects of their life should be affected by the move to give women equal opportunities in other facets of society.

The tensions are even clearer in the interview data. There, opinions ranged from one end of the spectrum to another, with some people shifting in the course of their own replies; others, given to liberalism more than to equality, were willing to see women have some new opportunities but not all possible opportunities.

One woman is categorically opposed to the women's movement. She said:

I'm not a women's libber. I think that some of those leaders in the women's movement are just really over in left field. I don't even know what their names are. About the only exposure I've had is when I watch their debates on TV. I don't think women should be drafted. If women want to join the services, that's fine, but to have all 18-year-olds sign up for the draft. . . . They want everything, but they don't want it equal. They don't want to put in their half. Not all women [are willing to be drafted].

A man worked his way carefully from point to point, from theology to reality, and was dissatisfied all the way:

I have to say that I don't believe in the E.R.A. I feel that my wife is a better person than I am. But, I feel that her [sic] and I are equal. In some ways, I excel over her, but in other ways, like in raising our children, I can't hold a candle to her. . . . Family is the highest institution in the world. And I feel that a woman's place, until her children are grown, is to be with them, with that family. . . . But I also realize that there are divorced women, their husbands are gone, and I feel that, yes, they should be in the work force, and they should get just as much pay as I do, if they can do the job. . . . I feel that women are much more qualified than men are to do a lot of these executive jobs. And the men should be out hauling rocks and fixing trucks. Really.

The reverse sexism here that comes with attempting to look at the world and the people in it afresh is burden enough. But in addition to that, there is no explicit attention given to the question of single women or to the parenting role or qualities of men. The confusion that comes with recognizing that something is theoretically true but socially disturbing is an obvious undercurrent in this statement.

The woman was equally stressed and explained her concerns, none of them theological, about changes in male-female roles. "There are so many men out of work," she said. "A couple of years ago they started hiring women. And it was a second job for the woman, but a man was losing a job that had to support a family." How this person feels about men losing jobs to men who hold two positions at once is not explored in the interview, but there is no reason to believe that this woman thought of that as a similar problem.

In other words the concepts of church, equality, opportunity, and role all contend and conflict when the question of woman enters the Christian consciousness. There is complete awareness that female-male equality is demanded by Christian faith, but there is higher support among this group of Christians (94%) for racial equality in the churches than for the developed role of women (64%). For many, women are equal, as long as they stay in their place. Less than a quarter of the survey participants (23%) are of a firm opinion that women should not be in the ordained ministries of the churches, but interview respondents spoke a great deal about the effects of the women's rights movement on family structures and the job market.

This emphasis leads one to believe that it is the social norms governing women, and not their roles in the church, that are the greater concern, even for Christians, when they find themselves confronted with the reconciliation of orthodoxy with practice in this area. They may realize that equality is a matter of faith, but they do not want it to upset their private lives. As the respondents pointed out in regard to the recognition and acceptance of blacks and other minorities, the economic effects of Christianity is a high price to pay. Nevertheless, it is Christianity itself which for many makes it necessary to keep testing the culture against what they believe to be the fullness of Christianity. A woman sounded the alert both to the church and society:

The women's issue is a big part of my life. I am an ardent feminist, and I don't see any incongruities in that and the Bible. If Paul and I were to meet face to face, we might have some problems. I think that he was a man and lived within the confines of his time and outlook. But I don't think he has done women any great favors. So I kind of ignore or pass over that. But nothing Christ said is offensive to me as a feminist, and that is all that matters.

Sexual Ethics

One of the most telling signs of a shift in social norms may be the disparity of the group's attitude toward traditional sexual ethics. The data show that distinctions are being made in regard to admissible kinds of sexual activity and that, in contrast to past expectations, some practices are obviously now considered more acceptable than others, even to members of Christian churches. What is even more surprising, perhaps, is the fact that some past standards have been rethought and found wanting; others, once absolutes, have been rethought and found unsure.

Folklore and literature are storehouses of a double standard in sexual mores. "Boys will be boys" and "It's a man's world" were the commonplaces of the culture. If those opinions are still the case elsewhere, they do not seem to prevail among Christians in Minnesota. Men and women, laity and clergy, respondents from the cities and respondents from small towns all rejected the permissibility of extramarital sex, calling it "always wrong or sinful" (85%). But that is where the clear consensus on sexual standards ends. Fewer respondents consider premarital sex (64%) or homosexuality (61%) immoral. And this is true of every denomination except Baptists and members of the Evangelical Covenant church. Or to look at it another way: 38% of the participants in this study, all formed in the Christian faith and still active in it, do not regard homosexuality or premarital sex as intrinsically evil, though many qualify their responses. Some, in other words, did not characterize such activities as "simply a matter of choice" (24%), but instead chose the responses "permissible for the engaged

(12%) or those in love (7%) or for consenting adults (8%)" or "regrettable but understandable" (32%). In these Christian communities old issues of intimacy have been opened again and changes have occurred.

In the face of all these pressures it is easy to understand why so many of the participants feel that their churches lack adequate programs to deal with race relations, the women's issues, and troubled family relationships. How the Christian church deals with pluralism may be the underlying theological question of the day.

Denominational Differences

Comparative analysis of responses by denomination indicates that, in general, it is Protestants and clergy who most believe that women should have an equal place with men in the ministry of the church. Here the strongest support comes from the United Church of Christ (80%), Presbyterian (79%), Methodist (74%), and Episcopalian members (68%).

On the other hand, it is only in Lutheran churches that a strain of thinking (5%) exists that men and women were not created equal. Though less than one-third of some churches—Roman Catholics (30%) and Baptists (32%)—are open to the presence of women in ordained ministries, the members of even these congregations are divided on the issue, with almost equal numbers for, against, or mixed in their opinions about women as clergy. One implication of the equality issue is that no church may for long avoid resolving what many members see as a contradiction between theology and practice concerning the role of women in the church.

For Protestants the morality of artificial methods of birth control and family planning is accepted almost without question, but among Roman Catholics one-third of the respondents are firm in their thinking that artificial birth control is sinful. On the other hand, perhaps what is most significant about the Roman Catholic responses is that in a church where the practice is categorically proscribed, so many respondents do not consider it a moral evil.

For Protestants, especially the clergy, abortion is no longer out of the question, but is judged as permissible, at least in extreme circumstances (80%). On this issue, though, Minnesota Catholics are firmly opposed (65%) by margins of two to one. This sharp distinction between the Catholic and Protestant respondents bears close inspection, since on other major aspects of human relationships the two groups show such similar patterns. Response to authority is surely not the answer. Roman Catholic authorities have spoken against the question of artificial birth control as well as against abortion. Nonetheless, these Roman Catholics have not embraced the church's position on birth control with either the unanimity or the enthusiasm reflected in their responses to the abortion question. What is the basic difference in orientation and attitude here? Is it social, or cultural, or theological? And what, if anything, does that have to say to other Christian peoples?

Demographic Distinctions

More men (48%) than women (36%) endorse the women's movement and, more men (57%) than women (49%) accept the place of women in ordained ministry. Whether these tendencies result from the lower self-esteem that is commonly found in peoples who hold secondary positions in any society or because women hold different theological positions on the subject is not determined here, but some of the interview data do give clues to the psychological dimensions of the question. One woman said directly: "I think the reason women have been treated like they have, and I do think they are a discriminated against minority, is, at least partly, because we, as women, accept it so much."

Differences in attitude among Christians according to educational levels, age, income, or living situation were rare but revealing. For instance, Christians in urban areas are significantly more inclined to accept abortion (urban—76%; rural—67%), premarital sex (urban—43%; rural—31%), homosexuality (urban—53%; rural—43%), sex education in the schools (urban—58%; rural—45%) and the women's movement (urban—69%; rural—50%) than people who live in rural communities. People whose incomes are above $20,000 per year (76%) are more inclined to consider abortion acceptable in some circumstances than those who come from lower income brackets (67%). But it is lower-income respondents (68%) in the Christian churches of Minnesota who look more to the church for help in securing better living conditions for American Indians, blacks, and Latin Americans than those whose incomes are above $20,000 (59%). Obviously, on these matters theology is conditioned by experience, perspective, and opportunity. Whether it should be or not is a different question.

What, then, may be said as a whole about the posture of Christians as Christians toward these great questions of human relations in our times? And what questions or directions emerge for the churches themselves out of these responses?

In the first place, if the Faith and Ferment study discovers patterns that run throughout American Christianity, then perhaps we must be alert to the possibility that lay people are especially looking to parishes for help in human relations, especially of troubled families. We may find, too, throughout this country that contemporary sexual ethics bear the influence of science and social pressure as well as of the biblical tradition and may need to be rigorously reviewed from both standpoints. We may realize, as well, that as feminist consciousness increases, church structures themselves will become more subject to scrutiny. We may come to see that for Christians the issues of minority rights and human development must entail more than an exercise in scriptural exegesis.

At the same time we may discover other things as well. Though the tension between theology and practice remains, there is a clear trend to equate all human rights with the Christian mandate. There is a struggle to integrate old and continuing family values with new understandings and imperatives of the equality of women, but our data show that "the spirit indeed is willing." It may be that Christians have come to understand that the theology of creation is a call to human rights.

2

Crucible and Measure

Suffering and Crisis

The world is devoted, at least theoretically, to the elimination of suffering. Medicine promises relief. Technology is relentless in its quest for ease and effortlessness. Legislatures debate how best to relieve people of their pressures. But suffering will not go away. So what is the Christian to think? If suffering cannot be eliminated, can it be claimed that God is good? If suffering could be eliminated, should it be? How is it to be understood and dealt with? These questions strike at the center of life, and the responses we received to these questions reflect the depth of the struggle they engender.

Not one of the interviewees in this study claimed to be free of suffering, and those who spoke of it spoke feelingly. They described the loss of jobs, the death of children, the pain of alcoholic homes, rejection by their families, great physical illnesses, deep psychological depression, the loss of meaning and support in life. "Scripture is very much alive then," one said. "But what I have trouble with is praising and thanking the Lord for [suffering]." Some spoke of suffering as a test sent by God and felt that sometimes they had failed the test. Others admitted the confusion and even anger that came with the conviction that they had always "been good," but that God had nevertheless dealt harshly with them. All of them talked about suffering and crisis as the crucible of faith, but they also spoke of it as the measure of faith. One woman explained:

I fight with the suffering business, [but] I don't think it is here for nothing. There must be a reason for it, and I think it is to help people become kinder—more compassionate and more understanding.

A man who had suffered the tragic loss of two wives but whose career had been almost without flaw was equally convinced that suffering was part of God's "plan" and meant to test his faith:

I guess you have to sort of resign yourself to the fact that everybody has a cross to bear, and maybe this is my cross. [There is some suffering in every life.] I can look back at some of the wealthiest people I know. Are they home free? No. They have problems. If it isn't some type of heartache or tragedy which confronts them individually, it's somebody in their family or very close to them. So I think that we have to have a certain amount of this in life. I don't think that anybody goes home free. So, on one side of the ledger, you are blessed and grateful, and if you're not, you should be. And on the other side of the ledger, you have heartache and you have to accept it. If you don't, you're not going to be happy. I accept it, should I say, not gleefully, but I accept it. I don't want to be fatalistic in things, but I can't help but think that certain things are patterned, and I think you sort of follow that pattern. Everyone does.

The Relationship of God to Evil

The greater number of respondents (68%) were strong in their opinion that the existence of evil in the world is not irreconcilable with the thought of a loving God. Very few (6%) found the two concepts totally incompatible. Furthermore, though surrounded by the presence and possibility of calamity and crisis, 63% do not believe that God created both good and evil. Some (23%) are convinced that "illness, calamity, and other forms of suffering and crisis are the result of sin," but 55% reject that notion. The idea seems to be that evil somehow is of human nature's own making. It is not created by God to tantalize, and it is not seen by most as punishment for infidelity. Apparently, evil is simply part of life, and though 63% do not believe that God creates evil, 88% do claim that it is faith in God that makes it bearable. One woman said quite directly:

I felt that [the suffering my parents went through before they died] was a preparation for their better life in the future. I just felt that there had to be an end to it. I didn't pray for them to die, but I didn't feel bad when they did.

What is more, it is the suffering Jesus, whom 97% believe to be the Son of God, that provides a model for them in times of their own difficulties. Eighty-three percent said that being familiar with the life of Christ enables them to deal with suffering more easily. To suffer as Jesus suffered is apparently a paradigm rather than a stumbling block, at least for the Christian.

But there are distinct differences in the degree to which members of various denominations hold these beliefs. Baptist respondents (85%) were most able to reconcile the existence of overwhelming iniquity with the concept of a God of love and goodness. Only slightly more than half (55%) of the Methodist participants, on the other hand, were as sure that the existence of evil in the world does not automatically preclude belief in an all-loving God. One wonders how the understanding of the faith in these two groups differs on the subject of evil and why. What special insight does each denomination bring to the understanding of the problem of evil? When between a third and a half of the church members of a Christian community in the United States, a people largely untouched by the survival struggles of most of humanity, question the relationship between God and affliction, then the question is certainly a central one.

The Purpose of Evil

At the same time, suffering is seen by these people to have its own kind of value. Christians of every denomination (88%) agreed that they become more aware of God when there is a crisis in their lives.

A pastor who had previously felt that "something like this is not supposed to happen in a pastor's life," went through a period when his family faced both marital and mental health problems. He talked about the effect of those crises on his spiritual life:

It was lonely. I have never been more keenly aware of my helplessness as a human being. It had the effect of shattering some prejudices that I was conscious of, and some that I wasn't so conscious of. . . . My children saw me weep uncontrollably. I saw them change from looking on with absolute horror and anxiety, to reaching out to Dad and hugging him and praying with him. . . . I met with my elders, and I shared with them what had happened. And I said that if in any way this seemed to undermine my credibility or competency as a pastor, I could understand and would resign.

And everyone of them hugged me and cried and said that they loved me and felt that I was the one the Lord wanted here at that time. . . . And I found out that all things work together for good to them that love God. At the time it didn't seem like anything was working out. But we have discovered that [it was for our best]. We have grown. My wife is more in touch with herself, with the Lord, and with people than she has ever been. Through this, she is a much more beautiful and loving person and an absolutely super wife. Our companionship intellectually, spiritually, emotionally, sexually, every way, is just deepened tremendously through this. And yet, I wouldn't have wished that, and I wouldn't want to go through it again at all.

Most of the respondents, especially the Baptists (68%), said that suffering had even strengthened their faith. Only the Episcopalians indicated in relatively large numbers (47%) that their faith had been taxed as well as confirmed by great struggles of life.

The tendency, too, especially for Catholics (57%) and Baptists (61%) is to believe that at least one of the purposes of suffering is to remind us of our dependence on God, but less than half of all the respondents together (45%) are firmly convinced of that. Others incline to this position but with reservation. The popular psychology that preaches the need to be in control of your own life may be affecting the traditional Christian definition of creaturehood, and feeling dependent on anyone may be seen more as a weakness than a virtue. At any rate, not all our respondents believe that suffering is God's way of reminding us of our creaturehood.

Suffering is an enigma in the Christian community. Why it exists or what causes it is not clear, or accepted, despite various explanations in the churches. Only one thing is plain: the intellectual problem of suffering is not a major issue in these peoples' lives, and suffering is not taken as a sign of God's hate or personal vindictiveness (92%).

Moral Evil

About half of these church members (52%) feel that the country is heading for moral disaster, but they do not seem to have deep convictions about the threat. Only slightly more than a quarter (29%) of the total group hold that opinion firmly, and of them, Christians from the Baptist (41%) and Evangelical Covenant Churches (47%) are the most convinced. The anthropologists discovered that some Christian groups were more worried about the effect of conservative Christian groups, with their emphasis on traditional moral standards, than they were either about social issues or theological questions. The anthropologists reported two groups they observed, one liberal and one conservative:

The participants in the liberal group, we found, tended to feel that they were particularly called upon to help counter some of this conservative challenge which, indeed, they feel distorts the Christian message. Thus, they felt they must not only respond directly to this challenge, but also try to help support others in the community who were under fire, such as teachers, school administrators and planned parenthood advisors. They were very much disturbed by the challenges to school programs. These members of the liberal counseling group were fighting to help people face social problems which were essentially generated by the nature of our society and the changes occurring with it. Now they were also faced with the need to help in a fight to deal with an increasingly organized action which resisted projects they considered socially useful.

Further, this conservative challenge was being promoted on broad ideological grounds which were increasingly conceptualized as Christian. Some said it was representative of a national movement often called the "Moral Majority," or the "New Religious Right." While many in the counseling group said they would agree with the argument that conservatives have a right to express their conservative religious and political opinions, they were concerned about the way these conservative Christians claimed to alone have God's truth and to "know the will of God" in political matters. This claim infringes upon the free political or religious expression of others, particularly the labeling of opposing opinions as unchristian, or ungodly.

In short, this counseling group noted that the U.S.A. is a religiously, culturally, and politically pluralistic society. Their own counseling group must accept the implications of this, but conservative Christians were calling instead for a return to absolutes. . . .

We have found one of the principal criticisms of the current flurry of social and political action by conservative Christians is that they are not dealing with the problems critics see to be the critical ones Christians are called to deal with: care for the sick, the imprisoned, the less fortunate, and the stranger.

Denominational Differences

Suffering, then, is part of the human condition, and whether it will always exist is no more certain than why it exists. However, one thing is sure as far as these Christians (97%) are concerned: as long as there is suffering, the church must minister to it. What is more, three-fourths (73%) of the group assert that their own parishes or congregations did indeed help them personally in times of hurt. Presbyterians and Lutherans most of all (80%) had found solace from their parishes in times of trouble; Baptists, Roman Catholics, and Methodists, on the other hand, felt least assistance (66%) at moments of distress. Nevertheless, only one-third (32%) of all parishioners clearly felt that the church has a greater obligation to the ill, the handicapped, and the suffering than it has to its less afflicted members. Apparently, ministry to the suffering is accepted to be an element of Christian community, but it is not its focus nor is it supposed to be.

Demographic Distinctions

Equally significant may be the fact that considerably more women (60%) than men (49%) contend that if for any reason they do not help someone who is suffering, they either would or should feel that by that omission they have failed Christ. Women (59%), more than men (52%), say that their faith is strengthened by suffering; women (58%), more than men (49%) consider suffering and crisis a result of sin; women (36%) find evil more difficult to reconcile with the concept of a loving God than men (26%). Women, more than men, it seems, do not simply take suffering in stride. They are more likely than men to find the cause inside themselves or to feel a responsibility to respond to the suffering of others.

There are interesting and significant differences in the way lay and clergy explain the existence or significance of suffering. The clergy (51%), far more than the laity (29%), recognize a greater obligation to the ill, the handicapped, and the suffering. Almost all the clergy (94%) can more easily absorb the idea that evil can take place in a world in which a loving God exists, but only 65% of the laity can make that reconciliation. The clergy (58%), more than laity (43%), see suffering as a sign of dependence on God, but the clergy (57%), more often than the laity (35%), reject the position that illness, calamity, and other forms of suffering and crisis are the result of sin. Obviously the gap between the clergy's understanding of the place and purpose of suffer- ing in life and that of church members is relatively wide and will affect the way each of them is likely to view the role of the church in both social and spiritual situations.

In general, it seems that most Christians do not blame God for evil, but they certainly do not have any single, clear explanation for it. They do not, for the most part, consider it either a punishment for sin or the result of sin. When faced with suffering in their own lives, however, they lean heavily on the life of Christ as a model for coping with it, and they often find their faith strengthened by contemplating the way Christ dealt with pain and hardship. They know the church must minister to those who suffer, but many do not feel that the suffering deserve the primary attention of the church or that they themselves are less Christian if they fail to respond to those in difficulty. In a society where social service agencies are a business and where progress is itself the civil religion, the positions are not without logic. Whether the church can be church under these conditions is another question.

If evil is something that God permits for our good growth or even as a sign of God's presence in life, then it is enticing to argue that evil is to be borne, as the man said, "not gleefully" but certainly willingly—even passively, perhaps. But if that is the case, and the responses to this study seem to indicate that most people think so, what then is the social gospel all about? Is it valid? Is it possible? If evil is its own kind of good, should anyone attempt to eliminate it? Given the data here and the present condition of a world faced with starvation, nuclear devastation, and economic imbalance, the contemporary church may have need to reopen the question.

3

Valley of Darkness, Valley of Hope
Death and Dying

"Not lost but gone before," Seneca wrote of the dead. "Like the foam on the river . . . Thou art gone, and forever!" the poet Scott answered. The thought of death as the end of life or as the entrance to a better life has marked the ebb and flow of cultures from the beginning of time. Whether life is destined for glory or condemned to eternal dust has been a central human debate. And correctly so, for it is precisely this concern that distinguishes the religious from the ethical, the essence of faith from the elements of what could otherwise be a simple concern for the social good. The problem of death is central to the very meaning and use of life itself. It is at the same time central to the meaning of church.

More than anything else, perhaps, the presence of death forces the human being to come to grips with the possibility that life is useless, that existence is absurd. It is death, not life, that cries for a sense of design. It is death that makes the human being accept limits and at the same time look beyond them. And it is the church that purports to speak to these great issues: the inviolability of life, the sacramentality of death rituals, the existence of life after death, the nature of salvation, and the centrality of the resurrection of Jesus Christ to the Christian account of the purpose of life and to eternal life itself. By custom or

49

education, consistent church members of all traditions have been formed in each topic. The results are mixed.

The Right to Death

For some years now various groups of citizens have pursued the legal right to terminate the life of the mentally or physically ill, for whom continued existence would appear to be without quality or creative future. Euthanasia (mercy killing controlled by law) has in fact been argued on the highest Christian principles — concern for others, human dignity, and the nature of life. Suicide, on the other hand, is seen by some as the ultimate act of human control, by others as a defiance of the lordship of God. Each issue is decidedly religious and has always touched Christianity at its deepest point. And the responses are not unanimous.

Suicide is overwhelmingly, but not unanimously, rejected. Most of the respondents (88%) agreed that individuals do not have the right to end their own lives any time they choose. For the others (12%) there can be mitigating circumstances that do give that right at some times. Although a clear majority now hold that life is to be left in the hands of the Creator, even among church members a noticeable proportion is not convinced that must be the case.

Of this Christian community 17% are inclined to agree, at least slightly, that "if its use is controlled by law, so-called mercy killing can benefit society." For the others (83%) life is to be lived to its final natural breath, regardless of the conditions affecting it. Human beings are not to tamper with its duration, not to obstruct its coming "to fullness of days." The data seem to show, however, that the relationships between technology, medicine, life, and Christian hope are yet to be resolved.

The Rituals of Death

The particular customs surrounding death are unique to every culture of the world, but every culture has developed some kind of rituals to deal psychologically and publicly with the termination of life. Consequently, peoples everywhere have more or less elaborate forms of dealing with death. In the words of one respondent to the study:

I think that ritual is a real important part of facing the reality of the death of the person you love. There are times when you just don't know what to do, and when a clear-cut direction is laid out for you, and you go to the funeral and do the things that are traditionally done; it's just a way of getting through that really difficult period.

Perhaps reflecting that same perspective, most of the respondents agreed to the importance of funerals. At least some of the respondents, however, make distinctions about the values that funeral practices provide. For 75% the importance is religious; for 67% it is psychological as well; and for 67% funerals are valued for their social implications. But whatever their meanings to various individuals, at least two-thirds of the population reject the notion that funerals should be discouraged by the church.

But agreement in principle does not signal unlimited approval of all rituals. Though Minnesota Christians today consider funerals necessary, many (43%) are also firmly convinced that they can be overdone and that elaborate burials should not be condoned by the church. Present funeral customs only camouflage death, 43% of the survey respondents reported. But it is difficult to determine from the data exactly what that means to people, because when the question specified items that commonly show unusual investment in the cosmetics of death—flowers, coffins, and headstones—only slightly more than a fourth of the study group (27%) were able to agree that the church should discourage that kind of expenditure on the dead. Although funerals are not an end in themselves in the Christian community and though there may be a trend away from the ostentatious or the excessive in mortuary practices, it is nevertheless extremely difficult for people to know what to cut back or to determine exactly the essentially religious dimensions of the funeral acts. What is most clear is that funerals are deeply imbedded in the culture, but not without question and not eternally fixed as a matter of faith.

Despite the country's long history of unrestricted graveyard interment, a luxury which nations where land is scare or the environment prohibitive do not enjoy, 60% of the answerers to this social survey were in firm agreement that it is not unchristian to cremate the dead—and this in the very generation in which some churches taught that it was a sign of disbelief in the general resurrection to do anything other than commit the mortal remains to the ground whole and entire, from which on the last day they, like Christ, might rise from the tomb glorified. This 60% believes that life continues after death, whether or not a person is cremated.

Life After Life

In their most concerted response on the entire topic almost every Christian from every denomination studied (91%) said that they are not indifferent to the question of whether or not there is really a life after death. What is more, they clearly believe in it. That life is not simply nondestruction or some kind of personal preservation; it is conceived as a continuation of life as we have known it here, a life to be lived in community with loved ones who have died before us. Almost two-thirds of the group (63%) agree that, "When people die who are close to me I do not despair because I believe that we will meet again." Yet, reservations are significant. Almost 20% of the respondents accept that position with only limited conviction, and almost as many (17%) at least to some extent disagree that they expect to be reunited with loved ones after death. In the Christian tradition those opinions cannot be quietly overlooked. If the notion of life after death is important to them, but tenuous, the whole question of what it is to be a Christian or to have faith emerges anew.

In the in-depth interviews people struggled with the questions just as honestly. The interviewer asked: "Do you believe in an afterlife? And if so, what do you think it is?" And people said things like this:

Whenever I hear the word "afterlife" I think of an old Woody Allen joke. He says, "I don't believe in an afterlife, but I'm bringing along a change of underwear just in case." . . . I do believe in an afterlife, but I really don't know what it would be like and that is probably the thing that scares me the most about dying.

The afterlife is a place for perfect communication. It is a place without language barriers. It is a place where we understand the consequences of our behavior.

I'm looking for life after death—not a physical life but as Chardin says, "There is a stream of life, circling the earth, a spiritual stream," and I would like to feel that I am in the spiritual stream, and going around . . . being at one with this great flowing of the spiritual life of all humanity.

But whatever their concept of a life to come, it was clear that it mattered to them, that church members rely on it, that by and large they try to deal with it, that it is seen as a better time to come. As one woman said:

If someone could convince me that there is no afterlife with God, I would be the most depressed person. There would be nothing to live for. I look at people who refuse to believe in God, and I wonder what they have to live for? What is in their life that could be interesting? What is there to hope for? Life is just a few years, and that's it.

At the same time that they believe strongly in another kind of life to come, or in the reunion of loved ones after death, a majority (60%) do not really believe that some individuals are able to communicate with the spirits of those who have died. Even so, a surprising number (32%) of people in an age of technology and the scientific method are not prepared to take a firm position against the possibility. On the other hand, perhaps it is precisely technology and the scientific method that leads so large a group to imagine the possibility at all. In a time when the impossible is commonplace and scientists get research grants to communicate with peoples in outer space, some of the great philosophical-religious questions of life may take a completely different slant.

The Meaning of Salvation

As far as churchgoing Christians of Minnesota are concerned, the good news is that they themselves are saved and will have eternal life. This high sense of personal salvation, however, does not apply equally to all people. A small minority (11%) believe that "God's love is so great that all people will have eternal life and no one will be lost." Universal salvation, the idea that God is either too loving to punish or that punishment is not eternal, is not part of the practicing theology of this Christian community. For those who do claim that God will not punish forever, though, the rationale is simple:

There has got to be an equalizer, somehow, someway. Everybody is a child of God; everybody is loved by God. And what is God? God is love. If God is really love, that includes everybody. Even Adolf Hitler. There is no rejection. I don't see how there can be any exceptions to that. It is God's desire that everybody will be with the eternal forever. . . . And I can't see how such a little thing as 27, or 13, or 3, or 78 years—however long you've had on this earth—will determine forever. That is a heck of a long time.

At the other pole of opinion, few (13%) accept the idea either that "no matter what people do, some will be saved and some will be lost." The doctrine that some souls are predestined to be saved has apparently very little acceptance in Minnesota. People can be "lost," but not because God has willed it so or even perhaps because of sheer imperfection. In fact, person after person, in direct conversation, took for granted that life is a continuing struggle against sin that will too often end in failure. In their minds it was not so much sinlessness but orientation—trying—that counts toward salvation. In one man's words: "Being Christian means that I can look forward to being saved, even though I am not a totally religious person. I don't go to church every Sunday, [but] I don't feel that I'm a bad person. I do feel that there is a place in heaven for people like me, too, even though we don't go to church every Sunday. I believe there is a God." For some people, obviously salvation is not directly tied to churchgoing.

Nor, it seems, is churchgoing uniquely related to the resurrection of Christ. Thirty-one percent, almost one-third of the church members sampled in Minnesota, agreed (19%) or agreed slightly (12%) that Christian teaching would be meaningful to them whether Christ had risen from the dead or not. The implication is that Christianity is meaningful without the resurrection of Christ. What would be the basis of the credibility of Christianity for these people is unclear, but one thing is relatively certain: no matter what the Christian churches think is being understood as the cornerstone of Christianity, for a sizeable segment of the contemporary Christian population there may be little understanding of the place of the resurrection in the concept of salvation. There is, moreover, a real problem about the resurrection and the belief in the afterlife. If 91% believe in the afterlife, but 31% do not see the essential importance of the resurrection of Christ, then what is the basis for their belief in an afterlife? Or is the "belief" of this kind simply hope against hope?

In questions about death we also come face to face with the problem of the role and nature of the church.

The Role of the Church

One of the more interesting discoveries in the study is that, as noted, people who believe in life after death, in the religious significance of funerals, and in a sense a personal salvation, are nevertheless diffuse in their opinions about the function of the church in relation to these things. Fewer than half of all the respondents (42%) think that one reason why the church must proclaim the gospel is to save those who may otherwise be lost after death. Whether that indicates that many church members do not see the church as the instrument of salvation or that they simply do not believe that the gospel of Christ is essential to salvation is not clear. One thing can be said: even to church members themselves church must be something other than a channel to the next world.

Life-After-Death Theology: Its Effect on Church

A large percentage (81%) of the respondents agreed that the teaching of the church about life after death is a consolation to them when someone close to them dies. Three-fourths said, too, that these same teachings of the church made them less afraid to die. Nevertheless, 40% were firmly convinced that "in church we should hear more about life here and now rather than life hereafter." Furthermore, if those who agreed slightly with the same statement (28%) are added to those firmly agreeing, we have evidence of a trend in the direction of church as revealer of the incarnate God rather than church as definer of the transcending God. The question then becomes whether such an attitude undermines or completes the gospel of Christ, whether theistic humanism or Christianity prevails in churches today.

In any case, half of the Christians surveyed are firmly convinced and another 12% are leaning toward the idea that the church is a necessary social institution, with or without life after death. If these positions are to be taken at face value and can be generalized at all, then the church has at least as important a role in the present life of Christians as it has in their preparation for the next. But in all these postures there are some significant differences of viewpoint among the traditions and types of people who do or do not hold what appears to be the collective Christian attitude.

Denominational Differences

More than any other groups of this study, the Roman Catholic and Methodist Christians (82%) were committed to the opinion that funerals have important religious functions for the individual, the family, and the community. The fact that people from these two churches seem to differ profoundly in their liturgical styles implies that it will be necessary to look beyond the meanings and effects of ritual to discover the basis for so clear a conviction.

Roman Catholic, Lutheran, and Covenant Church respondents were almost totally opposed (93%) to the idea that suicide is a human right.

In their opinion people simply do not have the right to end their own lives. Whatever their tradition, most respondents were against the supposition that human beings can have that kind of control over their own lives, but Pr< oyterians, Episcopalians, and members of the UCC (about 23% each) espoused suicide as an acceptable human option.

Catholics were opposed to mercy killing by a far greater majority (84%) than any of the other denominations, and they (69%) and Lutherans (70%) were less approving of organ transplants as well, factors which seem to indicate that there is in these traditions a fundamental suspicion of anything that tampers with the natural life processes of life and death.

Members of UCC congregations are less inclined (47%) than the other Christian communities represented here to consider funerals valuable. Presbyterians (59%), Covenant Church members (57%), and Episcopalians (52%) were not much more enthusiastic about the social worth of funeral rites or the church's acceptance of them than were Christians from the UCC.

Given what we have already seen, it is not surprising that far fewer members of the United Church of Christ (39%) than any of the other denominations, especially Catholics (74%), are consoled by the church's teaching that they will meet their dead loved ones again. Clearly, a sizable portion of UCC Christians are simply not committed to the thought that the associations of this life will be part of the next. Episcopalians and Methodists are also divided on the issue (53%); and Lutherans (67%), Presbyterians (65%), and Baptists (61%) are not much firmer on the matter. If the thought of life after death in a "communion of saints" is an element of the Christian faith, it is not universally held in any of the Minnesota churches, it seems. But if it is not a fixed element of faith, it is for most at least an underlying but undefined hope.

At the same time, UCC members (76%) and Presbyterians (73%) are most committed to the posture that the church is necessary for the development of faith, regardless of whether or not there is life after death. However, a higher percentage of the Baptists (83%) than of other denominations is convinced that if Christ had not risen from the dead, Christian teaching would mean very little.

Finally, Presbyterians (53%) and UCC members (59%) most believe that they should hear more in their churches about life here and now than about life hereafter. Since far fewer Lutherans (26%), Evangelical Covenant (33%), and Baptists (34%) hold the same opinion, the implication is that these groups may be more oriented to see spiritual concerns as outside the realm of historical experience than the other Christian groups around them. What is just as interesting, though, is the fact that Episcopalians and Roman Catholics—all with a keen sense of the transcendent dimensions of faith—are so open (49%-43%) to the insertion of the secular in the sacred, to the human situation as a vehicle for grace.

Demographic Distinctions

The clergy (69%), much more than laity (55%), look to the resurrection of Christ to make Christian teaching meaningful. The clergy (56%) think that elaborate funerals should be discouraged by the church and that present-day funeral customs are a camouflage of death rather than a reminder of it. But a majority of the laity (59%) disagree. They find funerals helpful and see elaborate presentations as an acceptable part of the Christian concept of death. Understandably, then, fewer laity (39%) want to hear more about life hereafter in their churches, while half of the clergy (50%) believe that life here and now ought to be as much the concern of the church as the life to come. More clergy (92%) than laity (74%) are inclined to feel that funerals serve an important religious, rather than social or psychological, function, despite the fact that the laity seem to support specific present practices more than their pastors do. And it is the clergy who most find the church's teachings about life after death a consolation in the face of death. The data seem to show that lay Christians have a considerably different mind about death than their clergy. What that says about either the clarity of the teaching or the depth of the faith today could be of utmost importance to the future direction of the church. The data suggest that we may well ask what will happen to the character of the church if the laity concentrate on one dimension of faith while the clergy emphasize another. If the promise of eternal life captures the contemporary imagination more effectively than the meaning of the resurrection, will the meaning of the faith for Christian life and service erode? For if that is really the case, then the power of non-Christian cults to take root in the Christian community may be more real than is usually considered.

Fewer women (45%) than men (55%) agree that present-day funeral practices serve to camouflage death rather than to enable people to face and deal with it. Men (60%) are more prone than women (54%)

to argue that if Christ had not risen from the dead, Christian teaching would mean very little to them. Women (66%) are more consoled than men (60%) by the church's teaching about life after death and believe they will be reunited there with those they love. Men, it seems, want a sound basis for their faith; women may be more inclined to believe by virtue of their respect for life itself.

People in urban areas (71%) are much more supportive of cremation as a proper way for Christians to treat the dead than are Christians who live outside metro areas. Only 54% of the church members from rural Minnesota agreed that cremation was proper Christian behavior. People in the cities, too, were also more interested (48%) than rural parishioners (36%) in hearing more in church about life here and now than about life hereafter. Christians from the nonmetro areas (71%), however, argue more for the value of funerals than city people (60%), perhaps because they are closer tuned to the cycles of life and death than their Christian counterparts in the industrialized urban areas. What is more, rural church members in Minnesota (63%) are more committed to the idea that Christian teaching would be meaningless to them if Christ had not risen from the dead than are the city-dwellers in the study (49%). Is this because traditional faith is stronger in rural areas? Or is it because urbanites, irrespective of the internal credibility of the dogma itself, may feel more pressingly the need for a social institution to bring a civilizing influence to their environment?

It appears from the data that, either because they are older or because they were born before the atomic era, older people are much more consoled by church teachings about life after death than are younger church people. Whether as life begins to shorten people become more receptive and hopeful about the afterlife or because the atomic era has made younger people more skeptical about religion or the acceptability of death cannot be determined here, but the associations may be worth pursuing. Older people, too, are less critical of expensive funerals, and older people (75%), considerably more than younger ones (42%), think that it is likely that some individuals are able to communicate with the spirits of those who have died. Older people imply that if they did not believe in the resurrection of Christ they would probably not be Christians or find much meaning in the teachings of the Christian church, but church members below the age of 35 insist that the Christian church would have value for them whether Christ rose from the dead or not.

All in all, then, the Christian community of Minnesota, like so many others, may reflect a deep need to believe in an afterlife. Funeral customs are important to it. For most, Christianity without the resurrection is meaningless, but for a significant proportion, the resurrection does not seem to be the basis of their faith. For some, suicide and mercy killing are acceptable options. Their personal salvation is primary for many, but life after death is not the sole or even the unrivaled aim of the church. In fact, there is little decisiveness among them about eternal life. The hope alone consoles. The enigma, of course, is whether or not this predominantly individual concern for salvation rather than a communitarian concern for the coming of the kingdom is authentically Christian and if not, what has happened to divert the tradition.

4

When the Lot Is Cast into the Lap
Control of Life/Moral Motivation

Even in the face of public ridicule, Noah held firmly to the conviction that God was directing his future and the intricacies of achieving it as well. Joseph, enslaved and sent to Egypt out of malice, announced later to his brothers who had done the deed, "So it was not you but God who had me come here" (Gen. 45:8). The book of Proverbs asserts: "The lot is cast into the lap, its decision depends entirely on the Lord" (Prov. 16:33). To these people God was an ever-present guiding force. And that is all well and good for Noah and Joseph and the writer of the book of Proverbs in the fifth century B.C. But since then the human race has discovered that a confluence of warm and cold winds causes rain, that grounding controls lightning, that surgery reverses illness, that helium gases enable us to defy gravity. Where is the God of dailiness in all of that?

People of this scientific age are faced with a different set of situations than were their religious ancestors. Now natural events or circumstances can be explained, if not controlled. The thinkable is possible. The unthinkable is probable. Rationalism is in its heyday, and God is debatable.

The contemporary Christian community is faced with a religious problem with which forebears did not have to deal. True, the Chosen People had to contend that there was only one God and that theirs was the only true God, but few, if any, questioned the existence of some god concerned with the daily affairs of the human race. That god was to be propitiated and praised, cajoled and flattered today so that tomorrow would be possible. But what does the Christian of the 20th century do with that? Is a human being free or simply a pawn of some great external, even if personal, force? In a scientific age what do people believe about the place of God in their lives? Is the God of creation also a God of providence? How free is free will?

Perhaps more important, in terms of the maturity and depth of contemporary spirituality, is whether or not providence, if acknowledged at all, is seen as a belief that everything must turn out well or simply the belief that however things turn out God's plan is being satisfied. As Christians in our study responded to these questions, three issues emerged most clearly: the nature of God's intervention, the nature of human responsibility if God is in charge of life, and the ultimate character of God's will. Intervention, responsibility, and determinism—key issues from earlier moments of human history—are apparently still important issues in modern Christianity. Perhaps, in fact, they may be more difficult problems for this generation than for the ages before it. The relationship between the sovereignty of God and the freedom of people who have built computers and explored outer space is a matter of delicate balance. The tension shows in the data.

The Intervention of God in Human Life

As far as Christians in Minnesota are concerned, God did not create them only to withdraw from them. Or, to put it another way, in this Christian community, to be human is not to be autonomous. Some Christian groups in Minnesota told the field study team that believing in miracles, in the power of the supernatural, is really required of Christians, because miracles testify to God's authority over creation. Individuals, lay and professional, spoke of the Lord leading them to their present positions because God has a purpose for them there. The researchers noted:

It may be that people who identify themselves as members of various types of Christian communities, who see themselves as Spirit-filled, charismatic, born again, or saved, are, right from the moment of their initial involvement in the movement, even more ready than members of the general public, or even than members of other movements, to act with a sense of personal power. Their religion gives them this personal belief system, and often prepares them to see the hand of God working in what they do. So while they are self-driven and motivated, they are also responding to a sense of higher direction.

The God who is everywhere is definitely with them. God "opens and closes doors [in life] for them." God provides "definite direction." God "provides a way." And when God doesn't, they assume that for some reason it is best for them.

A woman, forced to work outside the home in a job she liked, hesitated to take it while her child was still young. She explained:

I spend so much time praying, "Lord, if there is any way that I can stay home with her, if that is what you think I should be doing, or if that's what you think is going to be best for both of us, I know you will make a way. I don't know how, but you will." Well, God didn't, so I thought, "Well, I'll go to work. That's what I should be doing." And I accepted it that way. . . . And if I always have to work, if I have to go back next year, and the next year after that, until she is in school, I'm just going to say, "Well, that is what's best for us. And that is what God thought was best for us." And that's why I guess I can do it.

This belief in God's intervention was shared by 73% of the respondents. It is also confirmed in another part of the study by evidence of these people's reliance on prayers of supplication. However, the subject cannot be closed there. Though there is clear consensus that God intervenes in a person's life, fewer (63%) believe that God intervenes with equal clarity, directness, and immediacy in the affairs of society in general. Sixteen percent of this mainline Christian population do not believe that God intervenes directly in the affairs of society, and another 20% say they agree only "slightly" with the proposition that somehow or other God is guiding or effecting the direction of the human community. The implications of that for other facets of dogma —creation, free will, and providence—are obvious. For these people God is a God of personal salvation but much less a God of history. What that does to the Christian tradition or to the concept that God is the God of the whole human community may be something for contemporary Christianity to explore.

Personal Responsibility

At the same time that these respondents are not sure just how much they can expect God to work things out according to their private designs, they are nevertheless very sure that they themselves are responsible for what they do. Almost everyone (92%) in the survey agreed with the statement "No matter what the circumstances of my life situation, I am still responsible for what I do." But far fewer (75%) agreed that if they are not saved, it is their own fault. Salvation is something that cannot be earned or something that they may simply take for granted. In one man's words:

Salvation, I think, is a freely given gift from God. It was Jesus coming back for us and bringing us into a relationship with the Father. To say that my accepting Jesus—in the popular Pentecostal terminology—is salvation would be inappropriate, because then it puts salvation on me. It means that I am the source of salvation rather than Jesus, and I can either accept it or not accept it.

From one perspective, then, salvation depends on the coming of Christ and can be accepted or not but cannot be earned. For another, creation itself is the basis for salvation:

We were brought up to believe in heaven and hell, but I just don't believe in [hell] anymore. I think there is something good in anyone, no matter what type of life they lead, and that [everyone will come to see God].

Whatever the attitudes toward the basis of salvation, responsibility and salvation are not necessarily correlates. What is more, though the respondents claim a high sense of personal responsibility—even though distinct from the questions of salvation for some—they recognize factors outside of their control. Only a small majority (62%) are convinced that "life is what we make it." And even fewer than that (58%) feel sure that God created people with the ability to control their own lives. For these Christians responsibility is more the obligation to react correctly than it is the possibility to reshape the world.

Nevertheless, some of the most interesting parts of the study involved the attempt by Christian groups to do exactly that. The anthropological field study of the state discovered both "liberal" and "conservative" Christian activists engaged in organized attempts to control school curriculums, state legislation, civic programs, and public standards—all in the name of Christianity. Survey participants, too, spoke continually of the obligations of people to meet one or another Christian duty. Clearly, some kind of responsibility to alter the course of things is keenly felt, and the two facets of the problem—God's will and human activity—must be reconciled, or one or the other must be in vain. But it is precisely in this area that the data becomes ambivalent.

Determinism

Members of the Christian community sampled in the churches of Minnesota are divided over the question of whether or not it is possible for people to change God's plan for their lives. Forty-two percent of the respondents simply assume that such a thing is impossible, that God has a plan for every person's life and that it is predesigned and inevitable. What is more, only slightly more than a third (36%) of the population are basically sure that they are free to withdraw from the plan. The rest of the group studied are not prepared to take either position firmly.

One of the interview responses reflected the ambiguity of the survey data. According to this point of view, everyone has a pattern to follow. All do the best they can to control their destiny, but the sense of control is more psychological than real. He said:

You can't control your destiny. You don't control your destiny. And so you try to pattern, the best that you know how, with what you have been given to control that destiny. And some will control it in a good manner; some will not. I [just] don't think we have that much control. . . . I think that we try to lead ourselves to believe that we have a certain amount of control. And as long as we believe that we have that control, I think that life goes on, and I think that you have this constant incentive to do better, because you want to reach that end, you want to reach that goal.

From that perspective it is easy to understand the logic of activist organizing in the face of uncertain effects. It is even easier to account for the fact that a large segment (81%) of the respondents, though they differ on other significant positions, agree with the idea that it is their intention to do the best they can to cope with life and then leave up to God that which they cannot control.

All in all, then, determinism is rejected by these Christians, but not overwhelmingly. There is great uncertainty about whether or not they really have any control over what God wills for their individual lives. Thirty-one percent of the churchgoers in this study believe that they do not. Thirty-nine percent believe just as strongly that they do. The others are not ready to take any absolute position or are simply confused. At the same time most (68%) feel that they have at least some control over the circumstances and situations that shape their lives. Practically no one (2%) feels that they have little control over any elements of their own lives, that "no matter what happens outside of themselves, doing anything about it is out of their control."

The result of so much ambivalence about the role of God in human affairs is a certain uncertainty. Whatever their tradition, Christians feel sure that God intervenes in the human condition, but they do not know exactly how and they do not know exactly when: always or sometimes? In whole patterns or simply in the unplanned and unexpected events of their lives? In personal circumstances or in social events?

Nonetheless, no matter how they do or do not explain God's presence, they do not dispute it or regard it as malevolent. Whether that is enough faith for the Christian life is another question, but this is what the present moment has brought us to. As important, perhaps, as the theological questions involved is the awareness that, despite the climate of the present generation and their confusion about this persistent God problem, they simply accept the mystery of the question, without despair, even with trust:

Life isn't always terrible. There are good times, and if you make some wise decisions along the way, and think things through, the results are going to be livable.

Denominational Differences

In the melting pot called Christianity it is possible to draw what seem to be universal and relatively well-grounded assumptions from the data. It is possible to say, for instance, that it is of the Christian tradition to accept responsibility for individual actions, to reject determinism, to consider God an active part of the present life. And, when the data is undifferentiated, those assertions are both credible and helpful. At the same time a close examination of the data indicates the likelihood that on specific issues there may be considerable differences in the attitudes of various groups. This was particularly true of the providence/predestination questions.

Though none of the populations sampled was overwhelmingly committed to the idea that a sign of God's will for their lives was the occurrence of unexpected or unplanned events, more than half (53%) of the Roman Catholics in the study were sure this was so—perhaps because of the emphasis in that tradition on the lives of the saints and the history of God's strange ways with people. Presbyterians and UCC members are at the other extreme of the discussion. The large majority of these groups reject the idea that God's will is most evident in unplanned surprises. At the same time it is Presbyterians, Baptists, and members of the Evangelical Covenant Church (75%) who are much more convinced than Catholics, Episcopalians, and members of the UCC (53%) that God intervenes in the affairs of society. Whether this indicates that some groups tend to privatize the ways of God with persons more than others is unclear, but the considerable difference in the orientation on these two issues is worth noting. More than any other group, Baptists seem inclined to see the guiding hand of God in everything, personal life most (83%) but also in the public arena (71%), while members of the UCC seem most prone to feel that their responsibility in creation is to work things out as best they can without depending heavily on the direct control of God.

On the other hand, regardless of how instrumental they consider God to be in the course of specific human events, it was Catholics (88%), Lutherans, Episcopalians, and UCC respondents (84%) who took the attitude that it is a Christian obligation to do the best they can to cope with life and then leave whatever they cannot control up to God. But Baptists, who see the designing hand of God everywhere, were least in agreement with doing what seemed possible and letting God do the rest. Whether that comes from a conviction that nothing less than the perfect is acceptable to God or that God will do what has to be done without the efforts of people is uncertain from this data, but the implications of these very different attitudes toward the interaction of God and humans are important.

Roman Catholics and Methodists seem to feel most in control of their own lives. Catholics (74%) were most sure of the statement, "Life is what I make it," but more than half the members of most of the other Christian churches who participated in the study were equally sure that what they put into life would have a good deal to do with what happened to it. Only Baptists and Covenant Church members (49%) responded with less assurance that they could fashion life to their own designs. Apparently, for these churchgoers in Minnesota, life is not simply what they themselves make it. Perhaps it is what God makes it as well, judging from their conviction that God can be expected to intervene in a person's daily circumstances (85%) or, on the other hand, perhaps life is without any control whatsoever. Whatever the rationale, in matters of providence, control, and personal responsibility for life's results, Baptists and Covenant Church members seem to differ considerably from other denominations.

In the final analysis, two streams diverge in this data. In the first, God is present, in charge, and determining the development of life. In the second, God is present throughout life, but people have little expectation that God will program events. In the first, the person's responsibility is to cooperate with what God determines for them in daily life. In the second, people feel the responsibility to shape what happens to them daily and trust that God will, in the end, make things right.

Perhaps the streams converge again somewhere else, but at this point the two images of God seem quite distinct.

Demographic Distinctions

The various approaches to the God problems may certainly be conditioned by the insights, charisms, and formation programs of each denomination, but status in life may be a factor as well. If the differences that emerge in this population are reflective of other groups, then age, gender, and role in the church may affect the way Christians see God's activity in life.

For instance, men (45%) are more inclined than women (32%) to believe that people can change God's plan for their lives, perhaps because men have always been able to change more circumstances of their lives than women could. On the other hand, more women (78%) than men (67%) believe that God intervenes in the daily circumstances of their lives. It is women (84%), more than men (78%), who are most inclined to leave things up to God. But women (68%), more than men (56%) are more likely to take responsibility for the quality of their lives. Finally, many more women (53%) than men (31%) think that the unexpected is God's will for them. Whether these attitudes spring from cultural role definitions or a basically different religious orientation or formation deserves further study, or else the churches may find themselves espousing one version of the faith for women and another for men.

Age may also be a factor in the way people see God working in their lives. Whether those differences derive from changes in the nature of the society we live in or simply from the fact that experience changes people can not be determined here. Nevertheless, people born during or before the Depression think differently about the role of God in life than do people born after the Atomic Age began.

More younger people (91%) than older people (82%) tend to think that life will be what we ourselves make it. What is more, the feeling that God created people with the ability to control their own lives may diminish with age. Young people (63%) felt that self-direction was one of God's gifts; people over 54 (53%) questioned whether or not this was indeed one of life's prerogatives.

But older people were the ones more inclined to trust to God whatever they found beyond them (87%), while younger adults were less likely (75%) to do that. The gap in these responses is particularly provocative. Are younger people simply more sure of their own potential than their elders, whose strengths have already been tested? Are they less conscious of God to begin with? Or has the theology of divine providence actually shifted in the computer generation? Older people, too (81%), are more convinced that salvation is their responsibility and that if they are not saved it is their own fault. Only 67% of the younger respondents were as ready to take the same degree of personal responsibility for their own salvation.

At the same time the older (23%) and the younger (23%) Christians in the study were in agreement in believing God creates evil as well as good. Interestingly enough, each age group, in almost equal proportions, assumed that God intervenes in individual's lives (73%) and in the affairs of society (63%).

There are some wide differences between the way church members view the activity of God in their lives and the beliefs of their clergy on the same issues. In these Christian communities more laity believe that God is present in the unexpected; that life is what they make it (laity-65%; clergy-37%) but that they have no control over what God wills for their lives (laity-33%; clergy-15%). And the laity are more convinced that they should simply do the best they can and leave the rest to God (laity-79%; clergy-65%). The clergy (7%) have less room in their minds than their parishioners (24%) for the idea that a good God created both good and evil. Many more clergy (55%) than laity (35%) think that humans can change God's plans, and more clergy (77%) than laity (62%) believe that God intervenes in the workings of society.

But when all is said and done, the data on the subject are scattered, diffuse, and tenuous from every aspect, in every category of church-goer. Clearly the questions are real, the sure answers are few, the sense of mystery deep.

5

Contact with the Living God

Personal Spiritual Development

Goodness is possible without religion. A sense of social contract is no proof of a sense of God. When the search for a personal relationship with God is basic to or even supersedes a person's thought of social obligation or personal gain, a new life dimension develops. With the belief that God is a direct and present factor in all of life the human experience becomes an interpersonal relationship with God, a search for the God who is searching for us.

Contact with God is no small project, and we may ask whether it is a personal endeavor or a communal act. Is it something people do alone, or is it done only through the church? Over the centuries manuals of spirituality have described the process precisely. For some peoples at some times, encounter with God implied the most rigorous asceticism, the deepest mysticism, the strictest enclosure, the furthest retreat. For others, spirituality has been based on codes of perfection, on the imitation of Christ, on the creation of Christian community, on adherence to church law or personal piety. For still others, union with God has come through immersion in human needs. But in this age what is it?

One of the aims of this study was to determine who God is for some specific church members today. In Minnesota what does God look like? How do people relate to God, if at all? Where is God present in the lives of these people? And, finally, what is the relationship among a person's encounter with God, their relationship to the church, and their relationship to the rest of society? In search for insight into those relationships, we examined seven elements of personal spiritual development: prayer, community, faith sharing, sin, and concepts of God, the Bible, and church.

Prayer

Most (71%) of the people who participated in this research program described prayer as "very important." Almost three-fourths of every denomination, except UCC members, Methodists, and Episcopalians, report an equally deep commitment to prayer. The fact that even more (82%) say that they pray every day may be an indication that people make a distinction between prayer as essential to the spiritual life and prayer as simply a devotional exercise for Christians. The field study also suggests that people see prayer as deeply personal and integral to their spiritual development. The observers reported that church groups who were intent on creating an ecumenical bond or climate for dealing cross-denominationally with social issues did not, for that very reason, meet in any specific church or open their sessions with prayer. On the other hand, mixed groups intent on the preservation of personal spiritual values in society, rather than on bringing an ecumenical dimension to the implementation of social plans or projects, were more noted for the religious character of their assemblies. In other words, when the personal spiritual dimension of the subject under discussion was stressed, prayer was integral to the discussion. When the ecumenical aspects of the program were most in question, apparently it was not (perhaps because an ecumenical group has no prayer pattern in which they all feel comfortable). Prayer, then, as a key element of personal spiritual development was modeled in Christian study groups.

But though prayer was said to be important and daily prayer was common, it is not traditional prayers that these contemporary Christians consider best:

My definition of prayer is not the 10 or 15 minutes a day you spend on your knees with your hands folded. I do a lot of—what do you want to call it— quickies: "O God, let us get there," "I hope we have a safe trip," "Don't let it snow," and and that kind of thing. I'm not a prayer person, like a Dear John letter. I'm not like that.

For 40% of the respondents, prayer formulas are simply not necessary. But if these people pray often and spontaneously, prayer must be personal and immediate for them. Even more revealing, perhaps, is the fact that for these people access to God does not depend on ritual, nor does it have the overtones of magic. Prayer is a real communication process, a contact point between these individuals and God. What is more, even in this age of transcendental meditation, prayer is not seen as an activity designed to bring psychological satisfaction or a feeling of emotional well-being. Prayer is presence before God. As the participants explained:

I am a strong believer; when I need help, I pray.

God talks to us through his word, and we talk to him through prayer.

Prayer helps me accept things; then I can live with them better.

But what kind of God do these Christians pray to?

God as Present

One thing these Christians know about God is that God walks among them. God is a God who intervenes in life. God is close. God helps them make daily decisions. And God guides individual lives. In the 20th century, in the face of science technology, these Christians are not autonomous and they are not alone.

Eighty-eight percent of the sample believe in prayers of supplication. Furthermore, the fact that God knows what every person needs does not make prayer unnecessary, they say. As one interviewee put it, "God expects us to pray." And apparently the relationship is real. These people feel "close to God" either "frequently" (47%) or "always" (33%), and they feel just as strongly (83%) that God takes an active part in the direction and decision-making of their lives. The field study discovered, too, that Christians, especially conservative activist Christians, organize group "prayer chains" to support in prayer any legislative issues of concern to them and to "uphold Christian legislators in prayer" so they can work more effectively. One group the observers studied is designed so they can report with precision the results of their prayers. The field study reported:

Chain members, in a sense, "keep books on the Lord." They receive only two to three prayer requests per day, which are kept simply, specifically, and shortly worded so that each person on the chain can write them down, word for word, and then accurately pass them on to the next chain member. The coordinator of the prayer chain then follows what happens concerning the focus of their prayer requests and reports back to the chain captains what occurs. The captains then pass this on to their chain members, and everyone on the chain then also records how the Lord has answered their prayers.

For these Christians, God is not dead. On the contrary, God has entered human history in person.

God as Person

To 80% of these Christians God is real most of all as Jesus, God the Son. It is to Jesus that they pray most, and faith in Jesus as God the Son is nearly universal (97%). Only 2% of the participants describe Jesus as "the greatest prophet and teacher in history but not God the Son," or simply as one among the great teachers in history, data which though impressive or at least to be expected from active Christians may nevertheless be at variance with some of their other responses on the nature of the church. Though they believe that Jesus is actually the Son of God, a considerable number do not seem to relate the resurrection of Christ to the meaningfulness of the faith. A number (25%) are inclined to think, and others (18%) are certain, that the resurrection of Christ has little or nothing to do with the relevance of Christian teaching for them. Yet it is the dogma of the resurrection on which the entire credibility of Christianity rests. For people who claim to want and to have a personal relationship with Jesus, the resurrection seems a great deal less important to their appropriation of Christian teaching than may be rightly expected from a group who claim to be convinced of the divinity of Christ.

Less general but also strong (73%) is their relationship to God as Father, though many (63%) say that God simply as "God" or the "Holy Spirit" are equally important images in their prayer life. It is the Trinity, or one of its Persons, to whom Christians now most relate in prayer. These Christians do not turn for divine help to Mary the Mother of God or to the historical saints of the Christian community. Their God evidently is not a God who must be approached through intermediaries, who is so distant from the lives of these people that only through others whose worthiness has already been tested and confirmed can the distance be bridged. On the contrary, almost this entire Christian community (97%) believes that their growth in prayer life and spirituality depends upon the active presence of the Holy Spirit in them personally. Spirituality, it seems, is a very personal thing.

The Bible as Authority and Gospel

The participants' attitudes toward prayer showed that people talk to God. The question then became: do people think that God talks to them? And the answer to that question was equally clear. Almost every respondent (95%) said that the Bible is in some authoritative sense the Word of God and that this is a necessary belief for all Christians. It was not surprising, then, to find that a large portion of the Christian community (77%) felt strongly that reading the Bible is important for the development of their spiritual lives. Almost all the respondents (92%) credited the reading of the Bible as having at least some importance for their spirituality. Even 59% of the Roman Catholics, for whom Bible study has not been the focus of spiritual formation, were convinced that the Bible is essential to their personal spiritual development. However, that general endorsement of the Bible as integral to the spiritual life of the individual is more complex than it appears at face value. Though most of the participants say they read the Bible, they definitely do not all read it from the same perspective. Several interviewees articulated the different approaches with clarity.

One respondent felt that the meanings or messages of the Bible changed from situation to situation:

The Bible is the Word of God. It's how he wants us to live our everyday lives. . . . [But] I think you could have ten people read passages out of the Bible, and everybody would have a different impression of that particular passage. Sometimes I think it would be what mood you are in, as to how you would take it, also.

Another, a Lutheran minister, spoke of the Bible as a book of past experiences of God:

I think the Bible is a collection of revelations of people who have had a religious experience and recorded it. And there probably has been intervention by God, to see that these are collected, and that they have been an inspiration. Especially the coming of Christ.

Another minister was both literal and historical in his interpretation. He accepts every part of the Bible as factual:

I guess I believe in a very literal interpretation of Scripture. What I mean is simply this: Jesus speaks, to us today, throughout the Bible. Even though many of the events in the Scripture took place at the turn of time, human nature is basically the same today. And when he speaks, he speaks very literally and tells us what applies to people of all ages. . . . I believe that the world was created in a short period of time according to Genesis. In my opinion, everything was perfect, just the way God wanted it to be [when it was created]. I suppose some trees were growing and some trees had grown. . . . I have done quite a bit of study on evolution and creation. I have also taken courses like emergency medical technician courses, first aid courses, and so on. And the more I study these, and the more I study the human body, the more I realize that this body just couldn't happen. It had to be created, [so] that we'd have all the essential organs.

But he also accepts the idea that the Bible was written in one age and is being read in another. He went on:

I think you have to take everything into consideration [when interpreting the Bible]. I don't believe that we can interpret the Scripture just one way. I think Jesus has to speak to the 20th century, not the first century.

Consequently, though the acceptance of the Bible as Word of God is an incontrovertible element of the Christian tradition, its content and character are obviously subject to many interpretations. Forty-one percent of the respondents surveyed believe that in the Bible "people report verbally what God said and that the Bible in the original text contained no errors."

In the field research the observers identified groups who were engaged in certain public activities precisely because they believed that God had established the family unit and laid out definite guidelines in the Bible for its development. One organization they studied exists to mobilize people to resist public legislation which would destroy the family as it is described in Scripture. But many other Christians do not take the position that family life, or indeed any other facet of society as we know it, is so clearly mandated in Scripture. The remaining participants, who account for the larger part of the responses, believe either that the original text of the Scripture may have been eroded through mistranslations and copy errors (29%) or that, though the Bible communicates the Word of God, God spoke through fallible people and therefore the Bible contains errors because of the human element, and must be judged by reason (25%). A few Christian church members (4%) even see the Bible simply as a record of early moral and religious progress, a work that contains much wisdom from great human beings but which does not necessarily have a divine element.

Two problems arise out of this data. In the first place, the way the Bible is used will certainly depend on the way the Bible is defined. Those who see it as the verbatim Word of God will surely respond to questions of science or social norms differently from those who consider it a culturally conditioned guide to wisdom and righteousness. Secondly, though a large proportion of the people studied (75%) believe that the gospel of Christ is necessary for the salvation of all people, it is unclear what that implies. It may mean that to be saved, all people must accept the Christian Scriptures in order to know God. Or, the respondents may mean simply that the birth of Christ was necessary to the salvation of the world. Or, they may mean that Christian values are essential for the sanctification of the world, but not necessarily membership in a Christian church. The different postures dictate different world views and may be as essential to world development as they are to an understanding of world religions.

One interviewee explained the distinctions and found a dramatic rendition of the essentials of salvation more meaningful than educated accuracy in the Christian Scripture. He said:

As far as my religion is concerned, like I said, I have thrown out a lot of picky detail—things that are not, to my way of thinking, important to whether or not you are going to be saved. You're not going to be standing up there and they're going to say, "Quick, heaven or hell, when was Moses born?" They're not going to look at that. I don't know if you watched the Johnny Cash Special, but he had a Christmas poem on there that really said a lot. The sum and substance of the poem was that God had promised this innkeeper that he was going to visit him on Christmas Day. And at the end of the day, the innkeeper was lying in bed and praying, and he said, "Why did you let me down?" and God said, "But I did come. Three times I came to your door. Once in the form of a lost girl, once in the form of a traveling woman, once in the form of a salesman. And three times you let them in and showed them kindness." And I was crying here, I thought it was so nice. And that's the sum and substance of my beliefs. It's not what you believe about God, or what I believe, it's what comes from the heart. And that's why I think that the people who come from the backward countries and haven't heard about God are not going to be condemned. Because like I said earlier, the God I believe in would not do that. If you are basically a good person, and you are basically kind to people or put your best foot forward to do your best, without any thoughts of self gain, it doesn't matter which church or how you were taught about God. . . . You're choosing to lead a Christian life, a good life. And that's what I see.

Whatever their individual postures, however, there is no doubt that given the reliance on Scripture that these Christians reflect, it is their understanding of the nature of Scripture that is both a measure and a characteristic of their spiritual and personal attitudes, a clue to the way they deal with the world around them.

Community

In general, then, these Christians believe that God is present in time and that their lives are marked and managed by a divine love and will, that prayer and Scripture link the mind of God and the matter of life, and that the Christian message is determinative for the salvation of the world. Most of them recognize also the workings of God through the circumstances of their own lives and the lives of others.

Consequently, perhaps, their sense of personal accountability is high. They are strong in their conviction (92%) that a person's spiritual development requires an awareness of personal sin. God does not become present to people who are broken by sin, divided within themselves. The responses imply that spiritual development—coming to know God—depends on the decision either to concentrate on God or to concentrate on self.

At the same time, slightly over half (52%) have come to a greater consciousness of the dignity of all people as children of God because of the struggles of disadvantaged groups for their rights, by secular as well as by religious experiences. Their own spiritual awareness has been raised by a new sense of God in others—at least in theory. Although only slightly more than half say they agree or strongly agree that the liberation movements of other groups have had a positive effect on their own spiritual growth, another part of the population (30%) agreed, at least slightly, that the struggles of oppressed groups had had spiritual meaning in their own lives. In other words, a high majority (82%) say that the liberation movements of this period have given some new insight into their theology of equality. Yet when actual groups were named, these same Christians reported considerably less spiritual effects. The black power movement, for instance, touched 70% of the group; the women's struggle for equality of opportunity, less than half (49%). Whether the responses reflect a lack of personal involvement with either issue or a rejection of an issue is unclear. But the fact remains that the communal dimension of the spiritual life does not seem to come alive in either of the two great liberation movements in the United States, though the theory of God-in-others is a defined part of the spiritual experience of these people and social movements are given credit for the illumination of certain spiritual truths in their lives.

But faith is not a private affair in the lives of these Christians. Almost two-thirds of the group (63%) maintain that it is common for them to discuss their spiritual life with others. In the personal interviews we discovered that for some this is one of the values of prayer groups; for others, spiritual discussions are most common at the time of a retreat; still others are most comfortable broaching this subject with their wives or husbands. Whatever the situation, people from every denomination feel the need to share their faith with other members of the Christian community in order to strengthen it.

The group seemed to recognize, too, that personal spiritual development depends to some extent on being responsible to the entire human community. Seventy-two percent reject the premise that Christianity encourages people to attain as much material affluence as they can, so long as their methods are honorable. Things are not the end or the measure of the Christian life, nor is unbridled personal gain compatible with the Christian theology of community. In the Christian vision of these people everything is an avenue to God, at least theoretically. Withdrawal, passivity, privatism, insignificance, and helplessness are not the characteristics of their spiritual experience. Their faith dictates that the goodness of God is in everyone and everything, and, in their opinion, they have access to it. This accessibility to God through everything that has been created is, in fact, of the essence of Christianity for them.

But one thing is not essential to the faith life of churchgoing Christians, and that is going to church.

Church

One of the functions of this study was to determine, at least broadly, how church members feel about some of the most central questions of life and faith. It was only natural, then, to explore the elements of spiritual development and even more natural to pursue the effect of church on their genesis. What was less obvious was the opinion of church members about the relation of one to the other.

Most critical to the issue is the fact that these people say they do go to church. Half of them report that they go at least once a week. Another third of the population attend some church function more often than that. Almost half (49%) said that they also watch religious programs on TV at least twice a month. These are not people who describe the value of the church without going to any. Furthermore, these are people who show a strong belief in the church as an institution: "The world would be much different without churches from what it has been with them," they agree (92%). But, though church as church is important to them, only half are firmly convinced that having a good relationship with God requires their belonging to a parish or local congregation. What is more, though almost half (46%) feel that their church is the "true church of Christ," they apparently do not consider having Christian faith and belonging to a church the same thing. The figure is both significant and consistent.

In another part of the study the group was asked why they belong to a church: for worship, for fellowship, for moral guidance, because they see the church as "the body of Christ"? The greater number (59%) said that they valued church as an incorporation into Christ, not primarily as an instrument for worship or direction or social support. But if this is true, then church as "people of God" and church as institution may not be identical concepts in the minds of these Christians. Only 31% of the respondents, in fact, accept all of the teachings of the church as essential to their faith and 67% said they see no reason why they can't reject some church teaching and continue to have a deep Christian faith.

One woman said quite directly that she has come to the point where she judges the teaching of the church by her own standards:

I feel that in religious training, as in any other thing, you are taught the basics. From those basics then, you sort out what you want or pick it apart as you see fit.

A Catholic man indicated that even though he accepts the centrality of the pope, he does not accept what the pope says without reflection, discussion, and the authority of his own experience:

We read the pope's comments on certain things, and we discuss those. We don't always agree with what he says, but he still is the leader of the church, and I believe we should follow him. We do discuss that and things that are going on in our church, quite often.

Denominational Differences

Some of the churches show stronger strains of these elements of spirituality than others. Among the Christians in Minnesota who participated in this research, for instance, Roman Catholic (56%) and Baptist (66%) respondents were more likely than members of other denominations to attend worship services more than four times a month. It was Catholics, too (60%), who most felt that belonging to a parish is essential to the development of a good relationship with God, and Catholics (48%) who, more than any other denomination except the Episcopalians (51%), were most divided about whether or not the traditional prayers of the church are the best form of prayer.

On the other hand, it was Baptists (71%) and Evangelical Covenant Christians (79%) who say most often that it is common for them to discuss their spiritual life with others, and UCC members (60%) who apparently talk least about the spiritual dimension of their lives. Almost all the Baptist respondents (97%) in the study believe strongly that the gospel of Christ is necessary for the salvation of all people, while far fewer of the Episcopalians (52%), UCC members (53%), and Roman Catholics (60%) were as firmly committed to the position that eternal salvation depends on conversion to the Christian faith. At the same time, Baptists (63%), Evangelical Covenant (57%), and Lutherans (49%) are most convinced that the Bible is an actual account of the Word of God, which in the original text is without error. But Episcopalians (52%) feel most that though the Bible communicates the Word of God, God spoke through fallible people whose writings we may judge by reason. Only members of the UCC (58%) and Catholic Christians (59%) were less intense than other church members in the study (65%-95%) in their commitment to personal Bible reading. Finally, Roman Catholics (41%) and Lutherans (36%) are most inclined to consider the teaching of their churches as essential to their faith.

Demographic Distinctions

Interestingly enough, clergy were more likely than lay people to regard the Bible as the product of fallible human beings and so subject to critical judgment. At the same time more clergy (66%) than laity

(51%) reported that their own spiritual life had been enriched by the struggles of the disadvantaged groups in society.

Women (83%) more than men (76%) felt that God plays an active part in their lives, and women (53%) were more inclined than men (47%) to rely on the church as necessary to their relationship with God, though the men in the sample attend church as frequently as the women (77%-78%, four or more times per month).

More lower-income (87%) than higher-income (77%) respondents felt that God is actively present in their lives, directing it and guiding them in their decisions. Higher-income respondents (65%), more than lower-income respondents (53%) think that to reject church teaching is not to reject the faith.

It is easy to conclude that it is the powerful and the secure—males and wealthy people—who are least concerned about God. But the Christian churches may do far better to wonder why women and the less affluent are more likely to look to God and to the church for help and to inquire what the answer means for church teaching and the future of the church itself.

But whatever the shades of difference or the varying intensities of commitment, some qualities of the spiritual orientation of these Christians emerged clearly and may characterize the personal spiritual development of church members across the country. If that is indeed the case, then going to church may be a sign that a person's faith is strong, that prayer is common and necessary, that in every denomination the Bible is considered an essential element of the spiritual life, that the Trinity is fundamental to the Christian concept of God, and that church life and faith life are considered distinct.

The overall picture of the spiritual development of contemporary Christianity is a strange medley of individualism and institutionalism, but for people who believe in a personal and present God the integration of these two aspects of the spiritual life may be profound. But if, as the respondents assert in the data, seeing others as children of God and caring for them is an element of faith, then the life concerns which would support that theology are not found in this data. The equation "child-of-God is my equal" does not emerge here. Someone should ask again whether there is really any causality or correlation between Christian claims and egalitarianism. If not, it is not surprising that when the Christian community gets down to the specifics of supporting black power or women's rights gaps occur between what they define to be the Christian message and what they see as imperative to its presence. If so, then being Christian should have more to do with social issues than many of the responses seem to assert. The churches may need to assess how clear they have been or should be in linking the spiritual life to secular life.

6

Out of the Depths
I Cry to You, O Lord
Sin, Guilt, and Compassion

In the late 1960s, educational journals across the country carried the cartoon of a long-haired, unkempt, obviously belligerent youngster in a principal's office. The caption read, "And furthermore, you can't do a thing to me because it's not my fault: my father drank, and my ol' lady worked; we didn't have any money, and my first grade teacher never taught me how to read." Behind the cartoon lay years of speculation about the influence of environmental factors on the development of personality, a deep-seated suspicion about the nature and effects of guilt, a rising consciousness of the consequences of class differences, an almost universal rejection of the residue of the Victorian era, and a serious confusion of the moral, the immoral, and the amoral in ethical standards.

Pop psychology taught people how to "pull their own strings," how to get over guilt, how to take charge of their own lives. Some people asked, "Whatever happened to conscience?" A few even talked about "sin." But so many old rules had failed in the face of new situations—the genetics of racism, the corruption of authority, the indiscriminate or unlimited destruction of life through war—that the questions of what sin was and if sin was were simply reflected in other cultural shifts. People began to talk about "guilt feelings" instead of guilt, of social sin

as opposed to individual sin, of freedoms and unfreedoms. People began to make distinctions between what was legal and what was moral
in life, between what was a social or human right and so a matter of
individual conscience—like abortion or homosexuality—and what were
things intrinsically evil and to be outlawed at every level in every
institution.

The Christian community found itself at odds with its own tradition
in the new moral debate. This tradition has a clear perception of both
the personal and the collective character of sin, but different historical
epochs or different groups of believers had heightened or emphasized
one or the other aspects of responsibility. Individualism and its impact
on moral theology had come late to the scene. The early Christian community knew from the biblical tradition that sin was a community
matter. In the Judaic tradition sin was collective; justice was collective;
salvation was collective. But they also knew from the prophets that
there was such a thing as personal responsibility. When the New Testament talked about the search for a single sheep which had strayed, or
the father of the prodigal son waiting for the return of the one child
who had sinned against him, or the invitation to Peter to make a personal commitment, it recognized the continuation of the traditional
call to individuals within a community. So both the woman who had
sinned against the community by committing adultery and her accusers
with their more private faults are seen equally as sinners. With the rise
of individualism in Western culture, however, the person's private relationship with God grew in importance, often at the expense of social
consciousness. Clearly, the Christian tradition is threaded through with
questions of personal problems of conscience and covenant.

Given the pressure of the culture and the tension in the tradition
itself, it is essential to reexamine the place of sin, guilt, and compassion
in Christian communities today. Is sin a thing of the past? Has psychology replaced the idea of evil with the nostrum of neurosis? Is the
psychology of perfectionism the center of Christian faith? The responses of the participants in this study reveal the difficulty of the topic.

Human Nature

Any discussion of how people regard sin must certainly involve a
discussion of how people regard human nature. If human beings are
perfect, sin is impossible. If human nature is essentially weak, then

perfection is impossible. We ask in the spirit of the psalmist, "What
are we, O God, that you should take note of us?" (Ps. 8:5). For Minnesota Christians in this century, human nature is not a static thing, it
seems. Human nature is finite; it is part of creation and dies. But the human also transcends the finite and stretches for the infinite, developing
the natural and hoping to contact God. The human lives in hope of perfectability and, many say, Scripture confirms that hope. Three-fourths
of the respondents (51% clearly, 24% slightly) believe that if Christian
principles were applied to international affairs war could be eliminated; or, in other areas, that better social conditions are possible, that
justice can be achieved, that people can control their lives. In one
person's words:

Through education, self-understanding, and communication, we are becoming freed of those forces in our lives which cause us to do evil. . . . Human
nature is good. For the next million years, I see a continual process toward
growing into the presence of God.

But utopia is not the Christian expectation, even of church members.
It is definitely understandable, even excusable, to 45% of the study
population that Christians do wrong things. Less than a fifth of the
group (18%) are unprepared to accept moral failure from Christians,
but most assume that people can strive but fail. The question is why.

One explanation for human weakness is roundly dismissed by 83%
of the participants. In the minds of these Christians, human nature is
not totally depraved. In fact, some (28%) strongly believe that "humans are inherently good, and unless they are brutalized by savagery
will strive toward what is good."

But there are other explanations for the presence of evil in the world,
and they each carry weight in these Christian communities. One supposition is that evil is the result of social circumstances; the other, that
evil is the product of Satan.

Satan, Circumstances, and Sin

Almost every person who responded to the survey form (98%)
acknowledged that personal spiritual development requires an awareness of personal sin. But there clarity ends. Only 57% of the population
consider themselves, without reservation, to be sinful or believe that
it is of the essence of the Christian faith to believe that all people are

sinful. What is more, these Christians are almost equally divided as a group about whether or not external circumstances or an innate human tendency accounts for the evil that people find in themselves or in life. These people seem to be saying: "I believe in sin, and so I recognize that if I want to develop a deep spiritual life I must first recognize what needs to be righted or reoriented in my life, but the fact is that I don't feel that anything is that much out of kilter. In fact, I think that human nature is not sinful by nature. And if sin does exist, it is something outside of me—Satan or social circumstances—that accounts for it, and not the human condition itself."

In the field research a different voice was heard. These researchers came to realize that conservative Christian activists, who are often thought to be disinterested in the kinds of social service projects that are commonly associated with churches, do indeed provide aid for the afflicted and unfortunate. These conservative Christian activists do not attempt to deal through social services with problems seen by them to be self-induced. Situations which derive from alcohol or drug abuse, from inappropriate or excessive sexual behavior, from violence are, they say, a result of sin and thus need to be dealt with primarily in spiritual ways, by emphasizing personal salvation and individual transformation. The field research team was told: "If it weren't for sin, for disobedience to God, we could practically close down our welfare offices." Given this explanation, it becomes clear why conservative churches are often thought of as "other worldly" and as not dealing with the current societal issues.

The overall confusion about the nature of sin is as apparent as the sense of perfectability and seems to indicate that though people recognize that life is not perfect, they do not feel trapped by its dark side or necessarily responsible for it. People groped to explain to the interviewer how they account for evil, and the range of their explanations reflected what is apparently a general lack of consensus.

One woman perceived three sources of evil:

There are a couple of sources of evil. I think there is a supernatural evil. I believe that Satan exists as an individual personality. I believe that there are fallen angels that tempt and cause a certain amount of evil activity. I think man, however, is capable of an enormous amount of moral evil without any help from the devil. . . . Man is perfectly capable of making choices that are essentially informed, consenting, malicious choices. And so a lot of evil follows from that. I think there is a certain amount of evil that people experience because of the fall of man, in some way distorting the beauty of creation itself—Paul talks about creation groaning, awaiting the revelation of the sons of light—and we experience a certain amount of that in natural disaster kind of things.

There are three sources of evil in this person's mind: Satan, free will, and original sin. Not everyone talked about all three, but every one of the church members who discussed the issue in personal interviews related evil to one or the other source.

For the greater majority of the Christians who participated in the survey, Satan, who exists either as a personal being (29%) or as an evil force (59%), is almost universally accepted as part of the problem of evil. Satan is real, and Satan does evil, these people say.

But the belief that God allows people to choose evil rather than good in matters of moral choice is seen as another source of destructive behavior according to church members in Minnesota. One man said flatly:

I think most of the evil in our time doesn't necessarily come from external force. I think most of the evil comes out of people's greed and people's decisions.

For another, the personification of evil is the direct result of human choice; the two factors are not separate sources of evil but each is generated by the other:

There are spiritual personalities who have evil traits or attitudes. They live; they influence us; in some cases they can exert physical stress on human beings. They have, in some cases, the power of death. I know that because the Bible teaches that. It teaches that the personification of evil, the devil, is a personality. He is a powerful being who exerts influence over nations and national trends. He is the one who would like to be preeminent on earth. Jesus said that he is a murderer. We have the idea that the devil and his minions are funny little poltergeists who run around and play tricks on people. But that is not true. The truth of the matter is that he is a murderer, and Jesus said that he was a murderer from the beginning. He is a liar. . . . And evil, in my understanding, is an attitude that was born of the permission for people to make up their own minds, the choice of the beings that were at the beginning of time.

Original sin also plays a part in the existence of evil for others in the study. For some, original sin is understood as a kind of fundamental option for evil; for others, it is a blight on human perception that apparently weakens the human's ability to choose the good:

[I do not believe in Satan.] Evil comes from a lack of understanding. We
have a limited perspective. We are making big choices with very short-
sightedness.

These Christians have differing ideas about what sin is and what
causes sin. Almost half of the survey participants (46%) believe, at least
to some degree, that the circumstances of a situation shape people's
responses; the other half (54%) believe that humans have an innate
tendency toward sin. But on one thing they almost all agree: there is
such a thing as evil. Some think they inherited it from the first man
and woman and "became all dead in trespasses and sin; just basically
evil." Others believe that evil happens when people "veer from the
plan." Still others believe that evil "is an intellectual distortion." Most
prominently, however, their own sense of personal sin is limited. Fifty-
six percent see themselves without question as sinners. Over one-third
of the respondents felt (24% sure, another 11% slightly) that they "fall
short and make many mistakes but are not sinful." One participant
expressed the widespread sense of weakness without guilt:

The day I die I should only have to look up at my Maker and say, "Take
me." Not, "Forgive me." I'm not saying that I am perfect . . . but I have led
a life that I don't have to be ashamed of.

It is not clear whether the issue is what Christians today mean by
"sin" or the fact that as church members they consider themselves to
be in favor with God. What is basically clear, however, is that though
evil is a conscious part of their Christian formation and sin an acknowledged part of life, the idea of human sinfulness is in question for a significant portion of the group. When asked in conversation what sin is,
a woman traced what may be the underlying tension of the whole discussion:

[What is sin?] Well, I feel that waste, when somebody needs something, is
sin. That is one thing. There are a lot of different kinds [of sin]. Some things
that are sin to me, aren't sin to you. This is what being born again is, I
guess, and having Christ in your heart. It doesn't always mean the same
thing to you. Something can be wrong for me, but it's not for you. And I
can't say you are wrong because you are doing it.

Perhaps this very uncertainty about what sin is explains why these
participants respond the way they do to the subject of guilt.

Being Guilty and Feeling Guilty

The fact that the nature of sin is unclear in churches today is verified by the fact that the respondents make distinctions about guilt, too. As one interviewee put it: "There are two kinds of guilt, rational guilt and irrational guilt." And judging from the survey material a considerable number of people feel the same way. More than half of them (57%) distinguish between guilt and guilty feelings.

The response implies that whatever their concern about sin and evil, many Christians distinguish between a person's real failure to meet their own best standards or authentic possibilities and a pervasive feeling of "wrongness" that derives from an unconscious and ungrounded sense of inadequacy. One is specific; the other vague and free-floating. One has something to do with an objective conception of morality; the other with a sense of remote social demands or undefined expectations. One has to do primarily with religion, with the notion that God has expectations that humans are designed to fulfill; the other, with social or psychological development, with responses to expectations that are not universal or of the essence of God's standards for personal salvation but often confused with them. And though one of these factors may certainly impinge on the other (religion may effect personal development and personal development may effect an individual's ability to practice religion), one is not a substitute for the other, at least in the minds of these respondents. They see real guilt to be outside the realm of the therapeutic process and distinct from it. Guilt, they say (70%), need not always be handled by psychological therapy. There is, in fact, great uncertainty about whether or not psychological therapy can best handle guilt. Some (22%) are convinced that, when necessary, guilt is definitely best handled in the psychological arena. Another 39% disagree with that idea. The rest of the group (39%) either agree slightly, or they disagree slightly. In short, almost 40% are not firmly convinced of their position. The array of attitudes suggests that the Christian community may not yet have come to terms with the nature of guilt, any more than with the concept of sin.

Whichever position they may take on the relationship of moral guilt to the findings of psychology, there is a prevailing attitude that guilt is not always an indicator of fault. According to this attitude, real guilt is apparently both other than feeling and more than feeling. Guilt is not simply a mental disease. Without doubt, some guilt may be neurotic and devoid of moral meaning; that a person feels guilty is not necessarily a sign of genuine moral failure, the answer implies. On the other hand, the answer suggests that some things are intrinsically wrong and to be repented of. There is such a thing as valid guilt. Imbalance of appetites, or a failure to achieve full potential, or alienation from the best self is possible. Humans have potential for good or evil.

More important, perhaps, is the strong possibility that underlying all of these responses is the fact that large numbers of people simply do not know whether their moral world is made up of absolutes or of calls to make judgments in individual cases. They do not know whether guilt follows sin or follows cultural conditioning, or both. One respondent said: "Too often guilt is a superficial, cultural position," but then went on to say:

> But somewhere in all of that again is the divine plan that says when you understand the way things should be, and you choose to veer away from that plan, then you're going to be conscious of that and feel remorse.

But whatever "the way things should be" or how people feel when they have strayed from it, one thing these Christians are more likely to agree on is that none of us should deal unforgivingly with others.

Compassion

People who believe that human nature is not totally depraved, as 83% of the Christians of Minnesota do, might also be expected to believe, therefore, that good Christians should be perfect. As a matter of fact, that is not the attitude of most of the participants in this study, but there is an essential tension in the data.

In the first place 88% of the sample credit Jesus with having a compassionate understanding of the moral failures of his followers. In other words, Jesus—the Christian model and living sign of the mind of God—accepted human weakness, understood human failure, was patient with human efforts. It seems, then, that compassion must be at the center of the Christian character. The problem is that only 45% of the church members asked agree that it is excusable for Christians to do wrong things. The rest (55%) expect of one another a great deal more than Jesus did, it seems. A third (33%) of the Christian population sampled here are more or less inclined to think that there is no excuse for Christians who stray. Sin is apparently something Jesus can deal with, but which many people cannot. Whether a response like this reflects an excessive expectation of righteousness or an insightful respect for grace is unknown. What is sure is that this contemporary attitude toward sin and failure seems to be unlike what these same church members say is the attitude of Jesus, their model.

The ambiguity of this interpretation arises from the fact that the group makes a distinction between whether there is any excuse for failure in Christians and whether there should at the same time be a tolerance or understanding of it. The responses show a division on the subject of whether or not the faults of Christians are excusable, but they agree (83%) that Christians should not be very impatient with the moral failures of other human beings. What is meant by all of this? Do these Christians expect so much commitment and perfection in the Christian community that sin is unacceptable there, but yet do not expect either the same virtue or the same divine help for non-Christian people? Or are they simply saying that though there may be no excuse for moral turpitude in the Christian, nevertheless, Christian virtue calls us to be patient with the moral digressions of others, whoever they happen to be. This last meaning emerged poignantly in one of the interviews. A devout woman recalled her own sense of grace in life:

I think the time I realized or felt touched by grace was when I was nursing and I took care of a patient who had had an illegal abortion. And she came in with septicemia, total infection, and we did not know this. . . . She hadn't urinated, so I catheterized her one day, and just got total blood. Just all blood. And it turned out that her husband had been an accomplice to this—they were thinking about getting a divorce—and she finally died, about two days later. And during that interim time, her husband was brought up to see her with the police, because he had been taken into custody in case she did die. And I think they had a two-year-old child. And my heart just ached for those people, and at that point I couldn't sit in judgment on that situation at all. I think in terms of my own background, and what might have been, that I escaped from that. And I really thought that but for the grace of God there am I.

But perhaps the greatest proof that compassion, like the concepts of sin and guilt, is actually a cluster of connotations around a common theme in the Christian community rather than a clarified centerpiece of the faith is the fact that only 67% of the population could agree with conviction that it is also excusable for ministers or priests to do wrong things. If we knew whether the clergy, either by genuine commitment or by rigid self-presentation, have fostered an aura of sinlessness or whether the people in the pews refuse to expect less than perfection in their pastors, we might possibly know even more about the concept of sin and sinlessness in the Christian churches, about where it comes from and why.

Why Avoid Sin?

Whether a thing is objectively evil or not has a great deal to do with the nature of sin and the validity of guilt, but it is not the only measure of morality. Why people do a thing may certainly be as important in the long run as the behavior itself. "To do the right thing for the wrong reason is the worst treason," Alexander Pope said. Christ said: "The scribes and the Pharisees have succeeded Moses as teachers; therefore, do everything and observe everything they tell you. But do not follow their example. . . . All their works are performed to be seen" (Matt. 23:2-5), and "Blessed are the pure of heart" (Matt. 5:8). Motives, it seems, count.

Consequently, there are four dimensions to the question of sin: what it is, what it means, how it is to be regarded in others, and on what basis it is to be avoided. The final question is why these Christians—who do not consider themselves immoral or alienated from God—attempt to remain that way. What most motivates the contemporary Christian's moral choices? Fear? Reward? The social order? Personal integrity? What moves today's Christian conscience to control impulsive behavior and forego total self-centeredness, however that is defined? The survey results show a degree of independence in persons that might give lawgivers reason to think.

Anarchy is not a Christian virtue in Minnesota. On the contrary, study participants from every denomination agree in great numbers (82%) that it is generally part of Christian moral duty to obey the laws of the country. But having said that, they immediately begin to qualify their positions so that it becomes clear that if anarchy is no ideal for them, neither is authoritarianism. Only 20% of those surveyed accept the proposition that they have a moral obligation to obey a superior at all times. For these people, between the Christian and the law stands conscience.

Some of the people interviewed have thought through the problem of conscience and law and were able to express it clearly:

I'll tell you what else I do. I go in the spring, and I take enough fish to last me all summer, one time. That's a hell of a lot over the limit, but I don't take any fish all summer. I catch fish and throw them back. I go up there and enjoy it. But I have enough to feed my family. I don't give it to all my relatives. If they want to get it, they can do it. I'm not a fish factory. . . . That's what I consider prudent use. Since I am living here, I might as well get some of the benefits out of it. . . . Someday when I come home with a $50 citation for taking my snowmobile on the lake this weekend, maybe, they're going to say, "Well, Dad, isn't that wrong?" And I am going to say yes. And I'm going to tell them why it is wrong. Because a law was made. But I am also going to tell them that we have to follow laws; we have to have a degree of moral servitude towards the laws. But laws are wrong, and if you can sit down and really feel that something is wrong, then if you do it, you do it at your own expense.

For these people, law and conscience simply do not equate. Well over half of the respondents (58%) are firm in their opinion that no law is a substitute for personal conscience. To look at the same responses another way: very few of these Minnesota Christians (15%) disagreed completely with the idea that conscience is a higher guide than law. One person struggled to say why law, in itself, is an inferior source of moral principle:

You really have to come to grips with this: if a nation or a state makes a law that has nothing to do with morals, do we have to obey that? . . . From the law-enforcement angle, I would have a difficult time giving anyone a ticket going into a closed area with a snowmobile, as long as they were careful. I think that is a continuing controversy. And the use of only small motors, and after 1982, no motors [isn't right]. What do you do with a handicapped person? What do you do with an older person?

For these people law is not the definer of morality. At most it may be a carrier of order whose own quality must be continually evaluated and which Christians may be actually obligated to disobey in some circumstances.

What may be even more revealing in the long run is the fact that these people not only believe that conscience is above the laws of society, but they are also certain that conscience ranks above the laws of the church. Almost half of this group of church members (48%) said without qualification that sometimes they must obey their consciences rather than the teachings of their church or denomination. And if that weren't enough, they confirmed this understanding of the primacy of conscience over church in another way. Over half did not agree that people have the right to ignore or disobey the laws of the country (52%) or to withhold taxes (63%) on the basis of their religious beliefs. Perhaps they were asserting the separation of church and state, or perhaps they were attempting to declare the social order safe from the unscrupulous use of religion. At the same time, when they were asked whether they believed that people have the right to ignore or disobey church laws on the basis of their Christian beliefs, less than one-third (31%) were convinced that this was also wrong. Almost a quarter of the group (24%) agreed firmly that individual conviction supersedes church law. Another group (27%) at least tended to think that church laws and Christian beliefs may not be the same and, in that case, the rules of the church are to be ignored. A woman explained what seems to have been the thinking followed by many:

Even though the church's teaching was that birth control was wrong, I feel that if there are circumstances for the individual, he had a right to choose. I still say, objectively, birth control is by the church's standard, not the thing, but subjectively, an individual could [practice it], if he felt it was good.

What all of this portends for either the influence of government or church in the future is an important question for systems theorists or observers of institutional change and development. More than that, it is certainly a crucial question for theologians and professional ministers. Someone must ask why so many people think that their consciences must diverge from the church. What is going on, either in the people or in the churches, that leaves people with a sense of moral distance from the church? Has it always been this way? Should it be this way? How does this attitude affect the formation of conscience? Who or what forms conscience, if the church does not? And if the church is losing influence in the area of conscience formation or ethical definition, why is it losing influence? A lack of faith among the people? Social permissiveness? Cultural change? A lowering of moral standards? Hypocrisy in the church? Or the emergence of a more basic sense of Christianity than the institutional church provides?

Also evident in the data is the fact that punishment and reward are not considered high enough motives for doing good. Only a minority (13%) of the churchgoers studied were willing to argue that the primary reason for doing good is to get to heaven. And, less than one-third (31%) were firm in their position that Christians should obey God's law because after death God will punish those who have failed to do so. But the response pattern bears more scrutiny than that. Though it is true that few agreed strongly with either of those positions, if the number of those who agreed slightly with one or the other position is added, the picture changes significantly. More people (14%) were willing to "agree slightly" that the fear of punishment moved them to do good than were inclined to agree even a little (11%) that getting to heaven was their chief motive for doing good. If these figures are combined, then over half of the Christian population apparently links moral choice to punishment. Whether getting to heaven is interpreted as selfish but avoiding hell is considered essential to salvation cannot be determined, but the difference of response to two items that are apparently interrelated is perhaps a manifestation of the emphasis on the judgment rather than the love of God, a concept that could itself bear theological scrutiny.

But if morality is not simply an insurance policy for most Minnesota Christians, it is not considered a vending machine either. People are divided over whether to believe that if they live as good Christians, God will bless them with good things in this life. The largest cluster (33%) disagrees with that idea entirely. Morality, it seems, is something that is to be done for its own sake.

Consistent with all of this data is the fact that so many of the respondents (43%) say they would rather go to jail than violate their consciences on matters of equality, human dignity, and love. Internal standards and a sense of personal responsibility, not law, account for the moral principles of a considerable portion of the Christian community in this sample. The role of the church in mediating salvation is contested. Almost half (48%) say that sometimes they must obey their consciences rather than the teachings of their churches. Less than a quarter (23%) are of the convinced opinion that in order to avoid eternal punishment church members should do what their church or denomination teaches. Even fewer (15%) say that in order to get to heaven, they must do what their churches tell them to do. These people have a sense, it seems, that salvation is something between them and God, that integrity depends on more than legalism, that law may be neither the beginning nor the end of virtue.

But if that is actually the opinion of the people in the pews, then what is authority? Who has it, and where do they get it? When, if ever, is what the church says absolute? And how do we know?

Denominational Differences

Catholics (70%), more than any other group, believe that a Christian may be obligated to disobey civil authority in some circumstances.

Baptists and Lutherans felt most keenly (70%) their own personal sinfulness and the inherent sinfulness of others. Baptists, too, were far more likely (65%) to consider Satan a personal being than were members of other denominations, who by and large regard Satan as an evil force but not a personal being.

Baptists (84%) and Presbyterians (80%) were alike in their more pronounced rejection of the idea that the primary reason for doing good is to get to heaven. Roman Catholics (29%) were considerably more committed to the idea that achieving heaven is the basis of morality than were the members of any other denomination. UCC members, on the other hand, were more prominent as a group in rejecting punishment after death as a motive for obeying God's law (65%).

Protestant churchgoers in general refused to accept the idea that getting to heaven depends on doing what the church tells them to do. Roman Catholics tend to be more accepting of that position, though less than half (39%) were willing to accept that position without some qualification. No more than 12% of any Protestant group accepted the idea that salvation depends on adhering to church law.

Demographic Distinctions

Men (61%) more than women (52%), saw themselves as sinful and acknowledged an innate tendency toward sin, rather than circumstances, as the basic cause of evil. Perhaps because they are in a better position to see people who suffer from guilt that is without substance, clergy in the study (82%) are more convinced than laity (55%) that guilt and guilty feelings are not the same. At the same time fewer clergy (14%) than laity (23%) accept psychological therapy as the treatment of guilt, even "when necessary." Though not major, the difference may be worth noting if underlying it are two completely unlike attitudes toward guilt. These figures suggest some questions. Do the clergy make more technical judgments about guilt, that if it is real, it is moral and therefore cannot be alleviated by anything except conversion? Do the laity, on the other hand, make a distinction between "being forgiven or reconciled" and the continuing process of human growth?

More laity (34%) than clergy (22%) think that the avoidance of

eternal punishment is an important reason to obey God's laws, an interesting figure if punishment after death is a major facet of the Christian
creed. Have the laity been motivated to do good through punishment,
or do clergy have a different sense of morality or of God than is being
taught in the churches or understood by the people?

More women (63%) than men (52%) were committed to the idea
that no law is a substitute for conscience; more men (30%) than women
(18%) felt that people have a right to disobey the laws of the church
on the basis of personal conscience. These data suggest that there is
need to explore further the differing attitudes of women and men
toward the church.

Salvation, the teaching says, has to do with overcoming sin. The
dictum seems simple enough on the face of it, but there are many complexities underlying that basic Christian assumption. What is sin? Who
defines it? How can it be controlled and overcome? As one woman said,
both surely and tentatively:

What is moral is hard to define. I have told my kids this: you never have to
answer to anyone but God. You know what is right and wrong according to
religion, according to the Bible and the church's teaching, and you will have
to make choices. And if you do wrong, you will have to go to hell for it. It is
hard to say what is moral and immoral, but I think the church teaches it.

7

In Holocausts and Burnt Offerings You Take No Delight, O God

Social Justice

The man is young, a parent, a church member "who would even like to have a Latin mass once in a while." He has clear standards of self-discipline. He believes in hard work, in honesty, in sexual ethics. He knows himself to be a racist and a male chauvinist. He is angry about things which he believes are obstructing his claims to the good life. In describing his social morality, he said:

Why should I start cheating my neighbor and stuff? What the hell good is it? I don't need the money. Money isn't important to me. Status isn't important to me. [But I was taught by someone I really admired], a really moral person: "You be as honest as you can be. You be as straightforward and as loving as you can be. But if anybody ever gets you, you stick them right back. Because that is the way you exist today, and it's going to get worse." And you think about that.

From this point of view, life is all people for themselves. In a world that is getting smaller every day, we must indeed all think about that. A war in the East stops production in the West. Scenes of a famine in Africa are shown on the televisions in American restaurants. Decisions that enhance the corporations of one country imbalance the development of another. If in this environment life becomes a very private thing, then its religions may be simply a collection of household gods.

In both the Old and the New Testaments, however, sin and salvation are social values. The prophets remind Israel that fidelity to God means care for the poor, the proper distribution of wealth, honest dealing with the defenseless, a genuine concern for the whole people of God. In the New Testament, John sends to Jesus the question, "Are you he who is to come, or do we look for another?" (Matt. 11:3). The answer Jesus gives is not "See how orthodox I am," but "See what I have done to enable other people to achieve all the natural blessings of life." The Scripture reads: "Go back and report to John what you hear and see: the blind recover their sight, cripples walk, lepers are cured, the deaf hear, dead men are raised to life, and the poor have the good news preached to them" (Matt. 11:4-5). Over and over again the Scriptures claim that private piety or abstract legalisms are not enough to merit the kingdom of God. What is also expected is that people do something to make the world better for everybody else. But what? And how?

This study set out to discover which of these two ethics—personal security or general social concern—operates most clearly and the consequent implications for society. To do that we examined people's attitudes toward various Scripture texts and the theological positions based on them. We compared their responses on specific social issues to what respondents claimed were the essential dimensions of Christianity. We explored their opinions on the relationship of church to state. The data reflect the struggle of a generation that is trying to come to grips with its own best ideals by making those ideals possible for everyone. The problem is that they are reluctant to give up their own standard of living for the sake of other people's growth. Here theology confronts life.

To call for social justice is often to call for a new order of things, not only for others but also for ourselves. The venture is not without personal risk. The issues at stake in this study are: what kind of risk, if any, do contemporary Christians believe that Christianity demands? What does being a Christian have to do with the lives of others? Is Christianity private or public? Is Christianity to be a manifestation of God's mercy or of God's justice? Does being Christian imply that a person is bent on repairing the wreckage left by the system or of reforming the system when it fails? Does Christianity, in fact, mean any of these things to people? And why?

God of Mercy, God of Justice

The data from this research indicate that whatever their denomination, most Christians share a common understanding of Jesus' life and the Scriptural imperatives that flow from it, for them as individuals or for the church in general. For instance, there is wide acceptance of the idea that churches must be concerned for the poor and oppressed, that churches are to do works of mercy and charity, that the follower of Jesus is to take the side of the poor and oppressed. On the other hand, the acceptance has differences in degree that may be significant.

Almost all respondents (93%) felt strongly that the text "For you always have the poor with you" (Matt. 26:11) does not mean that the churches should neglect the poor and oppressed. On the contrary, most respondents (85%) believe that it is a mission of the church to make God's love present through works of mercy and charity. These people do think the church should be involved in the betterment of life in this world as well as concerned about the life to come. The consensus on the fact that the church must do charity is clear. The consensus on doing justice is less established.

There are not as many church members (76%) who are sure that following Jesus implies taking the side of the poor and oppressed and doing what is possible to secure justice for them as there are those (85%) who are convinced that works of charity are an essential element of the Christian gospel. More seem likely to believe that giving food to the hungry is of the essence of Christianity than would feel that taking a position on food stamp legislation is also required of the committed Christian. The distinction in the data might rest on the fact that one question asks what is required of *the Christian church* and the other concentrates on what is expected of *the follower of Jesus*. But if a line is being drawn between the obligations of the church as institution and the responsibilities of the individual Christian, it could also be asked whether this distinction is legitimate. But then two elements are introduced that clarify what is being said here.

In the first place, the consensus shatters over the item, "True Christianity requires that the poor and oppressed be liberated." Less than half of the group (43%) can be sure of this idea, though another portion of the respondents (30%) are inclined to agree at least slightly with this concept that by implication argues for equality of opportunity and a just distribution of wealth. Nevertheless, given the disparity of these responses, these church members seem to be relatively certain that to be Christian means to do charity, but they are far less sure about whether to be Christian means to do justice.

On the other hand, it is startling to find three-quarters (76%) of the population certain that following Jesus implies taking the side of the poor and doing what is possible to secure systemic justice, and to find almost half (43%) sure that liberation is an essential element of Christianity. The tension may or may not derive directly from the historical posture of the church, but it will certainly affect it.

The speculation is confirmed in another way. Over half of the group (59%) feel that the biblical affirmation, "Jesus is Lord" means that Jesus is master of all of human life, social as well as individual. The others (41%) cannot make that affirmation. From their point of view, it may be difficult to conceive that systems, like people, can be sinful and in need of conversion and reconciliation. One person thought the problem through this way in the interview:

I think the Synod of Bishops' statement, which is a classic that I use in discussing social justice, is that "the efforts on behalf of social justice constitute a constituent element of preaching the gospel." And we should adopt that policy. That is where the Moral Majority's church-state relations and I part company. Those people that reduce Christianity to Jesus' concern for how we are spiritually and no other way, I think essentially bastardize the New Testament, and the Christian message as a whole.

If Christianity cannot be reduced to a concern for individual spirituality, then other facets of life must be examined to determine what church members think they must do to make God's love present.

Attitudes Toward Life

Whatever the theology upon which their works of justice or charity may be based, the absolute value of life is not the keystone of these Christian communities. Euthanasia is permissible to 17% of these respondents. Forty-one percent consider the death penalty to be morally acceptable. In other words, life can be corrupted by evil-doing and by physical or mental deterioration to the point that the rest of society is not required to sustain it. Apparently it is some predetermined quality of life that directs the social judgments of the Christian conscience among the population sampled rather than the inviolability of life itself. Nevertheless, their responses to specific issues are often uneven, like the imbalance between the traditional awareness of charity as a Christian quality and the emerging consciousness of justice as a Christian obligation.

Attitudes Toward Specific Issues

For this population justice seems to have more to do with the particular issue being considered than with a commitment to share the fruits of creation equally or to promote universal human rights. Sixty-eight percent of the group, for instance, is basically firm in its assertion that the church should attend to securing better conditions for the elderly who are poor and discriminated against, but they are not nearly so committed to calls for justice from other segments of society. Less than half of them (49%) are willing to see the church take leadership in other social justice issues such as racism, sexism, and economic concerns. Not even half (48%) completely agree that their church or denomination should make a special effort to help insure that women have equal opportunity and rights with men in all aspects of church life and ministry. Finally, even fewer (40%) are firmly convinced that the church should work to insure the equal opportunity and rights of women in society. Although the trend is in favor of all these issues—another 20%-25% of the population agree in every case at least slightly—that is tendency, not tenacious conviction. In dealing with the question an interviewee explained:

We need to speak out against evil. I was involved here in a protest movement to a certain extent, but I wouldn't let that be the center of my ministry. I think many of the liberals of the church went overboard on social issues, perhaps to the neglect of personal salvation. So I am somewhere in the middle there. I also say that to have nothing to do with it is wrong. To have nothing to do with social issues . . . I think that is wrong. Jesus had both the social and the personal-spiritual. I'm amazed that on either side they can't see that in Jesus, that they would just have one side and not the other. I think they haven't studied Jesus very much. They take one side, or one aspect of his work and ignore the other. I can't understand that.

Attitudes Toward the Social System

The tension over whether or not Christian spirituality is a private or a public matter becomes evident again in the data on the political process and the economic system.

Not quite half (48%) of the church members contacted are sure that Christian faith implies that they should participate in the political process. Or to put the information another way: 27% of these church members are equally sure that to engage in the political structures of the society around them has nothing to do with their obligations as a Christian. This raises questions. Do different churches take different positions on this question? Have the people not internalized whatever the churches are teaching about it? Do the churches teach little or nothing at all on the issue of Christian participation in the public arena, leaving people to intuit their own positions?

The data are clouded even further by the fact that though only some of the respondents in the study (27%) say they most always or usually vote for those political candidates whose policies are endorsed by the church they belong to, a great many more people (73%) say that they consider Christian ethical standards and evaluate the candidate's policies in the light of those when deciding how to cast their votes. In the minds of these people, then, Christianity clearly has something to do with the public domain, whether they discriminate between denominational endorsement and ethical standards or not. Whether it is "anti-American" for churches to endorse candidates is only one part of the question; the other part is whether or not it is "anti-Christian." Our data indicate that for the people who participated in this study there is a great deal more in the social arena for the Christian to be concerned about than the pragmatics of politics.

At the same time, the relationship of Christianity to economics is much less resolved. The subject is serious for a group who live in an affluent society but have been formed in a tradition which says that "it is easier for a camel to pass through a needle's eye than for a rich man to enter the kingdom of God" (Matt. 19:24) or that, to share in eternal life, it is necessary to "sell what you have, and give to the poor" (Mark 10:17-21). But the answer is not yet clear, at least not to the Christian community in this study. What is clear, on the other hand, is that the question is a live one. The responses show that the Christian community presents three different and almost equally accepted positions on the implications of Christian teaching for the economic goals of a society. One segment (30%) says that Christianity implies a commitment on the part of Christians to the economic growth of the United States. Another fraction (27%) maintains that to be Christian commits us to the reduction of the material standard of living of the

United States. The largest part (44%) affirms no position on the matter. The only real meeting of minds on this item is the fact that almost no one (1%) takes the position that Christian teaching mandates a no-growth society.

Two things make the data significant. First, despite a heritage of the so-called Protestant ethic, economic growth is not regarded as a necessary reward for goodness. Secondly, the fact that so many people have no opinion on the matter raises the question whether, for many, Christianity has much to do with the economic goals of society.

The survey results imply that for some the association between faith, spirituality, and world community is real, and we are responsible for it. In the interviews people were very pronounced about the moral implications of wealth in a country that is "very blessed":

You learn [how blessed you are] very quickly when you go overseas. You don't complain about things at home anymore. Then you realize the difference that a Christian heritage makes. I am not saying that America is Christian anymore, but our heritage has made tremendous differences in the freedom of the individual, the value of life, the ability to be educated, to think your own thoughts and determine your own destiny. [But] all those things also have an accountability. [For instance] America with all her resources, ought to feed the rest of the world. Absolutely.

What is more, if the materials from this study have meaning among other church members of the United States, then a number of other people may be thinking the same kinds of things. Here a full one-third (34%) claim and almost another third (31%) tend to agree that Christianity requires a far-reaching change in the use of technology in American society and its economic system. Then they go on to say that in the present time a Christian way of life implies a discriminating use of technology to meet basic needs (37%), a discriminating use of technology to make life better (47%), and the development of simpler life-styles (37%). Some (19%) have no opinion on this question, but very few (6%) believe the ideal to be "the unrestrained, unrestricted pursuit and use of technology to make life better," despite a background of rugged individualism or a history of science unchained and unlimited in its possibilities.

The question for the Christian community that arises in this data is how to reconcile the fact that one-third of a group of people formed in the Christian religion feel that a commitment to economic growth is of the essence of their faith, while another third, formed in the same tradition, feel compelled by it to adopt a simpler life-style.

The point is that the problem of the relationship of economic growth and materialism to morality is very fluid in the Christian community. Perhaps that has always been the case, but this does nothing to diminish the importance of the question, either for the individual or for the church. For at issue, too, is the place of the church in the resolution of social problems.

The Role of the Church in Social Issues

Some of the most interesting pieces of information in the study deal with the place of the church in social justice.

Each of the local churches observed in the field study research was involved in some kind of social-political activity, but the goals differed radically. In liberal churches the observers saw study programs that focused on current problems and conflicts within society. They noted the organization of church boycotts of commercial products. They attended a four-day seminar to explore the relationship between church and political concerns. They observed classes which investigated current issues in order to inform the membership, add Christian perspective, and help equip people to become active in such issues outside the church. They participated in a meeting of conservative Christians who contended that Christians have been passive too long, content only to search for salvation or gifts of the Spirit for themselves, and who must now be active in political and social arenas. Furthermore, these conservative Christians were told that until now people in liberal churches and activists in various movements like gay rights, radical feminism, or the counterculture have dominated the political arena and that their activism has threatened family and Christian or American values. The churches are alive with social involvement, both from the right and the left.

Among respondents to the survey, only a few of the participants (10%) say they "do not care if their parishes or congregations treat social issues or not." Most (85%) think churches should deal with these questions, and almost three-quarters (72%) say that their parishes do. What "treat" or "deal with" means is obscured by answers to more particular items about church involvement. These items show less firm support. Little more than half (57%) are sure that their churches should be "involved" in social justice issues on a local level. Even fewer (45%) think that their church or denomination should be "involved" on the national level. Consequently, though these Christians look to the church for help in grappling with these matters from a Christian perspective, it is not clear whether they expect more leadership or more leaven. The interviews reveal many facets of the issue:

Should the church be leading the charge for social justice? I think they should be supporting that, but I am not ready to say that it should lead that charge, or any charge. They are all very important causes, but the church has limited resources.

To be listening to this conversation between these priests and staff excited something deep down in me. . . . It affirmed something that I couldn't define very well, that if the church had to be credible it had to be in the marketplace, on the streets, and in the apartment buildings.

I think the church should speak out against any regime that denies people their human rights. I think we are always on the side of the poor, the downtrodden, and oppressed. If we don't speak out, who will?

I was not active in that [protest] simply because I felt that being in the Christian ministry, this would have aligned me on one side or the other. . . . But I felt that as a Christian pastor, my responsibility was to share Christ with people, not to discuss a [protest] issue. My basic premise is to bring the gospel of Christ to people and to bring people to Christ. Then I feel that once they know Jesus as their personal savior, they can let him guide and direct their thinking. I see no conflict in [people's being for or against the same things] and still both be Christians.

The church has a responsibility as the body of Christ on earth, to act in concrete ways for the transformation of society so that society becomes a more just, more human society.

I believe that the church should just stick to the affairs of the church. God has provided us with politicians to handle all that. Let [the church] carry God's Word.

I think the church could start standing up for what religion is really supposed to be: standing up for the poor, the sick, the needy, the people in the Third World nations.

Whatever the church is supposed to be, almost half of these Christians (47%) think that churches are a help in establishing economic justice in the world, and another 24% tend to this opinion. Obviously, the church is perceived to influence the issues of the time. But the perceptions differ from issue to issue, and these differences are a challenge to the church.

Denominational Differences

Among the seven mainline denominations and varied independent churches represented in the study, Presbyterians and Roman Catholics (91%) were most committed to the notion that a mission of the church is to make God's love present through works of mercy and charity. It was people formed in these churches, too, who, along with people from the UCC, were most convinced (+50%) that liberation of the poor and oppressed is a mark of true Christianity. Church members who were least committed to this position came from the Baptist tradition (27%).

The Roman Catholics (54%) and Methodists (53%) in the study were quicker than other groups to endorse the idea that churches should be involved in social justice issues on the national level. Baptists (24%) least wanted to be identified as a denomination in public affairs.

When it comes to voting, however, it is Baptists and Roman Catholics who most claim (81%) that Christian principles are the criteria they use to evaluate candidates, but only Roman Catholics indicate to any extent (48%) that they always or usually vote for political candidates whose policies are endorsed by their church, a fact which gives credence to the continuing impression that Roman Catholics constitute a voting bloc in the country.

The Baptists in this sample were twice as likely (65%) to support the death penalty as any of the other participants; Methodists and Presbyterians, on the contrary, were more liable (35%) to consider the death penalty to be morally wrong.

Consistent with their position on abortion, Roman Catholics were more opposed (84%) to euthanasia than Christians from the other churches. The others were all more inclined to accept euthanasia in severe cases of physical or mental illness. This information may signal another social-moral change in the country.

Demographic Distinctions

The data also reveal that men (47%) accept the death penalty more than women (37%). At the same time, it is men (44%) more than women (35%) who value equal opportunity enough to believe that the church should make special efforts to insure the rights of women, particularly in the church itself. On the other hand, it is women (36%) more than men (30%) who feel that Christianity requires a change in the entire American socio-economic system. Though not large, the difference is statistically significant and may in some degree spring from women's innate or culturally conditioned sense of the needs of others, even when they hesitate to assert their own.

If the laity are looking for leadership in social issues, they have a clergy willing to give it. The clergy more than the laity see works of mercy and charity as essential elements of Christianity (clergy—94%, laity—85%), liberation of the poor and oppressed as a gospel mandate (c—90%, l—75%), a change in the American economic system as a necessary outgrowth of Christian principles (c—41%, l—33%), and participation in the political process as a function of Christian life (c—72%, l—46%). Most important of all, it is the clergy who most want to see the church provide leadership on the social justice issues (c—74%, l—46%). We need to ask whether the wide gap between the clergy and the laity on these issues exists because the church is not teaching what its clergy believe, or because the laity is resisting since prophecy disturbs, or because the clergy are wrong.

Finally, people above 55 are most committed to justice as a manifestation of "true Christianity." The older persons think that their church should be involved in social justice issues, and that Christianity requires a far-reaching change in American society and its economic system. People under 35 see churches as little help in establishing economic justice in the world. It remains to be seen whether the young like things as they are, or whether they would like things changed but have little hope that religion will do it.

In the final analysis what emerges is a people torn between principle and pragmatism, between ideals and culture. For the most part, the Christians in this study believe that, like Jesus, the church must have a public life. They believe that society needs Christianity, and that Christianity is not truly itself unless it is a living presence of God in history. These people want the church involved but are not sure how or where. They vote by Christian principles but do not look to the church for direction here. These persons want the world they know to stay basically the same but are beginning to have some misgivings about how Christian that really is. These people begin to withdraw from the application of Christian principles of equality and liberation as the issue gets closer to home. The more immediate the issue, the less decisive is the demand

for church leadership. Maybe they think very much like the interviewee
who said:

Would I like to see the church be more vocal or influential? I find that very
tough to answer. If things are going okay, I don't see a need for it. If the
government is doing what I or you believe should be done, and it is not
morally wrong, I look at that as progress. If there is a point in time when
they put the country into another skirmish like Vietnam, maybe for some
political gains for some people, to sacrifice some individuals for some personal gains, I think the church has an obligation to become involved in the
government. . . . I think the church has the same attitude towards those
things as people do. They should keep an eye on it, and when they see something going wrong, they should become involved.

In the meantime another criterion still stands: the measure with
which you measure will be used to measure you. The Christian community may have to look again at the place of justice in the church
of Jesus.

8

Put Not Your Trust in Chariots
Foreign Policy and War

It has been a long time since the living God reduced Gideon's army to a straggling band, a long time since a boy saved a people by confronting a giant alone, a long time since Judith and Holofernes made a national problem a private affair, a long time since a people believed that their safety was assured by the ark of the covenant. It has been a long time, too, since Jesus said, "Love your enemies, do good to those that hate you"; "Turn the other cheek"; "Peter, put away your sword." It is a long time since the early Christians refused to fight in the Roman armies because to do so would be idolatry. Those incidents are not the total record of the Judeo-Christian tradition. Before and beyond the figure of the pacific Christ is a history of the chosen people doing battle, of Moses with arms outstretched imploring the blessing of God on the armies on the plains below, of David triumphant, of the Crusades, of the Thirty Years War. In our own history there have been wars of independence, wars for civil unity, wars of self-defense.

Through all these times, Christian people have made rules for war, outlawed war, and developed its most devastating devices. It is mainly Christian people who have brought science not only to the point of universal communication, but also to the high art of planetary cataclysm. War has been theologized by churches, blessed by the clergy,

and fought in the name of Christian principles that were consonant
with the cultures out of which it grew: for the Führer and the father-
land, to make the world safe for democracy, for God and country, for
freedom, for security, for faith and flag. War has been fought for liberation and defense, for conquest and gain. People have sent their sons
to die bad deaths for good causes and been willing to send their grandchildren to death as well in order to maintain their values.

But war is with us still. The whole world races to defend itself
against the most indefensible of weapons at costs to the health, shelter,
education, and basic human survival level of every person in every
nation of the world. Perhaps at no other time has it been more imperative for Christians to ask what Christianity has to say about the morality
of war.

Against this backdrop of religious and cultural trends, the Faith and
Ferment study posed questions concerning the relationship of the
church to international affairs and war. The study set out to see how
Christians today regard war. What does war have to do with being
Christian? When is war acceptable? How should we as a nation deal
with other nations? What is the role of the church in foreign policy?
How should the church respond to war? In 1569 Martin Luther said:

War is the greatest plague that can afflict humanity; it destroys religion, it
destroys states, it destroys families. Any scourge is preferable to it.

But do Christians in general believe that? What informs questions
of war and international relations today? Does being Christian have
anything to do with the way people regard war? What kind of guidance
do churchgoing Christians expect of their churches in questions of
foreign policy and war? The survey responses reflect the struggle that
comes whenever the great questions of life meet the great ideals. With
earnest conviction and a tone of helplessness, one interviewee put the
problem this way:

I'm kind of a selective pacifist, I suppose you could say. . . . What happens
when you've reached a point where everything else has failed? A war is that;
it's the ultimate failure. And this whole nuclear business really drives me
crazy. . . . What I'd like to say is the simplistic approach—"We are just going
to get rid of our arsenal, and we are going to defuse our bombs"—but, again,
believing in the inherent evil in people, the kind of strength that one nation
can impose on another through blackmail and whatever else, being able to do
forcibly whatever they want to do, because they have more strength. That's
really a hard one for me to deal with.

The Formation of the Christian Conscience About War

Why is the question of war hard to deal with? From the data generated in this study it could be hypothesized that Christians see little relationship between the life and teaching of Jesus and the morality of war. The larger number of respondents to this study (69%) were of the firm opinion that it cannot be clearly determined from the teaching of Christ that Christians should not support or participate in war under any circumstances. But if Jesus' teachings against war are not absolute, then the Christian conscience is troubled by the matter, and the question of war is debatable in the church.

The diffusion of responses to another item in the survey indicates that this is precisely the case. Less than a third (29%) believe that the Bible and historic Christian tradition are clear and consistent on whether Christians may support war. Nevertheless, people look to the Scriptures and the life of Jesus as a basis for their own position. A spokeswoman for a conservative Christian organization observed in the field study explained that the group has been criticized for being in favor of strong military defense while claiming that it wants to save lives through the prohibition of abortion. People said that these were contradictory objectives. The woman, however, explained that "Not all killing is murder"; they believe that the Bible says that people have a right to defend themselves against aggression. At the same time, there are other opinions also grounded in the Bible. One man said, "I think Christ opposes war." He explained:

I think he exemplified [his opposition to war] with turning the other cheek. . . . I think we [must] try to avoid armed conflict as much as possible, because that destroys the very thing we are seeking to save and that is man, who is the image of God.

Other Christians (25%) do not agree that the Bible and the teachings of the church are as clear on the question of war. And even more troublesome may be the fact that a large part (46%) of the church members asked did not take a firm position for or against the idea that either the church or the Scripture give precise guidance on the morality of war. In fact, one of the discussants argued:

I don't think that there is any room for the church to get involved politically. If you look back in history, every war we've ever had, the background has been religion. [If the church] stays the hell out of it, we'll stay out of war.

Whether people believe that the teachings of Jesus and the church are clear about war or not, 51% are convinced that Christian teaching implies that if Christian principles are applied to international affairs, we can progress to the point where "They shall beat their swords into plowshares" and "One nation shall not raise the sword against another" (Isa. 2:4). Relatively few (16%) firmly deny the probability of that. In the meantime, there is little feeling that war is proscribed either by Jesus or church tradition. The Christian tradition is ambiguous, it seems, but yet offers hope for progress. One interviewee expressed the beliefs and perplexities which our data suggest:

I realize that people have different perspectives on peace. Most of the conservative people are not out after war, but see the road to peace as more armaments that somehow will deter Russia from attacking us. I can see their point, but my own feeling is that creating more weapons of war increases our likelihood of using them. But I think, even more than that, Christ would not be pleased with the way we are devoting so much of our financial resources into weapons of war. The whole "beating the swords into plowshares" is a meaningful part of Scripture to me. I'm very concerned about that. In terms of pacifism, I'm not so sure. Whether I think there is no such thing as a just war, I don't know. I am kind of struggling with that right now.

It is, perhaps, out of this hope and struggle that other more specific positions emerge from the data.

Foreign Relations

Most of the church members in this study (58%) believe firmly that interaction and coexistence should characterize the relationship of the U.S. to foreign countries, with the greater part of the respondents (84%) leaning toward that conviction. The thinking is that "the U.S. should make clear its opposition to nations that it really disagrees with (for example, communist or military dictatorships), but carry on with them as much as possible." The U.S., we must assume, is not to be isolationist, even over moral matters, nor, apparently, does this population believe that either intervention or international rejection have much place in our foreign relations.

Coexistence, even with Russia, is clearly (78%) affirmed. What may be more interesting is the fact that, in the mind of so many, neither Christians nor Christian churches are expected to call for a shunning of communist nations, despite the historical argument describing the incompatability between atheistic communism and the Christian West. One interviewee outlined that position:

I think that Christianity and communism are diametrically opposed to one another. And the only way [the communists] are going to have the world their way is to come into conflict with Christianity. . . . I think that the church needs to sound the alarm, needs to let us know, needs to point that out to us. I think that is one of the functions of the church, to be a prophet, not just for things of the Lord, but for things that affect its people. And I think communism definitely affects the people, and I think it definitely affects the ways of the Lord also. So it seems to me that the church ought to be a prophet, sounding the alarm that says, "Hey, the communists are a real threat to you. You need to do something about it. You need to be prepared to take measures." In that respect, I could see the institutional church doing something, and in some respects leading the nation back into a place of political and military readiness and preparation.

There are several questions to be pursued. Have Christians discovered communism to be less of a moral threat? Is morality being given short shrift in favor of economic pragmatism? Does Christianity demand something else entirely: a holy war, on the one hand, or peaceful coexistence, on the other, between nations whose moral values are considered contradictory?

Détente, whatever that may mean in the Christian tradition, is relatively firmly imbedded in the world view of most Minnesota Christians. The concept of economic aid to poorer countries and the effects of that on both the giving and the receiving nation is not. Individuals said:

If we go in and keep giving away food, as long as they are being handed what they need, they're not going to help themselves.

Is it God's will that we feed the world until we run out of food, and then everybody starves?

I think you should do what you can do to help the Third World countries, definitely. But I don't think taking hundreds of millions of dollars and giving it to countries without the assurance that it is going to be used for what it is supposed to be used for is the right way to do it. We're making more enemies. We made Idi Amin, let's face it. The American aid that went to that country made that guy, and he's a monster. So how do you do it? I don't know. That is a very difficult question.

The difficulty of the question was also reflected in the survey responses. Few (16%) were against the proposition that Christian values demand that economic aid to poor countries be given a higher priority in U.S. foreign policy than it is at present. Some (31%) were fully committed to the idea. More (34%) agreed, with some qualification. This philosophical climate, it seems, calls for the nation, as well as for individual Christians, to be concerned about the physical needs of people. But the lack of strong consensus may signal that the question requires a great deal more scrutiny, both by the churches and by the government, if consensus is to be achieved and U.S. foreign relations are to have integrity and effect.

Reasons for War and Weapons for War

On the other hand, these Christians accept that foreign relations may break down (94%), in which case they do not consider their religion a barrier to war. Two premises emerge from their responses: first, there are some wars Christians may wage; second, there are some weapons that should not be used. Whether both propositions can any longer be held is a question that the survey did not ask but which it seems these Christians will have to be able to answer to meet their own moral standards for war.

These church members are agreed (78%) that American Christians may support a war to defend the U.S. Fewer, but most (64%), also think that it is acceptable for a Christian to support a war to achieve or help others to achieve freedom from oppression. Less than half (44%) think it is equally acceptable for the Christian to support a war waged to assist an ally, and only one-third believe it is also morally defensible for an American Christian to accept a war that is fought to defend vital U.S. interests abroad. A small minority (6%) say that American Christians may never support a war. So small a representation seems to render the effect of Christian pacifism altogether negligible, without profile in the Christian community. But in conversation one of the participants took a different position.

I appreciate pacifists. I remember a professor of mine saying, "I am not a pacifist, but I am more than glad there are pacifists, because they keep the rest of us honest. I am glad they are walking that side of the street, and God bless them." And I would agree. I am not a pacifist either. I couldn't lay down our arms. I don't think we live in that kind of world. And yet, at the same time, let's put more effort into peace. Let's give it a try. We can do more talking. I'm glad to see Habib running around with his satchel in hand in the Near East. That's the sort of thing we ought to be working at.

Minnesota Christians will fight for many reasons, but they do not believe that it is Christian to fight for all reasons. As one person put it:

If I felt that there was a real cause or need and that my family or country were being threatened, I would go, even at this point in time. On the other hand, we went through a political skirmish in Korea and Vietnam, and I'm not so sure exactly what the causes or the reasons are . . . or that we are being told the exact truth about what the reasons are. I have a tendency to doubt our government. I would like to reserve the right to make up my own mind as to how I am going to commit myself and my family to that cause. . . . I definitely believe that sometimes it is necessary for a citizen and a Christian to refuse to obey the government.

These Christians do not believe that any kind of war machine is acceptable, that the government knows best about such things, or that there is no moral obligation on them as individuals to be alert to the character of international situations. A substantial majority (68%) felt certain that Christians should "strongly advocate negotiations between the U.S. and the U.S.S.R. to limit and eventually outlaw nuclear weapons." Others leaned in that direction, and few (9%) were completely opposed to the idea of Christians calling for the elimination of nuclear weapons. What may be even more significant is the fact that only a minority (33%) of the respondents are convinced that the U.S. must be second to none in military force; a quarter of this population flatly disagrees that the U.S. must have the most powerful military system in the world, and another 42% of these waver in their commitment to military supremacy from "slightly agree" to "slightly disagree." If this material has any resemblance to the American Christian culture in general, then the entire issue of armaments is in question in this country and the question is being linked to religion and morality: military dominance is suspect; the elimination of nuclear weapons is a Christian imperative; negotiation is a must. If the data are to be taken at face value, then Christians, these at least, want the world situation and our part in it to change.

In the interviews people said things like:

Communists are just as much a part of the world [as we are]. . . . The blame doesn't fall on all those people who live over there; there have got to be some good people over there. They were created like we are.

I think we need a strong, but not a bullish military force—just enough to keep things in perspective.

It's not that important to me to be number one. . . . If we get in a war, Russia is going to snuff us out, and maybe I'm going to die. But if I die, I die. If I don't die that way, I'm going to die some other way. I would much rather see more stress put toward harmony than all this money spent to worry about how fast you can kill off the next guy.

I think this business of preparing for war is the curse of our times, when you think of all the money that is poured into armaments, and all this training, and all the energy that is expended towards killing people.

The survey results support the pervasiveness of this thinking. Some people said other things that were equally strong and equally related to their religious beliefs:

If there is a possibility that we can get along with [the communist nations] superficially, or trade with them, all right. But I wouldn't monkey around with them too much. I am not so sure that they [can be trusted] . . . because of all I have read, and all I have heard on the radio and stuff. . . . I see them as a threat to our Christianity mainly. I think they could dissolve Christianity.

I think that it's sad that we didn't spend a little more money on the military way back instead of waiting. You cannot exist in a universe unless you are equally as prepared as your opponent is. . . . And I think that has nothing to do with religion.

I wish the atom bomb and power plants had never been invented. . . . America would be much better off, and mankind would be, too. But I guess it's in God's plan. In fact, I would say that the neutron bomb is in God's plan. . . . I often used to wonder how men's flesh could fall off their bones while they were still standing, but Daniel speaks of it. And I think that is probably the neutron bomb. . . . I feel that world events right now are leading up to the Battle of Armageddon. . . . Why should I doubt it now, when so many of the predictions from way back in the time of Daniel have come true already.

Obviously the churches have a role to play in all of this, but what?

The Church and Foreign Policy

The Christians consulted in this study are either uncertain about what influence they expect the church to render in foreign policy, or they make subtle distinctions about what that influence should entail. In two separate and vital places they shift the weight of their reactions. In the first, they give large support (69%) to the idea that Christian viewpoints and values relating to U.S. foreign policy should be expressed to the government by both individual Christians and their churches. But in a second set of responses, less than half of the same population (46%) accept the idea that churches should express themselves on matters of foreign policy. One reading of this information is that most people think it is right for churches to press the government to keep the Christian goal of human dignity at the base of our military strategies, but fewer would be willing to go so far as to have their churches criticize a specific defense project on the grounds that it costs money that should have been spent on the disadvantaged. The church, it seems, is being asked to function as standard bearer but not as prophet, to hold up principles but not to advocate anything specific.

On another matter, a similar problem of consistency arises. Almost half of the population (49%) say that no church should ever give unqualified support to any war, with the greater majority tending to agree. But in another place 39% say just as strongly that if the cause is morally right, the church should give full support to a war effort, with the greater majority tending to agree there also. There is obviously both dissonance and polarity in the data, not necessarily because the participants are inconsistent but just as probably because churches themselves have failed to give clear counsel or a certain sign about the place of war in the Christian community.

This is perhaps the basic point to be derived from this data: among the churches represented in this study there is broad feeling that Christian values should permeate U.S. foreign policy, that the U.S. does not need to hold military supremacy in the world, and that their churches should not promote that. But there is confusion about the role of the church in dealing with war. Perhaps the data indicate not only that the people in the pews are unsure about the relationship of war to Christianity, but that the churches may need to clarify their own place in a world where violence is a strategy for peace.

Finally, some of these respondents (15%) want their local congregations or parishes to do more about foreign policy and war than they do now. They say that little attention is given there to the implications of Christianity for foreign policy and war. Whether these attitudes stem from a feeling of remoteness from the issues, a natural apathy, or the conscious decision not to have Christianity brought to bear on so volatile an issue we cannot say. But it may be important for someone to find out why a group that says with such conviction that the church should be an influence in the creation of foreign policy also says, "But not in my parish."

Denominational Differences

Baptists (39%) and Lutherans (42%) were least likely to agree that Christian teaching implies that the application of Christian principles would lead to the cessation of war. Presbyterians and Roman Catholics (42%) were almost twice as likely as members of any of the other denominations to support the idea that Christian values demand that economic aid be given a higher priority in U.S. foreign policy. Baptists, more than any other group, are not only inclined to question the value of increased economic aid but are also much less likely (42%) to advocate negotiations with Russia for the outlawing of nuclear weapons.

Demographic Distinctions

Of all the topics probed in the study, more and greater gaps exist between the attitudes of the clergy and the opinions of the laity on issues of foreign policy and war than on any others. Three-fourths of the clergy (76%) believe that churches should express themselves on matters of foreign policy; far fewer of the laity (43%) think the same. The clergy (75%) believe that Christian faith has implications for foreign policy; fewer of the laity (51%) hold the same opinion. Clergy (75%) approved of détente and negotiations with the U.S.S.R., but laypersons (67%) were less enthusiastic about those policies. Most of the clergy (58%) said economic aid was a Christian obligation; few of the laity (27%) felt the same. Almost half (45%) of the clergy in the study said that the U.S. did not need to have military supremacy in the world; less than one-fourth (23%) of the laity felt the same. More laypersons (40%) than clergy (25%) were firmly convinced that the church should give "full support" to a war if the cause is "morally right."

This great discrepancy between laity and clergy on so many issues concerning foreign policy and war must be a sign of something serious in the church. Have people hardened their hearts? Are the clergy failing to speak on so important a subject, though they interpret the biblical message on the issue quite differently from the people? Is the ambiguity of the Christian message really ambiguity, or is it simply prudent silence on the part of the church? Are the laity more knowledgeable than the clergy about matters of public policy? Whatever the case, the world is left waiting for some resolution of these contrary positions, and in this century, perhaps to its peril.

Interestingly enough, Christian men and women differ very little in their attitudes toward issues of foreign policy and war, except that men (43%) think the church should give full support to a war whose cause is morally right, and fewer women (36%) are willing to support that. However, between the young (those under 35, who were born after the detonation of the first atomic bomb) and the older (those over 55, who lived and were formed in the preatomic age) there are also considerable differences in attitudes toward the influence and role of the faith in matters of foreign policy and war.

More older people (36%) than younger (22%) find the Scriptures and tradition unclear or inconsistent about war, but it is older people (61%) who hold a stronger conviction than younger Christians (46%) that the application of Christian principles would bring peace to international affairs. Older people (78%) believe that Christians should be strong advocates of negotiations to outlaw nuclear weapons; younger people (61%) think so too, but in considerably smaller numbers. Older people (43%) think the church should give full support to wars fought for causes that are morally right; younger people (26%) are much less inclined to believe that. More older people (38%) believe that Christian values require that economic aid to poor countries be given higher priority than younger people do (25%). At the same time, more than one-third (38%) of the older generation are firm in the conviction that the U.S. must be second to none in military force; only 20% of the younger people take that same position. Almost two-thirds (64%) of the older church members in the study are firmly convinced that Christian faith has significant implications for foreign policy, whereas only 42% of the younger generation feel the same.

The present unclarity in Christian perspective seems to introduce tension into the way people regard the present international and military situation, creating divisions between the generations, and between ministers and congregation members. An interviewee laid out the dimensions of the problem:

I suppose we could say that we had to get rid of Hitler because he was doing terrible things. But I don't know why we had to kill all the Germans and Russians, and destroy everybody in order to do that. It's a very total kind of way of taking care of a problem. And why we didn't see this when it was happening, I don't know. I don't know how much of this kind of stuff is really planned. You wonder about people who are in this business of making decisions about war, about what is being manufactured to promote war. And you look at Japan and their attack on Pearl Harbor. You think maybe they should have been put in their place, but with a bomb, and to destroy all those innocent people? It was a terrible thing to do. But they had nothing to say about it any more than that German mother who raised her kids. What did she have to say about whether or not they were going to spill their guts out here or not? She wasn't any crazier about it [than an American mother]. But then we have this propaganda about Gold Star Mothers and about defending the country and waving the flag. It is ingrained in us. And can't you be patriotic without going to war? What kind of patriotism are we teaching? Do we have to generate patriotism in this country by waving the sword around? Is that the way to do it? It's ridiculous. I think it is terrible.

What that implies for the credibility of the church or the Christianity of the future is impossible to tell, but there is no doubt that here faith and future meet.

9

The Garden of Eden Revisited
Ecology

Whatever Thanksgiving may now have become as an American holiday, it was certainly once a tribute to bounty. The United States was rich in resources. The land was broad; the people were few. To its north were the vast but cold plains of Canada. To its South the hot flatlands of Mexico. To the East and West ocean boundaries. America was rich and isolated. Progress became the civil religion, and there was no barrier to it. The scene was set for the Protestant ethic, technology, and the unending consumption of nonrenewable resources. Hard work would give us what we wanted; there would never be an end to it. There was no reason to be concerned—except that apparently Christians are. And furthermore, they say they are because stewardship is rooted in the Christian faith, part of the responsibility that came with creation.

Protecting the Land

Fundamental to their opinion that ecology is a moral issue is the understanding that the earth does not really belong to the human race but has been loaned to us for our use and so must be kept in good condition. One respondent said quite explicitly:

The earth is the Lord's; it's really not ours. . . . We have a responsibility to protect it and keep it beautiful and usable. I believe God gave Adam the garden to use. He didn't tell him to just stand there and look at it.

Another talked at length about the relationship she saw among nature, people, and things:

The land is to be shared, not to be abused. It is a gift from God. It is to nurture. The tie-ins between the world, the consumer, and the city are fascinating.

An 80% majority of the study group agreed that the teachings of Jesus are concerned with the care of the planet. The kingdom to come, it seems, is not their only concern as Christians. These Minnesota Christians are environmentalists who believe that concern for the elements of nature is a moral imperative. What they do not agree about is exactly what that means.

In interviews, some stated the belief that ecology involves the preservation of lands or animal herds in their pristine state. Others argue just as convincingly that ecology or conservation has more to do with the proper use of resources than simply their protection. One speaker explained the difference this way:

I lived in the mountains; I enjoy the mountains; I would like to go back there. But people are important, too. We don't need to live as extravagantly as we have. That's going overboard. But I don't think that we should let any one group have their say—not the lumber industry or the hikers. And I think there can be a way to work it out if there were less selfishness. . . . The Scripture says we are to subdue the land. Christians are God's agents in using the land.

For others the "tie-ins" are not so clear, the association between land and city not so fascinating. In their opinion the rape of the land is simply immoral.

To still another group, much smaller but virtually one-fourth of the respondents and therefore significant, the stewardship of resources is a necessary but not a religious issue.

Each of these positions was articulated not only well, but passionately, in the course of the in-depth interviews:

We don't want a copper and nickel mine. . . . About 40 years from now, there would be nothing here in this place. This way, if they'll just leave things alone, my kids and grandchildren might have something that they could still stay here for, and still survive.

For this respondent, short-term gain is an inadmissable use of land in the face of on-going human needs. And for others, too, the religious dimensions of the question are neither primary nor valid. They argued:

You don't necessarily have to be a Christian to be careful about the earth. It's not a Christian responsibility to do some educating about ecological concerns. I think that we don't even do the job that Jesus gave us—to go and teach others about Jesus Christ. Teach others that you and I have something that is important to us that gives us the desire to live, the want to do some good for somebody else—that's the Christian responsibility.

The issues of cultivation and control vie with conservation as deeply as biblical fundamentalism differs from a heightened cultural consciousness of the Scriptures. Some feel that the loss of nature in its primitive state is a rupture of humankind's relationship with God. Nature, they feel, fills "the need all people have to return to the earth and experience solitude." Other Christians argue just as strongly from the Bible that "nature isn't God; it's something we are to use to the best of our ability." Or as one put it, even more specifically:

I heard somewhere that somebody laid the rape of our resources to some kind of perverted Christian point of view where we are to subdue the earth. That struck me as a total misunderstanding of Christian stewardship. Christian stewardship is very comparable to forest managery. Conservation isn't preservation. It is wise use for sustained yield.

But though the approach to the issue may be unclear, it is nevertheless a serious matter and one which is basic to the future direction of the country. Because material progress as well as bounty have been hallmarks of the American culture, one is key to the other. The conservation question and the technology question are inextricably linked. To say that one is moral or essential to a full faith life is to take a position, at least implicitly, on the other. The question is, how do Christians who feel so strongly about conservation respond to the issues that surround technology? Is it possible to conserve resources and be a highly technical society? And if it is not, then which facet will these Christians surrender first? Is it necessary to choose between the two? Can one advance the other? And how? If the use of natural resources is a religious duty, what is to be said about the morality of possibility? When is that which is technically doable also morally appropriate?

Conservation and Technology

At least in Minnesota, if the two values of use and development meet head to head, the trend seems to be toward conservation. Half of the study population claimed to be strongly convinced of this, and another 34% tended to agree at least slightly that conservation should prevail over technology. But the tension is there nevertheless. When they were able to say more than the survey document allowed, respondents indicated that for them the issue reflected basic tensions in traditional church teaching.

For one person the interrelationship of issues and conflicts of values is deeply confusing:

I think ecology is important, but I also think it is in conflict with other moral issues. I see dilemmas; I see no easy solution. . . . It would be a very reasonable solution—to settle for less technological progress. We've had so much of it. Things are speeding up too fast the way it is. A slowdown would be good. On the other hand, the costs that are involved to industry, to become completely nonpolluters, are probably costs that industry can't afford without huge layoffs and other impacts on their employees. I don't know if Chrysler should be bailed out, but there are hundreds of thousands of other people that we've got to be concerned about. It's just a dilemma. I don't know what the answers are.

For another person the problem is how to care for the poor, itself a scriptural mandate, if the things of nature are not used to make a profit:

It is incumbent upon us, who are being ecological, to prosper or succeed in business. Because along with [being over the works of his hands] it is given in Scripture that we are to take care of the poor. We are to be successful; we are to tend to our business and be stewards of the earth that we have been given.

From the point of view of another segment of the Christian population who participated in this study, a new ecological consciousness is in conflict over older theological values:

I watched a film with Jacques Cousteau in the Mediterranean. I was appalled at the waste being poured into the Mediterranean and the effect on the balance of life in the sea. There is virtually little life left—whether it is plant life, or fish, or whatever. It's being systematically destroyed. And now we are talking about offshore things in California, and it's horrible how it is ruining the beauty of the environment. And we try to justify it any way we can. I'm very opposed to that. . . . I think too often, as Protestants in particular, we've taken the command of God in Genesis where it has given man dominion over the planet to mean that we have a right to exploit the planet.

But even though this Christian community is conscious of the complexities of the conservation and technology issues, the trend is to reverence the resources of the planet over the costs of industrial development. Eighty-five percent of the study sample indicated that Christians should oppose the careless and improper disposal of nuclear and chemical waste. But it is possible to wonder just how clearly they see or believe in the global implications of that statement.

Pollution

Though some individuals spoke eloquently about the effects of waste and pollution, they were, by and large, more aware of the impact of modern technology on their own locale than they were sensitive to the moral dimensions of planetary interdependence. But though they do not know how to assess or deal with the more cosmic results of modern industry, there is apparently a growing sense of global consciousness and some attempt to integrate a new world view with the parameters of the Christian faith. Over a third (37%) of the respondents to the social survey feel "as morally responsible for the quality of the air over Japan as the Japanese are." And almost another quarter (24%) agree that there is indeed some truth in that statement. All in all, a large proportion of the study group (62%) accepted some degree of obligation for the biophysical system of the entire planet and its unitary character. One woman described her attitude at length:

I think we have a real responsibility. The Third World nations are certainly in need of our help. And they say that our environment here is only part of the total environment of the planet. When they talk about pollution, they're worried about the acid rain up in Canada, but I'm worried about the cloud of pollution that circles the whole earth and that people will have to take care of it in terms of global pollution, rather than pinpointing one particular spot. And our great responsibility is somehow to cope with the whole pollution problem. It's probably more important than Russia and this nuclear warfare, or anything else. If we destroy our environment, we destroy ourselves and we destroy what God has given us to protect. So, in a sense, the battle becomes a spiritual one. We've got to protect this earth of ours at all cost.

These Christians spoke of the perils of nuclear waste and said it was a "sin" that nuclear materials were made before it was known what to do to neutralize the waste. Others blamed the government for past destruction of natural resources. "They wanted something started in Minnesota, and they gave them any kind of permit they wanted. They never should have given them that permit in the first place," a man said as he struggled with the technology and conservation issues and his own place in them. Another broadened the whole concept of stewardship and ecology to find a way to deal personally with the destruction of the planet or the misuse of resources, actions he felt powerless to control. He said:

We do have a choice to make. . . . The air I breathe and what I put into my body, those are the kinds of things that are real to me in terms of stewardship and ecology. . . . I have a great deal of difficulty understanding the Third World things. I haven't gotten involved in the boycott of Nestle and those kinds of things, not because I am not interested or don't care, but I haven't had the kind of experience that really grabs me. You talk about what is happening in our welfare system [here] and that is a whole different thing, because that I can relate to and deal with. It is not that I ignore the others, but I feel more helpless in dealing with that. . . . Those global issues can't excite me. I know my head and my heart say that those are concerns, but I face the frustration that other than the contributions that I might make, or the vote that I might cast, I really am not sure [what to do about that]. But I'll be involved about neighborhood things because that is my globe, my world. That is the world I live, I breathe, I share in. I think that if I were put in a position where the other would become more real for me and I could really claim it—I really support those issues; I don't ignore them—but they don't have the same claim on me in terms of who I am [as the issues that confront me personally].

What is most significant for the Christian churches is that less than half of the respondents (37%) were convinced that the quality of the air over Japan, or anywhere else presumably, has little or anything to do with the moral character of their own lives. The ramifications of this kind of posture for doctrines of personal, social or systemic sin are major but perhaps theoretical. A more pertinent question may well be what churchgoers who believe that pollution is a facet of morality believe that their churches should do about it.

The Involvement of the Church

Although most people (85%) who responded to the study questionnaire took the position that Christians should oppose pollution and that ecology is a moral issue, far fewer (63%) actually wanted their parishes or congregations to oppose pollution. Most important, those interviewed who looked to the church for leadership in this area and those who were opposed were able to explain why they felt that the church should or should not be concerned about the ecology issue. Some said, in essence, that the church as institution simply has "more important things to do" than to get involved in things of this nature. Another perspective saw the church as a representative body that "has to be so careful" to determine that it is "really speaking for its members." Some worried about the implications of something like this for the principle of separation of church and state. Yet still more thought that "rabbis and priests have to give us a push."

But whatever their concerns about the propriety of the church's public involvement in ecological issues, there is little or no question in the minds of these Minnesota Christians that it is their moral responsibility to confront the improper disposal of toxic waste (85%), to make changes in their personal life-styles in order to reduce waste (91%), to treat the human body with special care because it "is a special gift" (90%). They believe that regardless of who else does what, they ought to be concerned about the quality of the environment for the generations to come.

What is most compelling of all about the data, however, may be that the denominations and various categories of people differ on these issues hardly at all.

Denominational Differences

Catholics (58%) and Presbyterians (52%) seem to be most convinced that the proper management of the environment is a moral obligation and not primarily a matter of necessity; and Presbyterians (75%) and Catholics (69%) are most committed to the idea that the churches themselves should take a stand against the improper disposition of nuclear and chemical waste. It is Baptists (71%) who least support the idea that the natural order of things is a matter for church concern.

Demographic Distinctions

Although there is general conviction among the Christian population that ecology, pollution, the use of natural resources and global interdependence are more than simply prudential or economic concerns, it is the clergy (95%) who are more likely to relate these factors to morality than are the laity (78%). Moreover, people above the age of 55 see the use of resources as a Christian responsibility. Whether these data are saying that the church is not teaching the younger generation about Christian stewardship, despite the fact that its ministers believe in its necessity, or that this generation is no longer listening to that message is unclear, but the discrepancy is there.

The men of this study (51%) more than the women (41%) were conscious of the relationship between morality and ecology, but women (91%) more than men (85%) were convinced of the sacredness of the human body.

Finally, people in the rural areas of Minnesota were aware of the link between environmental concerns and Christian responsibilities, but people in the metropolitan areas were more keenly aware of planetary unity and interdependence.

All in all, the data on Christian attitudes and the biophysical system is clear, yet tantalizing. At first glance, the temptation is to assume that environmental issues are charged with moral overtones for the contemporary Christian. And that point in itself is indisputable here. But although Christians believe that something is of the essence of the Christian faith, they do not necessarily know what the churches should do about it. In the words of one respondent: "There are good people on both sides. All we can do as a church is to keep talking and not become enemies, keep the issue [in front of us] and keep working it through."

10

Here I Am, Lord; Send Me

Occupation

Scripture clearly teaches that discipleship includes a sense of mission and a certainty of call. Samuel is called by God to indict the very system that had formed him. Jonah was called to Nineveh. Judith was called to confront the pagan influence of the culture of her time. Esther was to use her influence inside the palace to save her people. Gideon was to do battle for the Lord. Work was basic to mission, part of the call, ordained by God, sanctifying, blessed, necessary and expected to be honest. Chosen ones were set apart by God in a special way and with special expectations, as both the Old and the New Testament indicate.

In those days the sense of revelation was common, the notion of urgency high. People worked while they had the light of life, never sure when the Messiah would come or, later, when the Messiah would return. The need to be ready was a conscious part of life; the need to spread the Word an urgent mandate. And good works were the key to it all. Life was to be spent doing the will of the Father, bearing good fruit, being the light of the world, not being idle, not being irresponsible (2 Thess. 3:6-12). All of life was intricately bound up with salvation and witness.

But that was before life became both more complex and more

sophisticated, before work was separated from the home, before people became separated from the product through assembly line processes or bureaucratic structures. Today when few people see more than isolated parts of the products they help to manufacture, and most do not understand the use of the things they work on, let alone feel influential in the multinational systems that regulate them, it is fair to wonder what part, if any, occupation plays in the faith of the contemporary Christian. The questions in this research were designed to probe the place of call, witness, and responsibility in the Christian community today.

Vocation and Ministry

Like the biblical figures before them, 68% of the population we surveyed firmly believe that God called them to whatever work they now do. An additional 18% profess some feeling that whatever professions or positions they are now engaged in are part of God's design or a response to God's call. For instance, the field research team attended various church meetings and conventions. At one, an exhibit of booksellers and publishers, they were told quite directly by the sales personnel and owners that the books, audiovisual materials, recordings, and cassette tapes were all produced to tell people how to lead better Christian lives, or how to manifest and use Christian principles in marriage, home, family, community, business, and education. They were engaged not in a job but in a ministry to which they had been led by God.

The prevailing attitude, then, is that God is directly involved in the work that people do, that their work is part of God's plan for their lives. At the same time, however, less than half (46%) indicated that it was Christian faith itself that guided them in their choice of occupation. There is no way to tell from the data whether those who responded this way meant that they themselves do not consciously use their faith to evaluate their work options, or that they do not feel that Christianity imposes any more obligations in this area than any other faith might.

What is clear, though, is that the respondents make a distinction between the presence of God in their decisions and the role of their particular creed or denomination in directing their professional lives. Over and over again in the interviews, Christians from all denominations described people as "sent" to influence their interests or decisions.

Almost everyone described someone: professors they had in college, priests they met when they were children, best friends who had made the same choices before them, the family minister, their sisters and brothers—all agents of the will of God in their lives.

What is more, for a large majority (83%), the teaching, counseling, prayer, liturgy, and Sunday worship of the church help, they say, with the problems they encounter in their daily work. So, though the church itself does not direct or define their vocations, it does apparently provide the support necessary to sustain them.

The interviews also show that the understanding of the Christian "call" or vocation among these people is not limited to the ordained ministry, either by ministers or laity. In fact, one ordained minister who had left the service of the church for a public service position explained that the heart of ministry is service, not role. He said:

Sometimes the Lord doesn't have to call us to a different congregation to serve. He can call us to a different vocation to serve, because we can do ministry in various ways. Ministry, to me, is serving people. And so, when these various job offers just dropped out of the blue, [I saw that it was here that I could] get right down to the grass roots of where people are having problems. . . . That simply says to me that the Lord is a miracle worker, and he knows what we need, and he will provide. He has promised to provide for all of our needs. And he does, really and truly, guide and direct us.

Other people talked of their "mission" as teachers or insurance agents or managers or business owners. But whatever their positions, they referred repeatedly to their obligation, as Christians, to serve others. And they were convinced that God would direct those intentions. A young participant, still in college and a regular churchgoer, spoke of his choice of academic concentration and its relationship to his future career. Each, he says, is inextricably linked to his consciousness of Christianity:

I think there are so many people out in the world that are just lost because they have tried to be self-centered and they can't because they have been beaten by other people, and we need to put them back together by love and Christ's love. And I would like to get some people together [in some kind of halfway house or in some kind of counseling]. The Lord will take care of it, if that is his will for me.

But how deeply people feel called or chosen for a position in life and how that feeling or call affects what they do or how they do it may be two quite different things. I may see the call as either a private or a public commitment. I may think of it as my way to save my own soul or as my way to witness to others. I may see it as a call to personal endurance and discipline or as the place for my own evangelistic efforts. In the U.S., where religious pluralism is a doctrine of the civil religion, that choice of attitudes could be crucial.

Work: Calling and Evangelization

In the minds of these respondents, work and faith are clearly interrelated. More than three-fourths of them (79%) see their work as being in harmony with their Christian faith. Some (13%) say that the work they do for a living has little or nothing to do with their faith. Few (7%) believe that what they do to earn their livelihood conflicts with their faith. But regardless of their answers, most of them see faith as an acceptable and intelligent guide in the marketplace. It directs their conduct in their daily work. Many (81%) try to be an example for Christ while at work. And in a society that urges people to keep a proper distance between their religious convictions and their public activities, faith requires a surprising number (39%) to tell others on the job about Christ.

If those convictions are actually the case, then for many American Christians faith is extremely relevant to their work. The question is, what do they mean by that? What does faith require of the Christian who works in systems that are now large, automated, international, and standardized? One person put it this way:

I think that all the years I have been working as a research engineer, God did not want me to be a poor engineer. He wanted me to be a very good engineer and to make as much money as possible, so I could give 10% of it back to him.

Faith demands that Christians take life's gifts seriously, not fritter them away, but use them to build the businesses they are in, to develop themselves fully, and to help others. But faith requires even more of some. It calls for principle as well as productivity.

The study asked people to respond to the following question:

If I discovered that my company engaged in or permitted degrading personnel practices or conducted shady or illegal financial transactions, obedience to God would require that I: Resign? Try to change the practice? Go along because I need the job for my family? Pay no attention because it is none of my business?

Almost every one of the church members (97%) who contemplated this question claimed at least some responsibility for the situation. The overwhelming majority (82%) said that "obedience to God" would require them "to try to change the practice." Another 15% said they would be required to resign. How many would actually do either, or for how long, or over what issues, or in what way is impossible to know. Nevertheless, the answers build a basis for social ferment. Systemic change may be as possible in the light of this century's excesses as it was in other periods of social tension or exploitation, no matter how comfortable people may find themselves. Furthermore, these findings may be as meaningful theologically as they are socially. Whatever the historical teachings of the institutional church, these data may indicate that most people do not believe that they are as required to "flee" evil as they are to confront and overcome it. And they seem to have common standards in mind.

Work: Morality and Aspiration

If the work they do is in harmony with their faith and if its practices are ethical, workers accept certain responsibilities as a result of their religious commitments. Unlike one who believes that the purpose of working is to make as much money as possible, 54% of our survey respondents do not believe that their faith encourages them to attain as much material affluence as they can so long as their methods are honorable. One speaker talked at length about the effects that sheer striving had had on him:

I took night courses [because] I couldn't afford to go during the day. . . . And I worked for a great many years in that field and got into supervision after a point in time and became a supervisor. [I went] from foreman on up to the plant managership. That's when I began to find out what the world was really about. And [my wife and I] began to become more and more aware that our jobs were good, the money was good, [but] we weren't enjoying our family or ourselves. And we were spending far too much time in the evening, instead of talking about things that were pertinent and relevant to each other, continually talking about our jobs. . . . And it was unbelievable, because the farther up the ladder I went, the worse it got. . . . And my wife and I made a decision that we had had enough of the rat race.

The speaker is representative. For most of these practicing Christians, money is not the primary object of their efforts. But fairness and sensitivity to others are common concerns (89%). For a large number, too (70%), the production of high-quality work is a Christian imperative. And examination of their own standards of behavior in the work place is a central Christian obligation in the minds of most (78%).

In summary, the data reveal respect for personal industry, justice, and sufficiency. The acknowledgement that work is based on faith underlies this respect. The fact that the church gives consolation, support, and guidance on career questions is affirmed. Whether the American churches have ever exercised the influence they seem to have on the American work scene is another question. But one thing is all but certain: whatever is going on in the American marketplace is perceived by Christians in Minnesota to be within the purview of faith.

Denominational Differences

The concept of "call" is highest among Baptists (78%), Presbyterians (76%), and Catholics (75%). By contrast, little more than a third (36%) of the members of the UCC believe that they are doing their daily work because God wants them to or because they have a mission to perform in that particular place. Nevertheless, though not all the participants feel "called" to their present work by God, most respondents—especially Baptists (95%)—feel that their work is in harmony with their faith. And most, especially Baptists (90%) and Presbyterians (89%), look to the church for help and guidance in the problems they encounter there.

Demographic Distinctions

Not surprisingly, clergy (93%) were far more convinced than laity (66%) that God had called them to the work they do, which may indicate that ordained ministry is considered a more sacred work than work done outside the institutional church. The clergy (94%) were also more likely to relate their choice of occupation to the Christian faith than were laity (40%) who were engaged in other kinds of work. Clergy (98%) were more committed than laity (80%) to the idea that they would be required to change unethical practices in the environment in order to be obedient to God. These differences in point of view between clergy and the people to whom they minister lead us to question whether the clergy fail to teach the kind of responsibility that they themselves feel about the application of Christian principles to the work environment, or whether a significant portion of the laity

(20%) does not accept the idea that they have a moral obligation to monitor the ethical standards of their companies.

Of the laity, though, more men (91%) than women (74%) agree that they do have a moral obligation to change unethical work practices. Do more men than women feel they would try to change immoral or unethical practices in their line of business because men are more convinced that this is a Christian responsibility or because women are more conditioned to consider themselves powerless? This question is particularly engaging in view of the discovery that a much larger portion of women respondents (23%) than men (5%) replied that in a work situation which they knew to be corrupt they would feel compelled to resign. In fact, a similar relationship exists between high- and low-income participants. High-income church members (89%) say their faith would require them to "try to change the practice"; somewhat fewer low-income people (78%) say the same. But more low-income (18%) than high-income (9%) people say they would have to resign in order to discharge their Christian obligations in that situation.

Perhaps the Christian churches need to look again at the relationship of faith to justice, of mission to ministry, of morality to work, and ask what the gospel link is and how it is to be made. Joseph worked for Pharaoh, we remember. And Levi remained a tax collector. Perhaps the answer has never been easy.

II

Between the Times of Christ
and the Kingdom
The Church

A modern parable reflects the problem of church:

There's a monk who will never give you advice, but only a question. I was told his questions could be very helpful, so I sought him out. "I am a parish priest," I said. "I'm here on retreat. Could you give me a question?"

"Ah, yes," he answered. "My question is, 'What do they need?' "

I came away disappointed. I spent a few hours with the question, writing out answers, but finally I went back to him.

"Excuse me. Perhaps I didn't make myself clear. Your question has been helpful, but I wasn't so much interested in thinking about my apostolate during this retreat. Rather I wanted to think seriously about my own spiritual life. Could you give me a question for my own spiritual life?"

"Ah, I see. Then my question is, 'What do they *really* need?' "

Is the church to be sign or countersign, priest or prophet to the people? If the church is where people are, can it call them to anything? On the other hand, if it isn't where the people are, is it church at all? It seemed important for any study on the church to ask, "What do they really need?" If the church is not providing what people expect it to provide, if the church of the clergy is not the church of the

137

people, if ministers want to give what the people say they do not want to have, whose millstone will that be? Do the people see the church as the institutional church sees itself? And, if not, how do we account for the divergencies?

This study concentrated on the church members of the Christian community, on people who belong to a particular denomination, on people who participate in the institutional church. The inquiry asked them to reflect on what they expect from their churches, what they believe the purpose of the church to be, what they see as the essential elements of Christian worship, how they regard churches other than their own, what they judge to be a proper relationship between church and state, how they relate to the parish church and its relatively new but fast developing electronic counterpart. The question, "What do they really need?" is a question for ministers and members alike.

In a nation that is historically Christian, free from religious persecution, and given to minting coins inscribed "In God we trust," we might expect the responses to be fairly uniform. In fact, clear differences exist in the way Christians of different denominations, age groups, and roles regard the nature and function of the church. What is more, a new movement among the Christian churches has emerged in response to these distinct perspectives.

At the same time, it is precisely these postures that either form or filter the Christian's attitudes about self, society, and the world at large. Some people, even adults in the pews, are living with questions and answers far more tentative than either their Sunday school or catechism classes allowed. One of the interview participants, a church member, admitted:

I still call myself a Christian. I guess it is just sort of a safe, secure thing. I almost think that I don't belong to any religion at all, that I am just completely dependent on myself. I don't know how much you have to believe to be a Christian. Just the fact that I believe in Jesus, and that I believe that he probably died on the cross and rose from the dead? If that makes me a Christian, then I guess I am. But I also believe that Buddha was probably very divine. And all these other prophets from all these other religions are equally as divine. They were all sons of God. And they just came to talk to the people in the way they could understand and be models.

But in the same church, in another pew, another churchgoer says quite confidently:

[The question of whether or not non-Christians will go to heaven] is a very unknown area. The Bible explicitly tells us that there is only one way, and Jesus said that, too: "I am the way." That is confirmed through the Book of Acts. The apostles held that so highly, that no one could be saved except those who received Christ as their Savior. He is the way. . . . I feel that those who reject Christ go to hell. I'm not sure about those who never had a chance to accept or reject him. Maybe there is an after-death experience. . . . I'm guessing.

And there the differences begin.

Personal Salvation

An interesting thing happened in the course of this data collection. A considerable number of people (78%) indicated that Baptism was not a distant event in their lives, that it affects them even now. In the personal interviews, however, very few mentioned Baptism at all. In conversation people talked instead about the basis of salvation being the need to make a "commitment," to be "born again," to "have Christ in their lives." As one person put it:

[The question, What must one do to be saved? can only be answered with] Paul and Silas' answer to the jailer at Philippi: "Believe in the Lord Jesus Christ, and you shall be saved." Actually, I believe that a person doesn't have to do anything to be a Christian or [achieve] salvation other than invite the Lord Jesus into the heart.

Though Baptism is meaningful, in other words, it may not be enough or, for some, even necessary for salvation. At any rate, it is not what people talk about when asked what is important or essential to salvation. This outward, visible form of initiation does not seem to be a sign of election as much as it is a sign of ongoing search or obligation in the Christian community. The implications of that position are far-reaching. If Baptism in the Christian tradition is not a requirement for eternal life, then the whole face of the church changes. Official inclusion in a baptizing denomination becomes a matter of spiritual impulse or social approval rather than an imperative. Being a good Christian, then, could have very little to do with being associated with an institutional church. Some active church members themselves have come to that conclusion. One described his movement away from the equation of denominational dogma with salvation or morality:

I was of the opinion for a long time, that the only ones who were going to heaven were Catholics. And this is what you were taught: If you're not Catholic, you're going to hell. I was thinking about that when I met my first girl friend. I was thinking I better get her over there [into the church]. . . . Now I don't think you [even] have to go to church to get to heaven. My brother doesn't go to church, and hasn't for years, but I think he is a very moral person.

A few people, all participating members in a congregation, were even more direct than that. One made a sharp distinction between the church as institution and the church as the people of God. He explained:

I feel that the church should have very little emphasis. The church is a place to go and worship that Christ who is on the right hand of God now. And it's a place where Christians who should love each other—and if they don't it's a poor church—can go and encourage one another, and if one of them has a need, pray for one another. . . . It's a sort of meeting place for Christians. . . . The church, as an organization, I feel, has no power. Whether it be the Catholic church, the Protestant church, or anybody else. Some churches, I believe, have taken on a responsibility that they shouldn't take on, and are exercising authority that they don't have as an intercessor between Christ and me, and that's not according to the Bible. . . . The real church is, like my wife said, the born-again Christians who walk this life daily and do the best they can.

Then why do these people bother to go to church? What do they see as its purpose and place in their lives?

The Effect of the Church on People's Private Lives

The question read: "Please check the one statement that comes closest to expressing your feelings about your church." The responses reflected some clear theological demarcations. In the first place, very few (7%) were willing to say that the primary function of the church in their lives is to be a place of worship. Apparently, in most people's minds, worship is not the most important function of the church. Even Catholics, for whom church attendance has traditionally been mandatory under pain of mortal sin, were little inclined (7%) to mark worship as the identifying basis of their relationship with the church.

Not many (15%) defined their church as "an important source of moral and spiritual values" either. It appears people do not go to church to be told what to do—its own kind of statement on the issue of personal conscience—and those who do may have very disparate expectations of what they expect of the church. One wants the law defined; another wants it subsumed under the single rubric, love. Each position was articulated in the interviews. One point of view argued at length for law, clear and common:

I think [the church] is a set of guidelines for right and wrong for people to live by. I don't think it is buildings or preachers or a place to go one day a week. A man always has a need for standing on absolutist ground. All man has searched for [some kind of certainty], something absolute, something final, something that cannot be shaken. People are searching for that, and they find it in a lot of different churches: the basics, the fundamental things, the Ten Commandments and things like that. . . . It would be awfully nice if you could just go someplace and they'd lay down the absolute law. It would be like an old Doris Day movie, just like Errol Flynn.

Not everyone's religion is made of absolutes, however. In another conversation, a participant explained that it was exactly the emphasis on law that had narrowed his image of God. He talked about the change in his perspective on the role of the church in the development of morality:

[My parents didn't have] a lot of gray in their morality. And I've had to kick some of that, because now as I look at these later chapters in my life, I see that there is a lot of gray in life, a lot of gray morality that they would have a hard time with. [My morality], all too Irish and Catholic, is sexual morality, but much beyond that is a kind of lack of definition around law and the areas between law and love. . . . I was raised in a family of law, and the church was law. [But] in the '60's, the church and the [Vatican] council were saying that if there is not love, then the law isn't energizing, isn't vivifying. And so that opened up a whole new spectrum by which to measure morality. Does it produce love? Does it come as flowing from a loving person? Does our behavior call us to love? Well, that isn't just a sexual thing. All of a sudden it expands morality to a social dimension: how to get along with people and family. And what kind of a God do we worship? Is it a God who is a lawgiver, or is it this tremendous lover? That whole expansion of morality broke me out into a new person.

A comparable proportion of respondents (19%) feel that, above other functions, the church is the place where they find support and fellowship among people who are seeking God. Those who took this position were clear about it. Church is where nice people gather to be a support to one another. They said things like:

Church should be a group of people who help each other.

The church isn't . . . so much what the religion is. I feel it's more of a place
that everybody goes to be together. It's fellowship more than worship. So
many people think that the only place you can pray is in church. I don't think
that you have to be in church [to pray].

Some people had entertained the same idea but then found fellowship an inadequate reason to go to church when other associations
seemed as able to fill that need, some of them even better than the
local congregation. One woman put it this way:

So many times when I attended church off and on, I would say to myself,
"I'm really involved in the community already. I have a job and a husband.
I don't need another club to belong to. I don't want to join the church and
make myself available for more work." One particular Sunday, the message
that the pastor was delivering was meant for me. He said the exact words
that I had used to my husband. He said, "What do you think that this church
is? Another club in the community to join? It's not. It's God's work here on
earth. And it's the most important cause you can join or become a part of."
And I knew there was no turning back.

The point of the inquiry was to find out whether people believe that
the church is an instrument of their spiritual well-being or whether they
believe that the church is a community into which they enter. For
some people (7%) church is synonymous with worship; for more (15%),
moral direction; for others, (19%) fellowship. For most, though (59%),
the church is "the body of Christ, a community into which they have
entered and in which they live their life as a follower of Christ." For
these people, church is the extention of Christ on earth. Church is
community, obligation, kinship, bondedness, discipleship—"the community of those faithful to God and the Scriptures"; "the body of believers"; "a physical body that has parts, functions, and tasks, joined
with Christ as its head . . . for direction, order, nerve center." For
these people, church is a life environment, a special people.

What may be of greatest note in these responses is not that the majority define the church as the body of Christ, but that many see the
church in more specific ways. The church is being looked to for many
things, perhaps because the church itself has claimed those prerogatives, maybe because it has not clearly claimed any of them. It may
be that people themselves heap their personal needs on the church,
possibly because the church, like the society in transition around it,
is undergoing fundamental change. Whatever the cause, if the church

is to be effective, if not unique, it appears that a major debate on the role of the church is pending.

The Mission of the Church

Aside from what people look to the church to provide in their personal lives, there is the question of what people see as the essential task of the church in general. Around this issue new movements have sprung up to challenge the traditional mainstream posture of the Christian churches. Why and how the movements have begun may illustrate best the impact of mission on the future of the institutional church.

In the field study that accompanied this research, we intended to concentrate entirely on the church as institution, its goals and public role. Originally, the research team fully expected to examine the capacity of churches and church life to deal with major social problems affecting Minnesota. For several years controversies and debates concerning land, water, and energy use had engaged the state and, in some instances, its clergy and churches. We assumed that the churches, through official and unofficial representatives, would interact with the structures of other public systems—business and government, for instance—to raise issues and affect public policy. The problem was to determine the process of church participation in public controversy and social debate. We expected that different groups might have developed different methods in the pursuit of public influence. That is not what we found.

Instead we discovered churches deeply involved in their own identity questions and face to face with a movement whose agenda and sense of Christian mission departed from their own. The concern was not whether or not churches should be involved in public issues, but which issues ought to be the focus of the committed Christian. Two streams of contemporary Christianity came quickly to the surface. The one saw its role to promote an incarnational gospel, the idea that Christ has broken into human history and so models for Christians the need to take upon themselves the human concerns of the day. The other feels that secular humanism is breaking down the scriptural authority of God, the dignity of the family, and the moral fiber of the United States, a country overblessed and therefore particularly obliged to be a sign and keeper of the covenant. Their agenda cut across denominations and traditional structures, was not centered in a monolithic organization, and challenged the role churches have played in cultural development.

In each case, the groups are actively involved in promoting what they consider essential to the Christian message. The problem is that they find one another's contribution to public life at least deficient, if not defective. Promoters of the incarnational gospel say that conservative activists fear change, are destructive of pluralism, and are pious but not prophetic in their practice of religion. Conservative Christian activists say that mainstream churches have allowed moral absolutes to erode and are more bases for social or political activity than they are for the denunciation of sin and the lordship of Jesus. In each stream, too, there are varieties and degrees of involvement.

The Christian community is alive with the role-of-the-church question. It is affecting ministry, membership, and public participation as well as Christian witness in the culture. Mission may be the church question of the day.

Ministry

Liberal Christian activists, the field research team reported, were involved in housing, health care, human rights programs, education for social change, economic development, and the peace movement. Conservative Christian activists, on the other hand, were concentrating on other issues, and were actually opposed to some of the presumably secular matters that the liberal Christians saw as essential Christian ministries. For instance, conservatives see human rights programs which support the women's movement and the civil status of homosexuals as a danger to the Christian family. In health care and public education they fear the breakdown of sexual mores and the secularization of life. In the peace movement they see a capitulation to atheistic communism and a threat to the American, and therefore Christian, way of life. These conservative activists are against abortion, sex education in the public schools, the teaching of evolution, the Equal Rights Amendment, and nuclear disarmament—all of which they consider a direct result of the infiltration of society by secular humanism. These Christians are for the teaching of creationism, for the traditional family structure, and for a strong national defense, all of which they see as basic scriptural mandates.

Two world views, both claimed to be embedded in Scripture and essential to the Christian message, underlie each of these contemporary currents of Christianity. Each is based on a different understanding of the mission of the church. Each transcends denominational distinctions. Each shapes ministry and the Christian witness in the world. Each seeks cultural change in the name of religion. Interview participants spoke about the mission of the church and reflected the tensions the research team observed in the church groups.

From the side of the incarnational gospel, a Lutheran pastor articulated what many people discussed in reference to a single issue.

I think God has never been so effective as he is in our time. The great things that we see and the concern for God's creation and the environment and the growth in freedoms . . . [Those are the things the church should be concerned with.] The gospel to me is, essentially, freeing people from hang-ups, and from one another, freeing people from all the [false attitudes] that have held women in bondage and other races in bondage, and poor people who are in bondage in Ecuador. So I think the church is at its best when it is freeing people.

Another person talked about trying to come to grips with what he considered two equally important aspects of Christianity: the incarnational gospel and a personal relationship with Christ. He said:

For a long time I was so into the social action thing, that maybe I was losing my personal relationship with God. I think I have grown to the point that I understand that there is a duality there that we need to foster, our relationship with God and with our fellow human beings. One's relationship with God and the whole aspect of prayer and meditation can lead to so much energy and strength for the social battles we face. . . . I think most churches really come down on the personal side . . . they might see their job as ministering to the people in their congregation, but [they do] no outward looking, whatsoever. . . . I think that it is an absolutely essential time for the church to be out there, to counterbalance this trend [Reaganomics and the conservative swing], and to analyze what is going on and see if it is consistent with our faith. I am on a social-action committee at church, and we've been concentrating on how we are going to minister to the local community. And that is an essential part of what we need to do. But what I brought up last time was that we need to also know how we should relate to our larger communities—state, national, and international.

Others recognized the place of charity in the works of the church but were careful to stress the development of personal spirituality as preeminent and basic to the Christian commitment. Good works without a personal relationship with Jesus, they argued, are without value. One person said:

We do focus in that area [works of charity] but first we feel that if they do not have the right attitude toward Christ, what they do will not please him, because he says that without faith it is impossible to please God.

Another facet of the Christian community is convinced that public issues have only an oblique relationship with religion. If people renounce sin and turn to Christ, they say, then social welfare will take care of itself. It is personal sanctification that is the mission of the church, they believe. One person expressed what was implied in many interviews:

I would like to see the church get back to try and teach their people who are sitting in those pews to be honest. Then, I would say let the people decide, not the minister, where their feelings lie about issues [like war, ecology, and human services]. We have a government, and I do not think that the church needs to be in it. The ministry should stick to ministerial areas [like] belief in God, telling the truth, and being as moral as possible.

Even with these differences in emphasis, people talked about the involvement in public affairs as having something to do with the mission of the church. The agenda differed from one end of the spectrum to the other. One group is concerned that the authority of God and the family is being destroyed; the other that the destruction of human dignity is a sin against the creative design of God. But, for the most part, both groups hold that it is the mission of the Christian church to be concerned about life in this world as well as about life in the next. One person put the argument in "conservative" terms, but the tone is general. (Substitute discrimination for prayer in schools, armaments for abortion, and military-industrial complex for the gay community, and the statement might well have come from some of the most "liberal" Christians surveyed and interviewed):

Christians have to get involved in politics, because the morals of the country are going down. The Christians are a sleeping giant that has to get involved, and they can control the destiny of the United States. It really made me happy when I found out about this Moral Majority. There is a lot of crying in the press right now, and politicians saying that the church is overstepping its bounds because they are involved in politics. I believe that's wrong. I believe they've got it backwards. The state, in my opinion, overstepped its bounds years ago when they started dictating [whether or not] people could pray in schools, or that I have to spend my money so that people can have abortions, or that I have to support the gay community, which I feel is totally against my Bible teachings, and the state dictates that I have to treat them as special individuals. I feel that they are overstepping their bounds when they dictate these things to me which are supposedly the church's jurisdiction. And the church is just beginning to fight back, and it's got a lot of people up in arms.

Because of this attitude, the membership patterns have altered and extrachurch associations have sprung up to meet the need.

Membership, Movements and Mission

Church groups and individuals reported the growing phenomenon of church shopping, both outside and within denominations, as people look for congregations and pastors that meet their own convictions about what the church should do and be. More than that, the "New Religious Right" has developed within churches of every denomination. The field research team discovered that, contrary to public opinion or media description, Christian conservatism is not a monolithic, neochurch structure with a designated leader. It is instead a movement that transcends denominational boundaries to work for what it believes to be the Christian message: that the activity and authority of God in the world has been obscured by the teaching of secular humanism; that pluralism has eroded the absolute value of Christian principles and Americanism; that the family, the unit divinely ordained and above all other human institutions, is under Satanic attack.

The movement is segmented rather than centralized in structure. Ideas, rather than membership roles, hold the group together. Small local groups attend to the core issues: sex education in the schools, legislators' voting records, the use of tax monies. National or regional figures act as information bridges among the various local groups. Networks form to bind the various local groups. Seminars, retreats, and publications acquaint local activists with their peers elsewhere. The field research team described it this way:

They are organized in a way best described as segmentary, polycentric, and integrated in networks. This gives us the acronym SPIN which also projects a kind of image of the organizational type. It spins out from its many centers, and it holds together around the pull of a central idea because of the way the various segments and leaders or center share information, cooperate, and interact to form networks of reciprocal exchange and common concern and stand against a common foe.

In the name of Christianity the movement sets out to spread the Word, commit people to its purposes, identify its opposition, and articulate an ideology which both motivates people to act and legitimates that action. That ideology is drawn from the church and a sense of its mission, but that sense, the social survey data indicates, is anything but uniform. The field research study concludes:

Our study indicates that as many, or perhaps even more, differences can be found among people in the same church or among churches in the same denomination [as might be found among people of different churches], not only in their political and social views, but also in their theologies. This has, perhaps, always been true to some extent. But it would seem that denominational labels served as better "lumpings" of this variety of faith in the past than they do now. If we are right, one of the implications of this finding is that churches and denominations are perhaps justified in being very cautious about taking formal positions, such as passing resolutions at official local church congregational or at denominational, regional, or national decision-making meetings, since the potential for effecting change through them is likely to be less than is their potential for risking divisiveness. Thus, action that goes beyond rhetoric is likely to be taken in settings other than within churches or denominations. It is with this premise that we have explored activities and ideas which, for the most part, informants call religiously or Christian-inspired or based, but which are carried on primarily outside the institutional church.

Because of the philosophical differences present in mainstream churches, movements within them may be more important for social action than the churches themselves. An interview participant described even more graphically what the anthropologists had already found in many groups:

Reality for me is that the church is not always at the same spot. The church is a whole gamut of people who are all at different levels. I am comfortable when the church speaks, even if it is only a minority. At least they can be the conscience for the rest. To try to get the church to speak en masse with some sincerity about any issue, as far as I'm concerned, is almost hypocritical, or unrealistic. They may be able to shove it through, but nobody believes it. What is more exciting to me these days, is to see people who are at the same level of the same intensity, or the same interest, coming together, and then speaking. Whether it is a fragment, or a minority, at least speaking. Then you know that X number of people are speaking with that kind of conviction, and they are doing it on the basis of the fact that they are Christians. Networking is a concept that becomes very real these days. . . . You keep getting plugged into people who are thinking the same things you are thinking, believing the same things that you are believing. And that may be within your own church body or ecumenically. And sometimes that can be a much better impact than trying to twist the arm of some assembly or district or synodical convention.

With that background, the social survey data becomes even clearer. Almost the entire survey population (97%) agree that the mission of the church is to preach or spread the gospel to all. Eighty-four percent also believe that local congregations and denominations should fulfill their mission by ministering to their own members. On two key points, however, the group divides. Half (50%) take the position that the first and most important obligation of their churches and denominations is to meet the needs of their own members. On the second issue, again almost half (42%) feel that the churches in the United States should influence government to a stronger degree than they do. To look at the problem from a different perspective, half want their churches to exert influence on public policy—as a mission of the church—and half do not. The tension between the private and public mission of the church is apparent. Furthermore, that tension could be critical for the future of Christianity in the United States. The question of the parable, "What do they *really* need?" is no small matter and one, it seems, that the institutional church must be able and willing to spend time thinking about if the church situation in Minnesota mirrors the church throughout the country to any significant degree whatsoever. The point is not that this study claims to have in any way determined the relative strength or quantity of either conservative or liberal Christianity. The point is that the monk's question is an important one.

The validity of the networking and of nondenominational groupings as new manifestations of the Christian church is confirmed by another facet of the data. Though almost the total population (94%) of the study was convinced that a main task of the church is to proclaim or spread the gospel to all the peoples of the world, not nearly as many (38%) would also contend that a main task of all churches is to convert all peoples to Christ. A few (5%) even said that the churches should not attempt to secure converts to Christ from peoples of other religions. Gone are the days, apparently, when conquering the world for Christ gets much endorsement.

Attitudes Toward Ecumenism

On the contrary, the desire for unity is high. Practically everyone in the study (95%) felt that churches should cooperate with one another whenever possible. More than three-fourths (77%) said churches should move beyond cooperation and try to achieve greater unity than they now have. And 65% even argued that in every church the sacrament of Holy Communion should be open to members of other denominations. So strong is the idea that the separate denominations are valid and valuable that conversion from one to another has become an uncertain value. So strong is the desire for unity that proselytism which encourages change from one denomination to another may have been virtually rejected. What is more, over three-quarters of the participants in the study (78%) felt that new converts to Christ should be encouraged to select a church of their own choice and not be pressured to join "my church." A number of people (41%) had reservations, too, about persuading members of other denominations to transfer that commitment even to their own churches, and less than half of the population (46%) were willing to claim that their church is "the true church" of Christ. Interview participants talked at length about these views. Their positions were unusually similar. A representative sample said:

I never have been disturbed about the fact that there are different denominations. . . . I don't expect everyone to have the same stance.

I was really upset when our pastor said that our good friends who were Catholic couldn't be baptismal sponsors for our son. Why he wouldn't think that a Catholic wouldn't raise my child if something happened to us as well as we would [I don't understand]. The views on religion weren't that different. There is only one God, and everybody believes in God. How our minister could be so narrow-minded to think that I couldn't have a Catholic sponsor just really upset me.

My husband said to the pastor, "I want you to know that I am going to join the church because I like you as a minister. And if you leave, or somebody else joins that we don't like, we're going to go somewhere else. Or by the same token, if we find that we are dissatisfied with you or the people in the church, we are going somewhere else." And that's it. It's not what you believe. I don't think any one religion has it in the bag—that if you are totally Catholic, you are going to be saved and the Lutherans are going to hell. I think each religion, whether it's Jewish or Mormon, or whatever, has some good points.

I met a Buddhist and became very fond of him. He would have given me anything. I've still got the Buddhist Bible he gave me, and I've read it. There's very little different from Christianity. The Moslem faith, which I am familiar with, is also not a great deal different. Mohammed is their Jesus.

It seems that freedom of conscience and a genuine appreciation of other denominations and religions now supersedes the theological warfare of the past, unless confusion and indifferentism have taken its place.

The Elements of Worship

Though few people were willing to say that it is worship that defines their relation to the church, church attendance and worship are important to them. Christians of all churches center the Christian community around the worship of God and contact with Christ. In fact, half of the respondents report attendance at worship services on an average of four times a month; almost an additional third of the population (30%) participate in some type of church worship from five to eight times monthly. Only 1% say they never attend a church worship service.

We wanted to know which of the following elements of worship these people found most fulfilling: the sacraments, preaching, or prayer. The social survey data suggest a trend in both Protestant and Catholic congregations. The greater part of the sample population (64%) indicated that worship at church puts them in contact with Christ most competely when the Eucharist is offered and the Word is well preached—and this from groups which until recently had emphasized one or the other element. More people see Sunday worship as an opportunity to receive strength and guidance for the coming week through private reflection and prayer (52%) than as an instruction in Christianity (39%), a fact which pastors might want to compare to their own expectations for the Sunday service.

There is ample evidence of support for their local congregations among the participants to this study. They maintain the church financially on an average of $10 per week, and 30% tithe to the church. They attend church regularly. Sixty-four percent consider the religious education programs of their congregations satisfactory. These people seem to value their churches highly.

The Electronic Church

Nevertheless, the same people do not look to their local congregations for Christian worship or direction. On the contrary, the data indicate that the electronic church is potent, even among these church members. Almost half of these respondents (47%) listen to a religious program on the radio or television from one to four times a month. Another 18% listen to religious broadcasts even more than that.

The information suggests that even the churchgoing population is open to the influence of religion through the mass media and that two-thirds of this particular population is being reached by the electronic church. Only slightly more than one-third of the group (35%) said that they never listen to religious programs on the radio or television. The implications of this phenomenon for the communal dimensions of Christianity, for ecumenism, and for theological formation bears exploration. Insularity is clearly declining. The question is, what is taking its place?

Denominational Differences

By and large, the sacrament of Baptism was most remote for UCC members; Lutherans were most keenly aware of the sacrament as a present and effective factor in their lives. The Eucharist was the most effective way of coming into contact with Christ for Catholics. Scripture well preached is the most important element of spiritual development for Baptists and Methodists.

Catholics, who give strong support to cooperation (83%), are nonetheless considerably more opposed (42%) than any other of the Christian denominations to the concept of open communion. Almost a fourth of the Lutherans (21%) are equally reluctant. Finally, it is the Roman Catholic respondents in this survey (54%) who support proselytism, the practice of persuading members of other denominations to join one's own church, almost twice as much as many of the other denominations in the study.

Roman Catholics (39%) and Lutherans (15%) felt more strongly than respondents from other denominations that, ideally, Christian commitment requires that their children be educated in schools operated by the church, a smaller margin than might be expected in denominations for whom parochial education is an established part of the tradition. Methodists gave practically no support (1%) to the concept of church-school education.

Almost half of the Episcopalians (47%), UCC members (46%), Presbyterians (44%), and Catholics (40%), who participated in this random sample of church members in Minnesota claimed that they never listened to religious programs on the radio or TV. On the other hand, almost three-fourths of the Baptist (73%), Methodist (72%), Evangelical Covenant (75%), and Lutheran church members (71%) said they listened to one or more per month.

Demographic Distinctions

Almost twice as many clergy (92%) as laity (55%) consider the church the body of Christ, a community into which they have entered to live their lives as followers of Christ. What is the explanation for the fact that church leaders, but not church members, look most on the church as community? Is it that the theology behind the question is clearer to the clergy, or simply that for them the church is, indeed, their life environment, while for most laity it may be family, not church, that is perceived to be the basis of their community life? More clergy (53%) than laity (64%) question the practice of proselytizing, and fewer clergy (53%) than laity (64%) hold their church to be the true church. Finally, more laity (53%) than clergy (24%) take the position that the first and most important obligation of their parishes or congregations is to meet the needs of their own members, which suggests clergy and laity may have different ideas of the mission of the church.

According to our survey, women (49%) are more likely than men (42%) to consider their church the "true church"; women (54%) said more often than men (41%) that the Eucharist is the most effective way of coming into contact with Christ; and women (53%) more often than men (44%) reported that the primary task of the church is to minister to its own members. But men (87%) more than women (32%) were markedly more supportive of persuading the members of other denominations to join their own. Whether these postures derive from the distinctly different socialization of men and women or from different theological insights cannot be determined, but the positions are sufficiently central to the faith to warrant further discussion.

One of the interviewees weighed the balance between personal faith and the institutional church and posited this as an explanation for trying to maintain the two together:

How can you divorce [faith or a personal relationship with God from the institutional church]? To say that I would rather have a personal faith than a church relationship [is impossible]. They're too tied together. . . . I guess that is what helped me get through some of my real feelings of indignation as far as the institutional church is concerned. I thought of someone who was living in Germany within an institution that was ignoring so much of the awful things that were going on at the time [of the Hitler regime]. And yet, he didn't give up on the church. You'd think that someone like that, with sensitivity and understanding of the world would have just thrown up his hands and let it go down the drain. And yet he had some belief in the possibilities of community and church. . . . It blows my mind. I draw strength from that. . . . The church has always been flawed. We've done awful things in the church, and yet there's been that thread, that small remnant, a small group of people who have stayed in touch with what it was meant to be. And that's why it survived. If the pope does these dumb things these days, we'll survive that, too. Because there are still those that ask the questions, that live the faith, that serve as the ongoing strength. And to draw away from that is something that I am not willing to do, although it's really hard often. In particular I empathize with women right now and what the institutional church has done to women. And yet I say, Jesus lived in an institutional church, and my God, there were more flaws then and he never gave up on it either. And that has to say something.

If the study has done nothing else, it has confirmed the dynamic, the changing character of church in our time, even among church members. Old absolutes have blurred a bit, a comfort to some and a loss to others. The scandal of division is breaking down, but the role of church is often unclear. Ghettoism and parochialism have diminished, but so have stable congregations. Nevertheless, church members continue to go to church—some for community, some for direction, many to develop in a relationship with Christ, even though the challenges seem greater than in the past and the mission more diffuse.

12

And They All Heard
in Their Own Tongues
Overall Trends

If churches teach one thing but people believe another, what does that mean? Should anyone care? If different people hear the gospel message differently, is either message still the gospel? Are the answers given by Christians in this research the answers that the churches expect them to be? And does it make any difference? Are the various denominations of the Christian church in Minnesota more different than alike, or more alike than different? Is the church of Christ in a state of Babel or at a new Pentecost?

On the one hand, the responses we have collected have been rich in differences. On the other hand, they have contained audible signals of transcendent constants. They have reflected a singularity of commitment, but its complexity as well. As a result, there is no guarantee that we have come to know clearly what the church is becoming, but we may well have discovered what the church is not: it is not monolithic. It is not a closed community. It is not a safe place from the struggles of the age. In fact, in many cases Christianity itself is the question that comes between these Christians and the culture in which they live. In other cases, the culture is a clear test of their Christianity.

What can be said, then, about the place of the contemporary church in Minnesota and its relationship to key points in Christian theology and human events? For it is exactly at the point of critical issues that the similarities, differences, and uncertainties of the church emerge most clearly. The following conclusions are based not only on those who are definitely committed to a certain position (as is the case for the presentation of the rest of the data in this study), but includes those who also agree or disagree slightly with the positions given. The purpose is to identify leanings in the Christian population, as well as determined positions.

About Life

Questions of life and death divide the Christian community. Euthanasia (mercy killing controlled by law) is still unacceptable to 84% of the Catholics and 65% of the Protestants in the survey. More than a third (38%) of the respondents believe that both physical and mental illness could be a basis for withdrawing or withholding life support systems. Most of these Christians (62%) accept the death penalty—especially the Baptists in the study (85%)—but 38% say that laws that provide for punishment by death are immoral. Barely half (54%) of the population think that the teachings of Scripture or the historic church tradition are clear and consistent on whether Christians may support war. Birth control is accepted (86%) and even more so by the clergy (91%) than the laity (85%) in the study. Abortion is acceptable, at least in some cases, to almost three-quarters (70%) of the population. Only Roman Catholics condemn abortion to any significant degree (65%).

The feeling is that in the Christian community life is not an absolute. It can be controlled and it can be taken at some times and under some circumstances, but exactly which circumstances govern its control may not be completely clear. Is this a cultural or an historical Christian interpretation of the use of life? If it is historical, what does that say about the nature of Christianity?

About the Church

Baptism is important to the greater proportion of all the denominations (87%) represented in the study. But the implications of that Baptism in a given church differ among the groups represented. Almost all clergy (92%) consider the church "the body of Christ." For most of the laity (55%) that is also true, but the gap here between the clergy and the laity is apparent. For many of the laity, church is most a place of worship (7%), value education (16%), or community (21%). Methodists (44%) look most to the church for support; Baptists (78%) are most accepting of the idea of church as "body of Christ."

Most (63%) believe that their church is "the true church of Christ"—the laity (64%) more than the clergy (53%)—and Roman Catholics most of all (89%). But over half (51%) think, too, that people have the right to ignore or disobey church laws on the basis of their Christian beliefs. What is more, most churches are almost evenly divided on the question. Whereas 65% of the Catholics take the position that in order to get to heaven they must do what the church says, members of the United Church of Christ (90%) dismiss that idea almost entirely. But Catholics (41%), more than any of the other Christians in the study, accept all the teachings of the church as essential to their faith. UCC members (88%) clearly do not. Most of the other respondents, too, believe that they can reject some teachings of the church but still have deep faith. At the same time, most of the laity (60%), unlike their clergy (44%), think that it is right to persuade other Christians to join their denomination. On the other hand, 92% of the laity, like the clergy (86%), say they would not pressure new converts to Christ to join their congregations.

These Christians believe in their churches, but they differ in terms of how tightly they draw the relationship between church and faith, between church and salvation, between church as people and church as institution. Both the theological and social ramifications of these distinct viewpoints are profound.

Finally, and perhaps consequently, the tensions in the churches show divergence. The clergy (92%) are apparently much more intent on the involvement of the church in social-justice issues—racism, sexism, and economic concerns—than the laity (74%). The clergy believe that the church should make a special effort to help insure that women have equal opportunity and rights with men in all aspects of society (81%); but the laity (62%) are not nearly so convinced of that idea.

Christians from all churches (89%) agreed that a mission of the church is to help minority peoples. But the laity (77%) argued that the first and most important obligation of their parishes or congregations is to meet the needs of its own members. The clergy were divided on this issue, with 53% agreeing, and 48% disagreeing.

The laity in Minnesota (74%) and even more of the clergy (84%) do not believe that the church should exert influence to insure that the United States is Number One in military power, or that the church should ever give unqualified support to any war (laity—64%, clergy—75%).

Clearly, the role of the church in social matters is an unresolved question. More than that, the clergy think one way and the laity think another. The obvious but not elementary question is, Why?

About Universal Salvation

If the respondents to this study are any reflection of the mind of the Christian church at large, then Christians (85%) believe that the gospel of Christ is necessary for the salvation of all peoples. They feel strongly (94%) that a main task of all churches is to proclaim or spread the gospel to all peoples of the world. Though most (89%) feel that not everyone will be saved, they do not accept the idea of predestination (87%), and most (54%) have a sense of their own salvation, especially Baptists (85%). Many (42%) believe that one reason the church must proclaim the gospel is to save those who may be lost hereafter.

The problem is that though most feel that the gospel of Christ is necessary for the salvation of all people they do not also feel that a main task of the church is to convert all peoples to Christ. To some Christians, Christ is necessary for salvation, yet not everyone has to be a Christian to be saved. Which of these two positions is most consonant with the gospel and within the tradition of the church is important, both to ecumenism and to the growing interdependence of the world at large.

About Evil

Most of the Christians represented in this study (70%) do not believe that God creates evil, but the laity (68%) are not as sure of this as the clergy (87%). Clergy, too (97%), accept with more ease than the laity (76%) that the mass extermination of human beings and other evils can take place in a world in which a loving God exists. However, though one-third claimed that suffering had both strengthened and weakened their faith in God at different times, over half (56%) said that suffering had actually strengthened it.

The question of evil is clearly still a question, but one which people accept relatively well. Nevertheless, Christianity is a religion built on the sufferings of Christ, not on nirvana, not on reincarnation, not on Stoicism. It seems that Christians, of all people, would be more agreed on the nature and purpose of evil and suffering.

About Sin

Christians (92%) believe, it seems, that an awareness of sin is essential for spiritual development. What they are not agreed upon is whether a Christian must believe that all persons are sinful (59% agree, and 21% disagree). Clergy (71%) take that position more than the laity do (58%). On this, far more Baptists (93%) and Lutherans (91%) agree that belief in sin is essential than is the case with other denominations; and Roman Catholics are evenly divided on this question.

People question the causes of sin, too. The clergy, by and large (82%), take the position that sin is caused by an "innate tendency," but almost half (48%) of the laity disagree; they say that "circumstances" are at base and that human nature is not evil. The clergy, too, are much more likely (81%) than the laity in the study (63%) to consider themselves "sinful" rather than given to making "mistakes." Clergy (64%) and laity (62%) are about even on Satan as a personal being rather than as an evil force.

To most of these Christians (68%), suffering is part of life. It will always exist, and the church must always minister to it. Yet the laity (77%) say that if Christian principles are applied to international affairs, humankind could actually "beat its swords into plowshares." The clergy (57%) are far less optimistic. But, then, the clergy (55%) believe that illness, calamity, and other forms of suffering and crisis are the result of sin, to which people have an innate tendency. The laity (67%) say they are not.

Either people do not understand or they do not accept what their churches are apparently saying about the nature and effects of sin. Either the laity have a poorly developed theology of sin, or the clergy are less intent than they on the equally Christian aspects of hope and conversion. At any rate, the gap between clergy and laity is so distinct on this subject that someone must ask whether the people are obstinate or the clergy are sin-ridden, whether the people are misinformed or the clergy ave overly pessimistic. What are the effects of both these attitudes on personal growth and social development, on church and on faith?

About Revelation

The Christians in this study almost unanimously (94%) accept the Bible as the Word of God and a necessary belief for all Christians. Baptists especially (63%) see the Bible as the direct Word of God, reported verbally, and without error. In fact, over a third of every denomination represented except the Methodists (27%), the Episcopalians (16%), and members of the UCC (16%) see the Bible as the literal words of God and true in every detail.

God is part of life to these people. God intervenes in the daily circumstances of their lives (86%); God plays an active part in guiding them and helping them to make life decisions (95%); and God intervenes in the affairs of society in general (84%). For the laity (72%) much more than for their clergy (44%), unplanned and unexpected events are signs of God's intervening will.

But people also reveal God's will to these Christians. Movements for black liberation, for instance, have helped many (70%) to realize that all the people of God possess human dignity. The role of the church in defining the will of God seems to be less clear than other facets of revelation: Scripture, a personal God, people. Less than a third (32%) believe that in order to get to heaven they must do what their church tells them. In fact, only 19% of the clergy took that position. Three-quarters of the laity and even more of the clergy (82%) said that sometimes it is necessary for them to obey their own consciences rather than the teachings of their churches. For the Catholics in the study the questions are apparently fraught with tension. Catholic responses, at least on the face of them, show a lack of resolution. Catholics (65%) say they must do what their church tells them to do in order to get to heaven; but 69% also say that they sometimes obey their own consciences rather than the teachings of their church.

That God is real for these people is clear. What is less clear is how important their churches are to their relationship with God, or in what way the church as denomination or institution mediates the presence and will of God for them. Is church a repository of revelation, a source of revelation, or a model of revelation?

About Christ

To these Christians (97%), Jesus Christ is the Son of God whose Gospel is necessary for the salvation of all the people of the world. To follow Jesus means to take the side of the poor and oppressed and do what is possible to secure justice for them (94%). What is more, churches themselves should take leadership in social justice issues, the laity say (74%)—but not as strongly as their clergy do (92%). Presbyterians (80%) and Catholics (78%), though, are particularly clear about this dimension of the mission of the church. Perhaps the discrepancy lies in the fact that laity (64%) were more inclined to see Jesus as "master of the personal and spiritual life of the individual Christian," while clergy maintained (81%) that the biblical affirmation, "Jesus Christ is Lord" means that Jesus is "master of all of human life, individual and social."

Nonetheless, they recognize equality as a keystone of the Christian way. They agree that in Christ "there does not exist among you Jew nor Greek . . . male nor female" (Gal. 3:28), at least in the kingdom of God. But though they say there should be no racial discrimination in the church (98%), they are far less committed to a nondiscriminatory role for women in the church (64%). Members of the United Church of Christ (62%), Methodist (53%), and Presbyterian (70%) congregations were strongest in their support of the role of women in the church. Other denominations are divided on the matter. Here, too, the clergy and the laity show a different bent. The clergy are committed to the fact that the church itself should make special efforts to insure that women have equal opportunities and rights with men both in church ministry (71%) and in the public arena (81%). The laity, on the other hand, are relatively as open to women in church ministry (67%) as their clergy are, but significantly less supportive (62%) of the idea that churches should help women gain equal opportunities and rights with men in all aspects of society. Whether the difference stems from the fact that the laity are less committed to the equality of women or to the involvement of the church in public issues is unclear, but the subjects need to be explored if orthodoxy and practice are to be consistent.

Life after death is an important concept of faith among these people (94%). But clergy (82%) more than laity (69%) link the resurrection of Christ to the credibility of Christianity. Most clergy say that if Christ had not risen from the dead, Christian teaching would mean very little to them. A third of the laity, however, seem to feel that Christian teaching and Christian churches are valuable for their own sakes, whether or not the resurrection established the divinity of Christ and the authority of the church.

It is obvious that great currents of thought are sweeping through the Christian community. Some of these currents may lead to departures from tradition. Others may be the resurgence of tradition at its best. Whatever the case, gone are the traditional Christian divisions. There are differences between the denominations, but there are also deep differences of world view within the denominations. There are also overarching truths and overarching questions which mark the faith-life of today's Christian. Perhaps it has always been so, but it is hard to believe that ever before has so much depended on the answers.

It is hard to know whose lives will be touched by this information. For some these findings may be only an academic exercise, a resource book among resource books. For others it may be a challenge. Surely for anyone it can be a cause for self-examination. "What is the church of Christ?" is certainly the question that has to stretch every Christian's life. Counselors, preachers, teachers, catechists, theologians, parents, and church leaders should all find something here, not simply to study as technicians, but to learn from as Christians. For to them falls the obligation to pass on the faith to future generations who may well demand to know about the place of the Christian church in these troubled times: the fidelity of its message, the relevance of its presence, the depth of its dogma, the clarity of its witness.

There is clearly more to attend to in the Christian church than simply its questions. The Sufi of Persia may have understood best the real power of religion, whatever its struggles. A tale reads:

A man on a camel passing the sage Zardalu called out at the sight of such a humble one who was believed by his followers to be a great teacher: "If the Teaching is designed to uplift people why is it that so many can be found who are cast down?"

The sage answered without raising his head: "If it were not for the Teaching, people would not, I agree, be cast down. If it were not for the Teaching, people would be extinct."

The controlling question of the study was not, "When the Son of Man returns, will he find clarity?" The question was, "When the Son of Man returns, will he find faith?" The study questions the theological clarity of peoples; it does not question the sincerity of their faith.

PART TWO

Historical
and Theological Analysis

MARTIN E. MARTY

Introduction to Part 2

Minnesotans who express their faith and its ferment have not appeared "out of the clear blue sky," even though their state has a great deal of clarity and blueness to its sky. All of them, including their Native Americans, who derive from Asia, have come from somewhere else. Most of them are of European, Asian, or African roots—roots which were pulled up within the last century and a half and transplanted to the soil of this northern Midwestern state.

Walking History

The citizens may not know it, but they are walking examples of history. Their own personal memories do not extend beyond their own lifetimes. Their elaborated stories may come from parents and grandparents, but oral traditions do not go back much further than two or three generations. They are subjected to constant bombardment by the "now" in mass media of communication. Some of them have a kind of amnesia, and others seek it, deliberately rejecting tradition in order to

Martin E. Marty, Ph.D., is professor of the history of modern Christianity at the University of Chicago, and associate editor of *The Christian Century.* Dr. Marty is a member of the Association of Evangelical Lutheran Churches.

be up to date, to belong to the moment. We cannot assume that courses on the history of the church are extremely popular.

To speak of historical analysis may, at first glance, seem to be importing questions from the university which have little to do with daily life. What are you thinking *now* about God and state and self? This seems to be the tone of the entire Faith and Ferment project. Yet the nowness is only apparent. The people may not always possess the tradition, but the tradition possesses them. The words they use, the phrases they employ, the images and models of church and secular life, all have pasts. They were shaped by people and transmitted through the generations by other people. "Faith" has a history, as does "ferment" and, even more interesting, so do "church" and "synagogue." Whoever belongs to the "church" is dealing with a reality that goes back at least to the time right after Jesus, and "synagogue" is a somewhat still older invention of Jews. They were not born yesterday and will not be exhausted with tomorrow.

How do people get their history? Just as it is borne along by genes or by lines of family, church, school, and state, they receive it from the chronicles of historians. Historians are not immediately relevant to the purposes of these Minnesotans. Keepers of the annals do their quiet work in dusty, undersubsidized, largely ignored archives and studies. Only when people do not know what to do, when they get stuck and have to "stop to think" do they give historians a hearing. Then the chroniclers open the book and show where the people have been, hoping to awaken an "aha!" or recognition, a "now I see!" about possible choices ahead. Whoever opens a Bible, a hymnal, a book of church or synagogue law or procedure, or the convention handbook of a denomination becomes a historian. What texts from the past disclose is possible ways of being today.

To provide historical analysis for the Faith and Ferment study, then, is to pull back curtains on archives, to open doors on studies, and to let a little of the dust and the light of the past fall on present-day believers. Such analysis provides points of comparison with other Americans, other Christians, other participants in the "Western" traditions of religiousness, even if these are today borne also by Africans and Asians. The easiest way to see how much roots, traditions, and history have to do with current life is to picture how different the responses to these questions would be were they provided by Buddhists, Hindus, or Muslims.

Minnesota Theologians

Similarly, the Minnesota respondents do not think of themselves as theologians, and a theological analysis may seem remote from their thinking, a bizarre application of intellectual tools to ordinary life. Theology, after all, is a very technical field, rich in jargon and private concerns, something carried on by professionals who check out their concerns with other professionals. Had there been questions about the image of theology, it is likely that most of the believers would have been characteristically American and asked for "just a simple faith," uncomplicated by creed, dogma, or theology.

In a startling number of ways, however, the respondents do show themselves to be theologians. The word, broken down, means that they have some words *(logos)* about God *(theos)*. Theology is not the direct experience of God; it is comment on that experience. It is not the worship of God so much as ways of clarifying what goes on in worship and other transactions with God. Theology is a discipline that employs tools from other disciplines—especially philosophy, literary study, and history—to illumine the understandings of humans in the light of God. Ordinarily it is a "plural" science. However much it applies to the lives of individuals, it is also devoted to the common existence of Christians. We might think of it as an interpretation of the life of a people in the light of God. This separates it somewhat from philosophy of religion, which deals more with ideas than with the community which holds them. Theologians, we might say, have little to talk about apart from the words of the believing community which provides the raw material for them.

If we keep this larger and yet formally apt definition of theology in view, the Faith and Ferment respondents are very much theologians. They ask and answer all the questions that the professionals ask, though in somewhat different language. One could take the answers of these Minnesotans, translate the terms a bit, and find outlines for textbooks on the hardest questions in theology, not least of all those that have to do with how and why a good God can cause or allow suffering in the world.

Theological analysis, then, here means an attempt to collate and clarify the answers in the light of the longer history of American and Christian theology. This is not a textbook on what Athanasius, Radbertus, or Jonathan Edwards—voices from the distant past—have said on the present subjects. It is a somewhat less formal application of norms from the world of historical theology to the attempts by citizens today to formulate visions of life lived under God.

If history is locating present-day people in their flow of past lives, and theology is locating their beliefs and ideas in the light of a transcendent or sacred reference, then this is a historical and theological analysis. Having mentioned something of what it is, it will be helpful to mention what it is not—four things.

What This Is Not

First, it is not a comment on the relative accuracy of the data. We shall not here question whether interviewers' tape recorders ran well, whether the right holes were punched and the totals properly totaled on computer questionnaires. Was the sample of the population gathered with sufficient care? These are important, of course, for they have to do with the data base itself. But we leave them to social scientists or to directors of the project. For present purposes, it is appropriate to have a kind of naive faith in the findings, to take them as they are, and to ask, in effect, "If this is a fair representation of a Minnesota sample, what does it tell us about their religious outlook and way of life?"

Second, this is not a critique of the questions or the way they were put. At times we shall not be able to resist scratching an itch of comment on the questions. We might, for example, have wished for many more topics. What do these people think about consumption of tobacco and liquor or the enjoyment of social dancing? These are questions that exercised and agitated the imagination of generations of religious Minnesotans, and responses to them would tell much about the ferment of faith in the state. The questioners and questionnaires overlooked many topics of historic controversy: what happens to the bread and wine in the central sacred activity of Christian worship? Does a question do full justice to the shadings of theology and does another one properly frame the historical perspective? Such questions are all also valid and should consume the parlor game time of some groups that make use of these findings. We must hurry past most of them most of the time in order to get to our central issues.

Thirdly, this analysis is not a detailed questioning of the viewpoint of interpreter and commentator Sister Joan Chittister. She is, of course, my major colleague in the production of this volume and has put in many more hours than I have. She is a professional in her field, and I am not prepared or equipped to comment on what she handles professionally. Here and there, however, I may be tempted to muse a bit about the way her ethos, outlook, and ideology might show in her presentation of the data. I shall do this not for the sake of "cutting her to size." Even if reduced by comments on these pages, her achievements would survive and stand on their own. The purpose would be, beyond scratching another itch, to teach something about even the most fair-minded representation of the findings of social science, and that something deserves brief comment here.

To some, social science is "objective," or purports to be. While historians are impressionistic and theologians comment on gaseous invisibilities, sociologists and anthropologists deal with "hard data," "thick description," and "behavioral variables" that get ranked in computers and other nonsubjective agencies. To quote the percentage of "yes" or "no" respondents to a question seems to place the one who does the citing on a firm ground away from the relativities of other disciplines. But is this the case?

I would argue that even the most cold statistical summaries come laden with ideologies and assumptions. One might argue, for instance, that to print the stock market reports or the batting averages in the newspaper is to be lifted far above the world of impressions and ideological baggage. It is not. To use several pages of the newspaper each day to print mathematical results of stock market transactions is to engage in historical and often theological exercises. The newspaper editors assume that there is a clientele which buys the paper in order to learn how a firm has done or to guess how it might do. The lists show that ours is a money world, that we have an economy which we endow with meaning, that people make sacrifices and give expressions of faith by the way they speculate about money and how they use it.

Similarly, the batting averages and other baseball statistics express philosophies of history. The long listings suggest that many millions of Americans in a world of hunger, poverty, and dancing find it important to contemplate what happens when one of 18 men throws the ball toward and, he hopes, past another of the 18. Citizens who read the box scores may be grim about their findings, but they are engaging in a "theology of play." They know with formal thinkers like Johan Huizinga and Roger Callois, that the human is *home ludens,* or with Josef Pieper that "leisure is the basis of culture." (See Johan Huizinga, *Homo Ludens: A Study of the Play Element in Culture* [Boston: Beacon Press, 1955]; Roger Callois, *Man, Play and Games* [Glencoe, Illinois: The Free Press, 1961]; Josef Pieper, *In Tune with the World: A Theory of Festivity* [New York: Harcourt, Brace, 1965].) We might even add that much of religious life, its ritual and ceremony and nuances of social existence, have a kind of "play" aspect themselves and are often undertaken on a day of rest and re-creation. No, box scores are not objective and neutral.

To the point: when Sister Joan Chittister prints the statistics that show how many Minnesotans in a sample believe this or that, she carries with her the ideas of her community and herself. She is a 20th-century person, an educated one trained in particular sciences, a woman, a member of a particular religious order, a believer through a specific community, a Christian, a Westerner, one given to certain causes.

For one obvious illustration, we can turn to the way she uses "liberation" as a theme in religion and theology. There is no question but that the Scriptures of the Old and New Testament proclaim the word of freedom and liberation—of God's people from *anomie*, nonpromise, Egypt and Pharaoh, Babylonian exile, their pasts, sin, bondage to the elements of the world, habit, custom, oppressors, or whatever. Yet many Christians can live out their lives not putting the particular modern political connotations on "liberation" that Sister Joan does as she interprets the data. More than she is given time to show, she is speaking out of the Christian tradition when she comments on liberation. She often sounds as if all religion is naturally interested in ethics, in social change, in the distribution of justice and the effecting of change. It may be that through most of history, religion—primitive, Mesopotamian, Egyptian, African, Buddhist, Hindu—has had almost no interest in ethics as she assumes it, in social change as impulsive modern Westerners seek it, or in justice as people in the prophetic Jewish or Christian traditions see it.

Many modern Christians were brought up in traditions of individual piety or pietism, or were taught that the faith was so otherworldly that it did not touch on affairs here and now. Others, and they are also in the Minnesota sample, believe in justice and might have understandings of revolution, but they were never schooled to connect these "political" expressions with their faith. Sometimes the interpreter criticizes them for an insufficiency or wrongheadedness in faith, for having fallen away from some ideal norm, when they had never shared her norm. On occasion she ponders how they can live on two separate tracks, reserving the word "salvation" for their own effort to be right with God and rejecting it for attempts to save people from demeaning and dehumanizing circumstance, and then implying a kind of bad faith on their part if they do not make the connections she makes. We have to remember that were they given equal time, many of them would charge that here her own ideology and political commitments show— and that these commitments are themselves quite possibly quite remote from those she herself would have known or shown a mere generation or two ago, before the Second Vatican Council and the entrance of winds of change into Catholicism. She is also shaped by traditions of democratic politics, welfare-interested economics, and certain kinds of calls for revolution.

To note this is not to say that her biases are wrong or that I do not share them, but only to urge upon readers the necessity of undertaking their own historical and theological analysis as they read the various authors, *all* the authors, of this study. Do not let the percent signs deceive you: they do not represent a world away from opinion and subjectivity. They are a different form of presenting the world of commitments, but the choice of questions, the suggestion that there is value in opinions, and the framing of responses to the responses by the authors, are all part of the interplay of ideology and opinion. We hope to be fair-minded; we cannot be disinterested, cannot leave our own hearts or skins behind.

Finally, this historical and theological analysis is not fundamentally a comparison between what Minnesotans today believe and what Americans elsewhere today do or might respond to questions in such surveys. For one thing, comparable data are not always available. It would be good to replicate the Faith and Ferment inquiry in 49 other states, so that we could engage in such comparison. May foundations and research centers be inspired to do such replicating and comparative work! But we cannot comment if there is not yet much to comment on. Similarly, to comment even where there is coincidence between these questions and, say, Gallup or Yankelovich surveys, demands its own kind of expertise, one which the present commentator lacks, or possesses only through years of dedicated amateur status.

This I bring up not to point to the invalidity of such comparisons but to suggest the unfinishedness of the present project. It happens that there *are* good reasons for such comparison. Not only is the United States not the whole world or the whole Christian world—

studies by Michael Argyle or S. S. Acquaviva among other names on bibliographies show vast differences between European and American faith and life—but Minnesota is not the whole United States.

One glance at the religious map and atlas shows some Minnesota distinctives. Three-quarters of a century ago, for example, more than three-quarters of Minnesotans who belonged to churches were Roman Catholic and Lutheran. The other one-fourth of the Minnesota pie was left for, in this order, Methodist, Presbyterian, Baptist, Congregational, Episcopal, German Evangelical, Evangelical, and "all other" believers. Except for the Irish, this meant that most Minnesota Christianity was of European continental derivation and not, as was the case of older or Southern stock, from backgrounds in the British Isles or Africa by slave transplanting to British Islanders' heirs in the American south. To the WASPS, the Minnesotans of 1906 were newcomers, outsiders, marginals, who played baseball on Sunday or drank beer or did not hold revivals or other good American things in religion.

How different was the world of 1906 for Alabama, for example. Well over half the Alabamans were Baptist, and almost all the rest of the other half were Methodist, with Roman Catholics having a small wedge of the circle, and Lutherans being invisible on the graphs. So it was in Arkansas, Florida, Georgia, Mississippi, North Carolina, South Carolina, West Virginia, Virginia, and other Southern states. The Utah world of 1903 was almost all Latter Day Saints, and no Baptists or Methodists show up on the chart alongside Roman Catholics and Eastern Orthodox. From what we know of Baptist, Methodist, and Latter Day Saint opinion, we could picture a very different world of religion there than in Minnesota in 1906.

Denominationally the map of Minnesota is more pluralist today than it was in 1906. Yet Americans do not have a "flattened out" pluralism. We do still live, more than many might think, in clumps, and our churchly contributions to American life are still in the form of lumps, not of simple strained out refinements. Minnesota still has its Catholic enclaves, its Lutheran counties, and its urban neighborhoods where one faith or another dominates. A quick glance at the map of 1971 shows that in all but 25 counties of Minnesota there were more Lutherans than members of any other group. One Baptist complained that in her county there were "more Lutherans than people," just as a Lutheran might say the same, vice versa, of almost any Southern Baptist county.

Of the remaining 25, Washburn had a Methodist plurality, but in all the others there were more Roman Catholics than anything else.

The Minnesota Faith and Ferment survey shows that there are indeed some denominational differences in opinion and practice, just as there are differences between the attitudes of men and women, aged and youthful, rural and urban. Yet these attitudes are not as strikingly disparate as one might expect. The effects of interactive pluralism, of one people's cheek living next to another's jowl, or Lutheran lions having lain down with Methodist lambs and produced Luthero-Methodist hybrids. More important may be the effects of common or public schooling, the interplay of playmates and, of course, the impact of mass media on ideas and opinions.

I have only two impressionistic illustrations of the erosive effect of pluralist life, but others will come out as we give historical and theological analyses of the survey.

Several years ago a Minneapolis newspaper included religious questions in its "Minnesota Poll" of opinion in the greater Twin Cities area. The editors asked me to comment on the findings. What impressed me was the skewing effect of the Lutheran subpopulation, which was many times what it would have been in almost any other American metropolis. Did this Lutheran presence, noted for its theological conservatism and moral squareness, also skew the findings of Minnesotan opinion? Hardly at all. Wherever I could compare, the percentages matched those in national Gallup samples and showed little distinctiveness.

The other illustration is more impressionistic and derives almost from the world of gossip. A half dozen years ago I dined with a young woman who momentarily—until her form of conscience and her low morale almost overwhelmed her—counseled in an abortion clinic. As she complained of low morale, I sympathized and said that I knew such demoralized counselors elsewhere as well. It was hard, I knew, to keep up one's spirits in the abortion service centers in American urban ghettos, where teenage pregnancies, apart from familial contexts, were so frequent. She fired back that she was not in the inner city, that my remark had more of a racist and perhaps sexist undertone than I knew I was conveying or wanted to convey, and that she never saw poor teenagers. In fact, she said, she never saw anyone who had not gone to certain colleges—and then she rattled off a sequence of Roman Catholic, Lutheran, other church-related, and private and state-supported colleges.

What is more, that clinic in its interviews asked the religious affiliation of the women who came to it. She sent me a computer print-out with its tabulations of a month's clients. The figures matched almost perfectly the religious percentage of the Twin Cities population and the percentage of women of that faith seeking abortions. Thus if, for example, an area was 35% Lutheran, 35% Catholic, 3% Jewish, 4% Baptist, the women coming for abortions were 35% Lutheran, 35% Catholic, 3% Jewish, and 4% Baptist. Clearly the formal teachings of formal bodies were not shaping the practices of women in crises or stress situations. The legal effects of *Wade v. Roe*, the women's movement, the liberalizing debates in schools and books, or the free enterprise that people show in common circumstances of stress, did upset the impact of religious traditions.

The particular denominational map of Minnesota, then, tells us something of the particular opinions revealed here, but we may be just as surprised to see how much Minnesota is like other states. We cannot let curiosity over this subject, important as it is, preoccupy us or distract us from the tasks at hand. A few words are in order about Minnesota particularities, however. It is necessary to paint with a broad brush.

Although Minnesota includes major cities, they are always at the edge of lake and prairie. Not a few observers have noticed how people of plains, prairie, lake, and open sky country have a kind of openness and optimism not matched by people cooped up in urban America. The cities of the East, crowded as they are with Eastern European Jews or great numbers of Catholic immigrants, Orthodox, and others were marked not only by persistent and sometimes grimly ambitious new Americans, but also by people who have a strong sense of the limits of life. The plains and open sky people are less aware of these limits. They may have some of the spiritual barrenness or blandness that novelist Sinclair Lewis claimed was pervasive in Minnesota. But they also have been generous, venturesome, open to the world of the neighbor, and trusting. As we read this data, we might keep in mind this character of the Minnesota past.

Second, Minnesota, known before many other parts of the country, thanks to pioneering exploration by French Catholic missionaries, was settled late and did not set the terms for American politics, religion, or ethos. That had been preset by the New Englanders, Virginians, and middle colony people who started the Protestant traditions, or by Spaniards centuries before in the Southeast or Southwest, and by French in the Canadian northland. Characteristic American ways of thinking about religion came from Plymouth and Williamsburg and Philadelphia. Like much of the Midwest, Minnesota does not have a "history" in the way that Massachusetts or New York does, religiously speaking.

A book on *America's Religious Treasures* by Marion Rawson Vuilleumier (Harper and Row, 1976) includes 37 sites in Massachusetts. These include Plimoth Plantation, the Salem witch country, Boston Common, Old North Church, the Christian Science Center, Harvard University, Cape Cod churches, Brandeis University, Stockbridge Indian shrines, Shaker Village, and other "shaping places." The same author pointed to but 12 Minnesota spiritual shrines, four of these being Lutheran or Catholic colleges. How many Americans feel religiously shaped by anything that went on at Fort Snelling, Bethany Fellowship, the Episcopal cathedral at Fairibault, or the Mille Lacs Indian Museum at Onamia? I am not saying that Onamia was less important than Massachusetts or Jamestown, but only that it is not part of the American myth and legendry.

This means that Minnesotans do not have so much of a history. Few novels outside those of Ole Rolvaag have chronicled the lives of hardy Scandinavians. Their days seemed all alike, as they adapted to a preset history and context. The Irish, Germans, and Scandinavians did not initiate history, were not part of public consciousness, did not leave theological texts with which others now have to cope, as the scholars do with those of Jonathan Edwards or Horace Bushnell. When the Germanic people started having an impact—people named Schaff, Rauschenbusch, or Niebuhr—they were not, in the public eye, tied to the experience of Minnesota Protestants, the German Baptists or German Evangelicals. They made it "at large" in the WASP-based pluralism of Rauschenbusch's Rochester (New York) seminary or the Niebuhr's Morningside Heights and Yale.

The Faith and Ferment study makes a virtue of the necessity of studying people who do not leave the major documents in sourcebooks of American religious history. Perhaps we have here a fresh glimpse at what common people think, however uncommon they are, apart from the norms of people with well-known last names or formal historical recognition. They may provide some continuities which more cooped, explosive, and experimental peoples in the older, more worn-down America of the East or the upsetting pluralism of a California or Hawaii may not represent. We have to leave much of this to speculation.

Similarly, it is not possible on the basis of this data, to see what effect the rather open and malleable political traditions of Minnesota have on religion. The state has been able to assure measures of economic security and produce affluence unknown in much of the Old South, pre-Sunbelt days. Did this relative comfort have an effect on views of God as benign? We have to leave this to the speculation of the reader, lacking as we do comparative data. But it is worthwhile to plant these inquiries in the mind of readers, since Faith and Ferment wants to inspire "do-it-yourself" projects of interpretation.

Finally, by way of introduction, let me introduce the five main themes or tools for analysis that grew out of my reading of these findings against the background of history and theology. I did not come with these categories in mind, but let them form in response to what was here. Admittedly, other readers could have come up with others, but I believe these five themes provide useful access to the material.

Social Behavior

Readers may wish to be alert, with me, to see the ways in which these findings show that Minnesotans are "typical Americans" because of the way they fuse belief and behavior. We can hypothesize that humans have always done this. It gives a false impression to write purely intellectual history about Christians of the past, as if they were really informed by or lived by the dogma or formal belief systems of the church. Historians find it easier to unearth and expound canons and decrees of church conventions or leatherbound books of doctrines than to find out what people actually believed or how they lived. We might find less disruption of continuity between belief and behavior in the past if we knew more about behavior then, as we are coming to know it now.

This point may momentarily seem to take us far from Minnesota in order to draw near it again. I am assuming that Faith and Ferment, though it draws data from one province, is not a provincial document. Just as the great universal literature is always particular—Dostoevski's Russia belongs to all of us because it belongs first to Russia, as does

Faulkner's to Mississippi—so good social scientific surveys are specific, designed to tell us something about the human condition, the Christian situation, the American context, and not just—for instance—about churchgoing in Minnesota. So it is valid to dwell on some of the universal implications of a local study.

Let us suppose that a thousand years from now historians of Christianity would stumble upon but one preserved document on birth control from late 20th century Catholicism, the papal document of 1968, *Humanae Vitae* of Pope Paul VI. An astute reader would easily gain an awareness of the fact that not all Catholics were following papal teaching, for the document breeds a sense of nervousness or worry about lapse from the practice of abhorring and shunning "artificial" birth control as being against natural law and the law of God. Yet one could easily gain from it the notion that Catholics were not in favor of such forms of population limitation. (Similarly, because we have the "high-culture" documents of ancient ecumenical assemblies, we get the impression that men and women of the fourth and fifth centuries chatted easily about *hypostasis* in the Godhead, or substance and essence and accident in the Lord's Supper—which they might very well *not* have done!)

If one had a fifth-century equivalent of Faith and Ferment from the open sky country of ethnic Byzantium or Ephesus or Nicea, there might be a considerable gap between the Trinitarian or Christological formulae of the theologians and the lived lives or believed opinions of the people for whom they were formulated. Whatever the snoopier historians of our day are discovering suggests the gap. I have heard a colleague report on the 15th-century Council of Basle in these terms. He was not interested in the way the Council dealt with Hussite questions of the ratification of the Compactata or how it dealt with the polity of conciliarism and the problem of schism. He dealt with the folk and show business aspects of Basle's life. During the Council the little city housed more prostitutes than professors, more camp followers than theologians, and a good time was had by many. But were it not for my lewd-minded historian colleague, we could easily carry the impression that the confessions and decisions of the Council itself represented the life of Baslers, the Swiss, the European Catholics of the day.

To see how much an intelligent observer can miss by looking at formal belief without connecting it to social behavior, we might note a book like Father John Hardon's *The Protestant Churches of America* (Westminster, Maryland: Newman, 1956). This preconciliar document does not know that there are prostitutes, jugglers, livers-and-diers in the Protestant world. It knows that at the head of each tradition there are some formal creeds and confessions, and the author uses these not only to measure but to display the life of these churches. One gets the impression that a visitor could use the Augsburg Confession to understand Lutherans or the Westminster Confession for comprehending Presbyterians. Hardon takes the *Articles of Religion* of 1784 to depict American Methodism. Clearly these documents have *something* to do with these churches, but it would be nothing but a cause for confusion or embarrassment to use them as guidebooks. Such a circumstance is not new; historical examples abound.

For instance, one of the two or three greatest evangelists of 19th-century America was Charles Grandison Finney, an upstate New York lawyer who, upon his conversion, had to join something so he joined Presbyterianism. Those who licensed him to preach assumed that he had read that church's Westminster Confession and was prepared to let it define the boundaries of his proclamation and biblical interpretation. He later claimed that he had not read it. Enemies on the revival trail, Universalists and their kind, challenged him: how could one so humane as he believe that God damned to hell unbaptized babies? Finney averred that God could not. Well, came their taunt, his own church's confession did have these rigid Calvinist decrees on many pages.

Finney acquired a copy of the Confession and was shocked to find what it said. "I was absolutely ashamed of it. I could not feel any respect for a document that would undertake to impose on mankind such dogmas as those, sustained for the most part by passages of Scripture that were totally irrelevant" (Quoted by William McLoughlin, *Modern Revivalism: Charles Grandison Finney to Billy Graham* [New York: Ronald Press, 1959, pp. 23-24]). If that gap could be present with evangelist Finney, what might we expect of the laity of Eighth Presbyterian Church in Duluth 150 years later. This citation is not designed to demean Hardon, Finney, or Duluth, but only to point to the gap between formal documents of Christianity and the social behavior of its practitioners.

Is the gap between the proclaimed teachings of the church and a set of informal teachings, acquired through changes in practice and behavior, something new on Christian soil? Hardly. Most Christians look back on the Middle Ages as a time when everyone knew the church's teachings and had orthodoxy beamed their way weekly if not daily. Yet Jean Delumeau in *Catholicism Between Luther and Voltaire: A New View of the Counter-Reformation* (London: Burns and Oates, 1977) presents a different picture.

The Reformation and Counter-Reformation, it turns out, were not so much the reform of Christianity as its introduction to the lives of many longtime members of the church. For centuries they had had the Christian message directed to them, but their "real" religion was a kind of superstition, a belief in the power of relics. The old paganism lived on under a thin Catholic veneer.

The point of bringing that up is not to say that Minnesota Christians are secret pagans. Instead, it reminds us that lay people—and parish pastors as well—keep on adapting and smuggling in practices that may or may not be close to what the books of dogma say they believe or should believe. There is a kind of free enterprise in religious opinion, in conservative as well as liberal religious groups. Most change occurs because the teachings have to square with the lived experience of people.

A second non-Minnesotan illustration of faith in ferment is Bernard Groethuysen, *The Bourgeois: Catholicism vs. Capitalism in Eighteenth-Century France* (New York: Holt, Rinehart and Winston, 1968), a classic study of the ways the French middle class emerged without help from the dogmaticians or doctrinal-minded priests of their day. The people thought they were good Catholics; they gave alms and often went to church, and they prayed. But Groethuysen showed that these Catholics were bemused by clerical ignorance of their needs and ways, and simply paid no attention to official proclamations that did not inform or touch their lives. He is not saying that the laity was always right but that it was seldom ignorant. Instead it improvised to fill the gaps between what had to be done or thought and what the church kept suggesting should be thought and done.

A third example is John Bossy, *The English Catholic Community 1570-1850* (New York: Oxford, 1976). Bossy studies how for two and a half centuries English Catholicism had to go underground and how it devised modes of existence that had little to do with the formal or official teachings—all in the name of gentrified loyalty to Rome. When English Catholicism came out into the open again and found its hierarchy restored in the middle of the 19th century, John Cardinal Newman in the high culture interpreted this as "a second spring" or "miraculous rebirth," born of his and others' new intellectual apprehension of the faith. Not at all, says Bossy, who shows, as have others, that the restoration of the hierarchy was often motivated by merely practical concerns.

To cite Delumeau, Groethuysen, and Bossy against Hardon is not to celebrate non- or anti-intellectualism or to be against the history of ideas. Nor is observing the gap between formal church authority and Minnesota faith in ferment a rejoicing in the disparity between confession and act. It is a celebration of intellect and ideas that points to a different set of ideas and a different location of ideas in the life of the church.

My *A Nation of Behavers* (Chicago: University of Chicago Press, 1976) is a book-length mapping of American religion in the light of social behavioral change, and the first two chapters suggest, as does *Faith and Ferment*, that denominational lines have less to do with religious opinion and practice than do ethnicity, separate histories, or social location. It draws on Suzanne K. Langer's observation that humans' symbolic behavior has roots which "lie much deeper than any conscious purpose . . . in that substratum of the mind, the realm of fundamental ideas." Similarly, George Boas is cited for his observation that "when an idea is adopted by a group and *put into practice,* as in a church or a state, its rate of change will be slow *[emphasis mine]."*

People in Minnesota and elsewhere live by *creencias,* Ortega y Gasset's Spanish term for the German *Grundideen,* which "are not ideas which we *have,* but ideas which we *are."* They connect with *vigencias,* the binding social observances that present themselves to us "as something that [does not depend] upon our individual adherence but, on the contrary, is indifferent to our adherence, it *is there,* we are obliged to *reckon with it,"* and, contrariwise, "at any moment we can resort to it as to an authority, a power to which we can look for support." This is the zone of laws, customs, language, extant social obligations, and taboos. On these terms, we can hypothesize that Minnesota Methodists may very well consider that they are acting in good faith as Methodists, but without reference to *Articles of Faith* imported from John Wesley's England in 1784 so much as promulgated by the bowling team of First Methodist Church somewhere in Minnesota. "That isn't done . . ." or "We Methodists, or we Minnesotans ought to do this . . ." are sentences that often connect "binding customs" with "the ideas that we are."

Development

While George Boas cautioned us to notice that rates of change may be slow when a group puts a belief into practice, "slow" is a relative term and disguises the fact that change is constantly present in even a relatively conservative circumstance such as that embodied in Minnesota Christianity. Our fifth theme will note the presence of two basic families of Christians in Minnesota. One of these, often code-named "mainline Christianity" and especially Protestantism, is committed to a tradition that allows for development and change. Its members are not necessarily faddish or modish, but they are sufficiently open to modernity to welcome the moderate changes that erosive and corrosive times work. They do their accommodating not necessarily by deep inhalations of a heady *Zeitgeist* but by an interpretation of the faith that goes back to Separatist Puritan John Robinson (who waved off the Mayflower company from England toward New England): "The Lord hath more truth and light yet to break forth from his holy Word."

In that spirit, to speak of development is not shocking. Such Christians welcome development of faith in the light of scientific discovery and new inquiry. While they may not know the term, they tend to be "process theologians" who see God "consequently" emerging from each new context and complexity. They are in Bergson's term "creative evolutionists" who welcome the movement toward complexity in the light of the Word of God and church tradition. Tell them that they have "developed" beyond the norms of biblical constriction, traditionalism, dogmatism, and the confessions of their own church, and they are likely to feel congratulated. The letter kills, but the spirit gives life, they well might add.

A moderate camp, catholic evangelicalism or evangelical catholicity, present in Roman Catholicism, Episcopalianism, many kinds of Lutheranism and Presbyterianism, is more responsive to what is fixed in tradition—be this in apostolic succession, creedal formulae, the confessions of a church, or liturgical practice. Many Christians in these traditions were dragged screaming into the era in which developmentalism is recognized. Some Catholics got there through the ministrations of intellectuals like Newman in England or Johann Adam Möhler and Tübingen semi-Hegelians in the 19th century. For 60 years papal decrees against Modernism suppressed this developmental sense, but since Vatican II (1962-65) it has made its way. Pierre Teilhard de Chardin was only the best known of these evolutionists. Some scholars have seen in some Vatican II decrees, among them the one on religious liberty, a definite development of doctrine accompanied by an implicit —and, one might add, debated—suggestion that previous teaching was superseded. (Had it been "wrong"?)

Similarly *Nostra Aetate,* a Vatican document on world religions, definitely has a more winsome and charitable view of non-Catholic Christianity and non-Christian world religions than one associates with earlier Catholicism. There is in it no repudiation of the idea that "outside the church there is no salvation," but there is a definite development of recognition that something positive may well be going on among people of good will who do not know Jesus Christ.

A third camp is very uneasy with the notion of development, and likes to picture itself literally faithful to a literal and always rationally clear Scripture. If it draws on a confessional tradition, this kind of Lutheranism, Presbyterianism, evangelicalism, or fundamentalism, sees that tradition as "fixed," and "right," if of lower status than the inspired and inerrant Scriptures. Here there is resistance to the idea of development and a strong impulse to claim that there has been no change. Yet the close reader of *Faith and Ferment* will have no difficulty seeing how deviant and developmental the laity's perceptions and practices are. Understandings of divorce, we shall note, are prime examples. Such churches have not yielded an inch in their basic understanding that only adultery on the part of a marital partner is grounds for divorce. Yet the findings are clear: people who divorce on other grounds are understood and accepted as they would not have been 20 years ago. While this may look like a practical or pastoral adjustment, there are already evidences of a kind of "doctrinal" coming to terms with change. The old views are being nickeled and dimed to death as new ones become official.

This principle of lay development connects with a helpful idea proposed by sociologist J. Milton Yinger in *Sociology Looks at Religion* (New York: Macmillan, 1963). He protested against those who saw religious change as "secularization" when it was nothing more than— religious change! Secularization should not become "synonymous with religious change." What we are seeing is persons acting religiously in a way that does not express directly the faith they profess. "It is one thing to have many of life's decisions carried out without reference to religion—the usual dictionary meaning of secularization. It is another thing to redefine one's religion while disguising or obscuring the process by holding, somewhat superficially, to many of the symbols of the earlier religious system." He goes on to say that "religious change is usually a latent process, carried on beneath symbols of nonchange." Minnesotans are constantly improvising, making faith come out right to meet circumstances, as this study makes clear across the board. Some may bring assumptions that lead them to regret this; others may well see it as a sign of vitality and validity to faith.

Three attitudes toward development and change are present in religion. One is John Newman's proposal that to grow is to change and to have changed often is to have grown much. A second is Richard Hooker's suggestion that all change is inconveniencing, including change from worse to better. Third is Edmund Burke's conservative argument that if it is not necessary to change it is necessary not to change. The first is characteristic of those moderates toward liberals who find God in the process; and in the process and stress, an immanent Christ. They want development, though always in context—otherwise they would develop out of and apart from their faith traditions. The second group of moderates toward conservatives are willing to admit to change, though they want a strong hand in monitoring and interpreting the process and feel uncomfortable even when the developments are manifestly positive. The third group works hard not to change and is not likely to welcome change. Its upholders often criticize the very idea of taking social scientific surveys of religion. Thus when it was shown that Catholics (in Minnesota as everywhere) in decisive numbers do not follow the logic, theology, or injunctions of *Humanae Vitae*, the newsbearers were treated as subversives who might undercut official Catholic teaching.

Faithfulness and Continuity

Peter Berger is not alone among sociologists of religion in pointing to the fact that the general tendency of religion in society is toward the conservation of values. The very notion of tradition is integral to religion, and tradition means "handing down." Even the prophets, in the tradition dear to Sister Joan Chittister, acted in the name of tradition and covenant, as she does with those who share her assumptions.

They do not want to be seen simply as innovators. Some scholars regard most of the ancient prophets as articulators of the political views of the minority parties, those out of power. They do their judging not in the light of utopian norms disguised under the symbols of "the day of the Lord" or "the kingdom of God." Instead, like the "primitive rebels" in Marxist historian E. J. Hobsbawm's worlds, "they looked backward." Max Weber argued that in the context of religious symbols there are basically two ways to change the world: the charismatic and the virtuoso. The charismatic is messianic. He can say, in effect, "It is written, but I say unto you. . . ." The virtuoso says, "It is written and I insist."

Those who connect "liberation" with gospel message, do not want to come at us from the future, though they may derive their views of the future from ancient documents that see God being "I will be who I will be," and Christ "the power of the future," the "first fruit of the new creation." They invoke ancient prophets who were faithful to older traditions and covenants, saying, "It is written, and I insist." In a sense this whole religious debate has to do with who is going deeper into the tradition. In Charles Peguy's sense, there is a *ressourcement,* a deeper dipping into resources. Thus one may argue that Catholic theologians like Hans Küng and Edward Schillebeeckx are often in trouble because, in their view, they are posing the world of A.D. 70 against the world of A.D. 1870, and prefer the older tradition. Their views of ministry, authority, and sacrament, they would say, derive from the archaeology of evangelically Catholic biblical views, not from late and freezing developments from the reactionary times of Vatican I in 1870.

The respondents who make a sharp breach between private personal Christian faith and the secular world of politics and social change believe they are being faithful to a tradition, *the* tradition. They draw selectively on some biblical texts and church confessions to support their sense of continuity. Their critics will say that theirs is a young tradition, not much older than Catholic Venice or Protestant Geneva of five centuries ago, when capitalism took new form. They fuse and confuse Christian faith with that of Adam Smith and *The Wealth of Nations* of 1776 or the Social Darwinism dog-eat-dog laissez-faire free-enterprise capitalist connection of religion and economics of 1876. They are the innovators.

The economic conservatives, alias liberals, reply in kind. To them the "liberationists" are not drawing authentically on the Q'hal Yahweh, the social congregation of the Lord of the prophetic era, or on the *ecclesia,* the bonded fellowship of early Christianity. Theirs is not a social view modeled on monasteries or craft and guild life in Christendom, as they claim. No, they deviate from the tradition of Christian individualism and are really innovators inspired by Karl Marx and other 19th-century radical social prophets.

Our present purpose is served only if we notice that spokespersons for both sides make the claim that they are being faithful to traditions with continuities. Development there may be, but deviation this is not. These leading representatives belong to elites. They speak up for, but are statistically a very small part of, the Minnesota sample in Faith and Ferment. But we can find in that larger and largely lay sample clear evidence of a generalized if soft orthodoxy, an astonishing willingness to be bearers of the tradition. All the erosions of modernity and corrosions of mass communications, all the impellings to be up to date and impulses to belong to the "now" are qualified by the respondents' evident and constant willingness to check out their faiths against patterns from centuries ago. They develop within the broad banks of streams. They do not want their faith to be poured on the sand any more than most of them want it to form stagnant pools. The dialectic of development and continuity makes up much of the plot of the book.

Toleration of Ambiguity

In general, people have difficulty handling ambiguity. In a stunning chapter on "Conflict between Belief Systems," Sebastian de Grazia in *The Political Community: A Study of Anomie* (Chicago: The University of Chicago Press, 1948), shows that people belong constantly to spheres which emit contrary beliefs. Thus our capitalist-cooperative culture sends out contradictory symbols. In economic life there is a constant demand to "shove thy neighbor" in the world of competition. Yet that same world produces the Chambers of Commerce and Brotherhood Weeks, where the message is "Love thy neighbor." The young person, torn between these directives, may fall into *anomie*.

The Minnesota sample lives with the worlds of "love" and "shove." These come their way from their Christian and their economic systems, from church and state, throne and altar, land and liturgy. Because of these tensions, they have to tolerate some ambiguity.

More striking, however, is a tension that shows up again and again on these pages and leads to some creative musings by Joan Chittister.

That is, the Christian faith, born in the face of and at the edge of
mystery, comes at its adherents with a strong sense of inner contradiction. The root one of these has to do with a God always described as a
God of love (even: God *is love!*), yet this God, putatively all-powerful
in most of the traditions' statements permits or maybe is the agent of
suffering, pain, and evil in the world. How do clergy and laity live
with this ambiguity? Do they get *anomie* and become "dropouts"?
Evidently not, according to this data. They have a faith that prepares
them for ambiguity, and they continue to function in the face of it—
or in spite of it.

This ability is often seen as a mark of ignorance or bad faith. Thus
historian Sidney E. Mead, a master of his subject, expects rational
consistency and clarity in expressions of faith. In comment on a study
that parallels Faith and Ferment, Mead is implicitly, perhaps explicitly, amused by and critical of lay expression where it has not been
perfectly consistent. He refers to *A Study of Generations,* sponsored
by three large Lutheran bodies. In *The Nation with the Soul of a
Church* (New York: Harper and Row, 1975) Mead says that "among
the [findings] were discoveries that there are differences between the
generations, and between clergy and laity, and between the synods!"
That exclamation point is to express derision over social scientific
naivete and astonishment. "But to me," he adds, "the only significant
'finding' reported by the reviewer was 'that three out of four Lutherans
said that all religions lead to the same God, yet three out of four . . .
[also] stated that belief in Jesus is absolutely necessary to salvation.'"
What was astonishing, he noted, was "the implication that around 50
percent of Lutheran church members in the United States find it
possible simultaneously to hold two theologically contrary views, each
rooted in age-old antagonistic theological traditions." Mead believes
this situation came to be because these people wanted to be *both*
Lutheran Christians and loyal citizens of the commonwealth. The commonwealth presumably taught tolerance of all faiths, while Lutheranism was exclusivistically Christomonistic.

Mead may be more than half right, but he is not wholly satisfying
in his observations. *Nostra Aetate* was produced by Catholics, most of
whom did not have the experience of republicanism in the American
commonwealth, which Mead sees as the root of tolerationism. Many of
the bishops and theologians would say that Mead's "religion of the
republic" of America was as sectarian and exclusivistic as many other

faiths, certainly as classic Christianity. How do these people keep from being schizophrenic, he asks, because the belief systems collide?

Here one must note that the problem, or the creative source, is within the Christian, in this case the Lutheran tradition itself, and this problem or creative potential shows up again and again in this Minnesota survey. The Lutheran child, as much as the Catholic in the era of *Nostra Aetate*, is taught that there is only one God. Lutherans go back to Paul's address quoted in the book of Acts, a speech on Mars Hill in Athens. There Paul looked at the many altars and an altar to the unknown God and announced, "What therefore you worship as unknown, this I proclaim to you" (Acts 17:24).

Being an Athenian and being accused of ignorance is not necessarily flattering or satisfying, but it did provide a root connection for tying together God the Father of Jesus Christ with the God behind the gods of Athens. Paul did this in his own writing in Romans 1, where he found a moral potential in the pagan conscience, one unformed by attachment to God in and through Jesus Christ. Somehow the various religions may "lead to the same God," but they may not fully arrive.

There are a thousand possible variations in the minds of Lutheran and other churchgoing respondents to surveys. Their answers may not come out fully neat, but they are able to live with them. Here again some conflict may result from the tension between development and continuity, the two immediately past-present themes of our discernment in this study. Yet the people seem to be able to function with these somewhat contradictory ideas. Christianity, after all, was born of paradox.

Sister Joan often stops to wonder, as would Mead, as must I, about the degree to which people seem not to have thought through these ambiguities. Yet on second glance we may note that what they have not thought through they have lived through and with. They have kept the vigil in the sick rooms and pondered the "why?" of a good God, yet few left the faith because of suffering, and this study shows that they anticipate ways to connect pain and divine goodness. One must recognize the limits of all terse questions on such vast yet subtle subjects, see the problem for the respondents who are not allowed nuanced or delicate answers, and not expect any more neatness here than in the economic and social worlds of "love thy neighbor" and "shove thy neighbor," or of life in a world of nature that appears to be both beautiful or benign and at the same time threatening and malignant. The Christian praises God for the whole of creation, in the face of contradiction, paradox, and ambiguity.

Two Church Clusters

We have already noted and often shall in the pages ahead that on many issues there seem to be two broad clusters of Christians in Minnesota. On many themes there is a gravitational pull toward a "conservative" response by evangelicals-fundamentalists-pentecostals, many kinds of Baptists, some kinds of Lutherans. Similarly, another kind of Lutheran teams up with mainline Protestants toward a more open-ended affirmation of change and a somewhat more liberal cast. Catholicism is often a "swing vote," siding now with the putative conservatives in opposing abortion and then with liberals on many social issues. The patterns are not always consistent. But they do show the line of division within Minnesota Christendom and often the line within church bodies. We might speak of these as the "open" and "closed" churches, but these may be regarded as pejorative terms by people on both sides of both issues, or all sides of all issues. The distinction merely shows the uselessness of using Hardon-type handbooks to locate one's self in church traditions as these live on today. The theme is so obvious that we may spend less time with it than with the others, to which we now turn.

13

Social Behavior

The beliefs and behavior of people, Christians, and Minnesotans interfuse. Belief gives birth to behavior and behavior to belief, in an endless circle or symbiosis. The proposition is less interesting than the particulars as these are revealed to a historical or theological analyst in the chapters of *Faith and Ferment*. The demographic sections of chapters are most helpful and revealing in this respect.

Men and Women

Thus in Chapter 2, "Suffering and Crisis," there is a significant difference (women—60%, men—49%), between women and men in their recognition that should they fail someone who is suffering, they would by that omission fail Christ. Women more than men consider suffering and crisis to result from sin, and women more than men—always by ten percentage points in these cases—have more difficulty reconciling a loving God with human suffering. "Women more than men, it seems, do not simply take suffering in stride."

This is as good a place as any to point to this significant and rather constant ten-point difference between women and men on substantial issues. Sister Joan frequently speculates over the reasons for these

189

differences, and finds them rooted in both social circumstances and in different teachings about submission to God, to males, to authority, and to the idea of suffering. Both the social behavior of historic women's role models and the belief systems conspire to cause women to have these different views of suffering in the scheme of salvation.

The data do not permit too much exploration or extrapolation, and one must do some speculating, because of the way the question is asked and because of the tempting clues in the answer. The difference would not be remarkable at all were it not for the fact that both men and women read the same texts and hear the same sermons, but, given their behavioral circumstances, they clearly get different meanings from the preachments and writings. One could be a literalist about the interpretation of the parable in Matthew 25 and say that 100% of Christians should feel that they have failed Christ if they have failed to serve suffering neighbors, yet less than half of the men feel this, while 11% more of the women do. What causes more of them to have ears to hear?

To the historian, there are social circumstances that have to do with roles. E. J. Hobsbawn in *The Age of Revolution 1789-1848* (Cleveland: World, 1962), describes how in that period there was a kind of "secularization of the masses" that showed up chiefly as "widespread dechristianization of males in the polite and educated classes," which spread through the work force as well. With the rise of industrialism and the modern city, men moved out of the home to the factory (in the United States, pre-Minnesota, until 1829 more goods were manufactured in homes than in factory work places). In this process men were progressively moved from a "wholistic" world in which suffering was addressable in one-to-one terms.

Women as mothers, teachers, nurses, whether they stayed in the home or found employment without and whether they were "seculars" or "religious," members of orders of nuns, were drawn more and more into the sphere where they were encouraged to minister to the sufferers. They saw the pain up close. In *The Southern Lady: From Pedestal to Politics 1830-1930* (Chicago: The University of Chicago Press, 1970) Anne Firor Scott studied diaries of mistresses of slave plantations. Their image was "queen of the home," and to them were given the duties that went with love, marriage, work, and family life. Out of this grew great discontents of a sort they dared express only in their diaries. Much of the discontent that made them "secret abolitionists" was born of husbandly drives to make the wives, in effect, heads of large corporations without training for the task. More of it came from the fact that women knew domestic slaves as persons and came to know and see the sufferings of disrupted families. They learned to care.

Minnesota was too late and too northerly to be a slave state, so Minnesota women did not have that experience, but they had similar ones. The men left for field or factory in the morning, and the women dealt with children in the crisis of disease. If they entered the work force outside the home, they often became nurses and were close to suffering in the hospitals in the hours after the usually male surgeons had moved on. They stayed behind in the wars to console mourners who lost someone far away. Churchly auxiliaries assigned them tasks to relieve suffering everywhere in the world. Missionary societies called for their sentiments and talents on behalf of people in need far away. One might even be cruel and say that in their circumstances they had time to dwell upon their own sufferings, as the men who moved into the excitements and tense worlds of office or marketplace did not. Whether or not empathy for suffering is somehow innate or a predisposition on the part of women, their modern cultural roles poise them to be closest and they are therefore most likely to have ears to hear religious injunctions men do not know.

Today the women's movement is discontented with seeing relief from *suffering* as central to the revolutionary cause. Today relief from *oppression* is prime. Oppression as a motif better helps the perceptive and miltant woman locate the enemy, often in the structure of the male world, or the quiescent and submissive, religiously trained subordinate female world. Oppression can be thrown off by defiant and revolutionary activity: it is pictured as removable and removed in socialist states, though evidence to the contrary seems overwhelming in most such states.

Suffering, meanwhile, does not go away. Let it be reduced through the introduction of a pesticide which produces more food, and the world finds that the chemical also may contribute to the spread of cancer and, hence, more suffering. Let an affluent society allow for medicines and longer life, and the lengthened span only creates more years for stretching out miserable marriages whose suffering leads to the pain of separation, the trauma of divorce, and the consequent loneliness—a poor substitute for the advertised freedom of women alone. The circles and cycles seem endless. Physical suffering, diminished, is replaced by spiritual and psychic suffering, and the woman knows that no age of progress removes it, while oppression can, at least in theory, be decisively countered.

It may well be that the data here suggest something for the militant women's movement, in that women may have caught something essential to the Christian faith in somewhat greater numbers than have men. "Christianity is suffering," historian Jakob Burckhardt has written, and to lose that theme in a cosmetic or illusory society is to lose something essential to the faith. This does not mean that the restriction of insight into the meaning of suffering should be continued in the male world, but rather that what more Christian women already know, the men must learn. It does not mean that women are well served by bad consciences for their failure to serve all in suffering, but it does mean that they have a grasp on something that a callous, computerized work force, until recently largely male, screens from view. The issue in a future which includes an ever-increasing number of women who have entered the secularized public world of males who made this move a century ago is not how to keep them interested in suffering. The question is, "Is a *humane* technological order possible?" and how can men and women be agents of humaneness, using Christian symbols and impulsions?

Sex Education

A second illustration on social behavioral change that forces response in religious circles is in Chapter 1, "Changing Relationships." The curricular attention to sex education of children has moved beyond the confines of the family. Only 6% join the Protestant fundamentalist militants in saying that "sex education in the public school is 'always wrong and ought to be eliminated.'" Yet, as the commentator notices, there is much skirmishing ahead. Many parents do see schools contradicting their teachings, and they feel that "cultural pluralism is eroding the absolutes of Christian, and American, family life." History courses, science, and sex education alike are seen as producing tension.

Several years ago anti-sex education militants focused on a social scientific text which portrayed an Eskimo tribe. The book was designed to teach elements of cultural anthropology, to get children to think about how different they are because of their cultural context. The portrait of the Eskimos was generally accurate, as even the critics had to admit. The choice of the tribe caused the scandal. The sexual practices of these Eskimos ran counter to those of other North Americans. To become aware of these others was to remove the distinctiveness of Christian viewpoints, it was charged.

As easy as it is to dismiss the militants, so necessary is it to see that they have a point and what the point is. They are striking out at cultural relativism in the form of pluralism. To become aware of other world views is to risk loss of confidence in one's own. To see that what one regards as "normative," as part of "natural law," as written in the hearts of "the Gentiles who have not the law" (Rom. 2:14), to see all these as arbitrary, the product of cultural accidents and taboos, is devastating to the absolutist. Because reaction to such change and erosion is growing and resentment over it is skillfully manipulated by a coterie of fundamentalist Christian leaders, one may expect that in several years the 6% in opposition will grow to 10%, or more, and that the ambiguous may have more who will turn militant.

From some angles it is possible to say that "the game is over," in many respects, for the fundamentalist opponent. Television reaches into all the homes. While Christian television is designed to help people screen out worldly views of sex and education, to hold an audience it must replicate many features of the world it recently opposed. The necklines are low, the hairdos are high, the tuxedo shirts blue and ruffled, the beat is soft rock—once the devil's music—and the aura is one of packaged gospel as another entertainment product. The intentions are valid, but it is clear to any late-night listener, the effort is not successful. Performers and audiences are sometimes jocular about and sometimes disapproving of what happened on earlier and more suspect worldly prime-time television. The norms of the secular world creep in.

Similarly, to further the sex education theme, the best-selling sex manuals of the 1980s are written by and for evangelicals and fundamentalists. They have discovered sex with a vengeance. The books by the LaHayes or the Shedds have found a market among people who duplicate every feature of the sexual revolution but confine it to marriage. Where once there was a strong suggestion that even within marriage lust was possible as a distraction from life with God, now "whatever turns you on," so long as it is approved by both marital partners and not disapproved by an explicit biblical text, is permitted and encouraged. Oral-genital acts, which were perversions a decade earlier, became allowed or supported in the conservative manuals. These changes are not good or bad, but they are changes and they are occasioned not by ecumenical councils of Christians calling for change. They occur because the laity are part of the sexual revolution and will follow it apart from Christian norms unless inventive Christians cater to their tastes and markets.

Pluralism does produce essential problems in these intimate zones of life which once were the preserve of church and family. It may be only a romantic or nostalgic view that sees children protected from outside stimuli until recently, but there is no doubt that the stimuli have increased. Most Minnesota Catholics and Lutherans do not send their children to parochial schools. These Christians get the same jostlings and signals that their liberal Protestant and secular compatriots receive. They become aware of the fact that they and Jews and Methodists and Unitarians and others "do it" differently, and they find some attractions in these differences.

The evidence of these pages, then, is that the laity and parish priests and ministers are not only victims but are in some ways the agents of enlarging the boundaries of the sexually permissible. While it is true that some church bodies have established commissions and task forces to study theology in the light of these changes, it is also clear that the commissions result from the pressures and from a desire for the churches to keep control or speak relevantly. It is hard to think of more than a pioneering few writers on sexual revolution or awareness who were moved only by the perceived inner norms of the Christian faith. There were few if any Christian councils convoked to determine what the tradition was and then to see how behavior would relate to it. The change came the other way around. People next to unlike people found other practices attractive; the media packaged their lures; Christians began experimenting and going their own way. The churches tried to retrieve initiative.

What I have written is not supposed to be a judgment on the changes but rather a recognition that social behavior tells us as much about doctrinal shifts as do studies of pages by theologians in their formal moments. Pluralism will continue to work its effects. For some this has led to a new tribalism, to Christian "Yellow Pages" and Christian cable TV, and dealing only with "our kind." So it has been in Iran and Lebanon and Northern Ireland, and so, some think, it should be in the United States. Let tuition tax credits make it possible for more and more parents to draw back from public school pluralism. Let Christians try to minimize pluralism by proposing legislation that makes religion and even Christianity into a privileged viewpoint and faith. Fear as one might such moves and tendencies, or smile as one will at the pathos of such efforts or at the ironies of adaptation, the observant analyst must also pay these Christian groups the compliment of noticing that they read change well and are trying to adapt by reacting.

Control of Life

Elsewhere in the study there is evidence of tensions between the social behavior of Americans and the theology that was once supposed to be characteristic of their elites. In Chapter 4, "Control of Life," we read that almost everyone (92%) agreed with the statement, "No matter what the circumstances of my life situation, I am still responsible for what I do." Far fewer (75%) agreed that if they are not saved, it is their own fault. We read further that while people see salvation as a gift and the control of destiny in no small measure in God's hand, yet they recognize a need to engage "in organized attempts to control school curriculums, state legislation, civic programs, and public standards, all in the name of Christianity." Here, as so often, the laity is not ignorant. It recognizes that the norms of a culture do much to determine the character of faith, so they work to change the cultural norms.

Yet the whole impulse does not square completely with the elements which accent divine sovereignty in historic Calvinism and much of Augustinian Catholicism, strands that remain strong in the background of Minnesota church people. I am well aware here that in brief compass and perhaps given a whole seminar, library, or lifetime, the non-Calvinist cannot accurately reflect the inner life of this once-dominant and still somehow shaping American tradition. Every professor of Calvinist theology that one will find winces to hear the efforts by non-Calvinists to reframe that theology's central positions. The attempts to attribute all initiative to God, to speak of creative determinisms, foreknowledge, or foreplanning, all eventuate, in the mouths of non-Calvinists, in simple determinisms. The non-Calvinists cannot figure out why Calvinists—or Augustinians—have been so busy rearranging the *civitas terrena*, the earthly city, if God has it all arranged anyhow.

However hard it is to get close and speak from within, it must still be said that these dominant traditions do force some hard intellectual choices on believers who stand or have stood within them. Shall one work so hard on cultural change that it appears that one is Pelagian, a busy earner of salvation, producing good works through constructing a congenial culture? Hardly. Yet that is evidently what has gone on in the American centuries. H. Shelton Smith in *Changing Concepts of Original Sin* (New York: Scribner's, 1955) traced the challenges to determinism and the rise of responsibility in the main line of New England theology, from John Taylor through the Unitarians, from Horace Bushnell into liberal theology. Throughout there was a softening of the old ideas that God determined all that went on and that individuals could do little to arrange circumstances for salvation.

More than anything else, the practice of revivals in Protestantism undercut the determinist notions. American Protestants soon came to learn that religion would not be passed through the loins of godly parents to their children, as had occurred for ages. Here people were as free to be nonreligious as to be religious. As moderns they could choose to be what they wanted to be or did not want to be. If the covenant was to continue, the new generation had to be converted, as did the marginal people within the nominally Christian culture.

This meant, beginning with the First Great Awakening of the 1730s and 1740s, that the old Puritan notion of "the heart prepared" had to be enlarged upon. Ministers began learning techniques of conversion. They set up circumstances, including an "anxious bench," which led to warrants for and psychological impulses toward conversion. The evangelists would always say that God did the converting, that grace was all-inclusive and sufficient, that people did not earn salvation—and they meant it. Yet the social behavior encouraged at revivals produced another set of ideas. The speakers pursued what Perry Miller has called "the rhetoric of sensation" to induce change. They tied conversion to social control, and on the frontier they formed elites on the basis of who was converted and who was not. Everything about camp meetings, sawdust trails, and stump speaking contrived to produce what Paul Tillich has called a "revelatory constellation" conducive to conversion. Thus people would "get religion," and a new generation would gain the faith. No self-respecting body of Christians that wanted to grow on the frontier could expect to reproduce itself, compete with others, and gain against "nothingarianism" in religion, unless its leadership took new measures or used special means to create a cultural environment. The poor, the sinful, the deprived, the declassé all took some responsibility for their changes. The revivals and their counter-

parts in Catholic and Lutheran or other supposedly nonrevivalist traditions, did their part. There is a long behavioral history behind the
Minnesotans' 92% assent to the statement, "No matter what the circumstances of my life situation, I am still responsible for what I do," even
in the most grace-stressed circumstances of life, acquiring salvation.

These behavioral conducements did have intellectual corollaries, also
in folk culture. Eugene Genovese in *Roll, Jordan, Roll: The World the
Slaves Made* (New York: Pantheon, 1974) reproduces an anecdote
which shows how a typical slave pondered circumstance, determinism,
responsibility, and salvation. The slave asked a white stranger "Massa,
may I ask you something?" The stranger watched the slave dig a grave
and said, "Ask what you please." The question: "Can you 'splain how
it happened in the fust place, that the white folks got the start of the
black folks, so as to make dem slaves and do all de work?" He had a
younger helper who feared the wrath of the white man and broke in:
"Uncle Peter, it's no use talking. It's fo'ordained. The Bible tells you
that. The Lord fo'ordained the Nigger to work, and the white man
to boss." Then came a very reluctant and momentary theological ac-
quiescence from the older gravedigger: "Dat's so. Dat's so. But if dat's
so, then God's no fair man!" Theology had to make God a fair man,
and the social behavior of Christians met God half way by taking
responsibility and being willing to blame God for not coming through
with other halves of bargains. The process still goes on in the minds
of Minnesotans and wherever faith is in ferment.

Death and Dying

In Chapter 3 on funerals we gain another insight into the impact on
belief of social behavior and religious practice. Few rites of passage
are more connected with religion in more cultures than are funerary
ceremonies. How people dispose of the dead, how they ritually recall
the meaning of their life and death, and how they celebrate remembrance tells much about the culture. Philippe Aries in *The Hour of
Our Death* (New York: Alfred Knopf, 1981) illustrates how developmental, culturally circumstanced, and fluid have been Christian practices and understandings in the West through the ages.

Satirist Evelyn Waugh in *The Loved One* and social critic Jessica
Mitford in *The American Way of Death* have contributed to the
legend of American practices in this area. They show that a funeral-

home culture develops largely apart from Christian norms. There is nothing in Christian understanding of dust and ashes that commit believers to have lavish funerals or to engage in cosmetic acts that prolong the illusion of present life in a dead body. Yet for a believer to go against social convention in the name of faith calls for acts of defiance that are almost incomprehensible to all except the culturally mobile or unconcerned. At least two-thirds of the respondents reject the notion that funerals—and the data makes clear that here is meant the modern American funeral—should be discouraged by the church. Then come criticisms: of overdoneness, elaborateness (42% want the church to react), yet only 27% wanted the church to discountenance high expenditures for flowers, coffins, and headstones. For the most part, here is cultural conformity unmarked and unmoved by specifically biblical or Christian standards. Whatever comforts, let it comfort, so long as it is not an explicit denial of Christian understandings: this seems to be the humane adaptation of most respondents.

The improvisation based on changed practice is revealed where 60% of all the people felt that it was not unchristian to cremate the dead. Not many decades ago it would have been closer to 6% because current practices—agnostic people favored cremation to taunt those who believed in resurrection-by-reconstruction—led to beliefs against cremation. Catholicism had historic prohibitions which many Protestants copied. But more recently the extravagant use of urban area land for burial, the high costs, and the acceptance of the practice by many Christian pacesetters has led to a reevaluation. People "do it," the church reexamines the record and sees few or no present reasons to oppose the practice, and adjusts.

Sin and Guilt

Chapter 6 on guilt shows how the practice of psychiatry has produced behavioral norms that lead to adjustments of faith and belief. We may assume that once upon a time, in the spirit of the Psalms in the Bible, believers easily and simply connected guilt and guilt feelings. In the modern world of psychiatry and clinical therapies, healers have engaged in practices designed to separate the two. Now in the Faith and Ferment sample, 57% of the people separate guilt and guilty feelings. The former has to do with religion, while the latter is the result of social or psychological developments that do not belong to the universal character of humans. Real guilt goes beyond what therapy alone can handle, say 70% in a spirit that reflects the long Christian understanding of ontologically based flaws. Here orthodoxy persists, as a substantial number of respondents wonder whether psychological therapy can well or best handle guilt. In any case, thanks to the findings of psychology, "there is a prevailing attitude that guilt is not always an indicator of fault." The respondents do not want to minimize real guilt, but therapy more than the Christian tradition has taught them to make less of guilt *feelings*.

One of the most knotted and webbed connections between belief and behavior in the West has to do with what one literary critic called "the decline of hell." Here, as so often, no ecumenical council convened to repeal the threat of hell. Charles Grandison Finney did not call a Presbyterian gathering to repeal the Westminster Confession on the threat of damnation, also of infants. He was too busy, or was ill-equipped to pull it off, or he simply produced circumstances for behavioral change which led such damnation to die the death of a thousand qualifications or to die in ten thousand conversions. By the end of the 19th century America was sufficiently boon-filled and promising that urban revivalists could downplay "fire and brimstone" or the threat of hell and begin offering heaven.

So it has been subsequently. Hell remains "on the books," but except for nominal checks of orthodoxy, it remains no literal threat even to the clienteles appealed to by the more raucous evangelists. Any content analysis of their sermons reveals that hell may be a threat to the Soviet Union, secular humanists, or Elizabeth Taylor. But to win conversions one must offer heaven, preferably beginning with heaven on earth, in the form of improved domesticity, success, glamor, fame, material gain, beauty, and health. Americans have seen too many "nice" nonbelievers whom they cannot picture in hell. They have begun to share too many of the good things of life to picture God standing by to punish them with hell in the afterlife. The revivalists by their practices, the evangelizers by their comforting pitches, the suburban priests with their new value systems, all conspired to adapt to perceptions of believers and accent the positive afterlife, not the negative, and often even to accent this life, not the one to come.

Only 13% of the respondents argued that they did good chiefly to get to heaven. Less than 31% believed that one should follow God's law because God would punish after death those who failed to follow.

Only 14% "agree slightly" that fear of punishment moved them to do good. Clearly evangelists would have slim pickings if they had to frighten one in seven who "agree slightly" to such a proposition. About half the sample find some way of connecting moral choice and any form of punishment. We lack sociological surveys from the past; but the sermonic and tractarian evidence shows that it was once a much bigger weapon in the preachers' arsenals than it now is.

Economics

In a more mundane area, economics, American practices keep leading to change. Christians are very divided, with 30% believing that Christianity commits Christians to the economic growth of the United States, 27% think that Christianity calls for reduction of the material standard of living, and 44% have no opinion at all. Here is an area where the economic behavior patterns do not lead many to identify a specific policy as Christian. The split becomes most clear when the surveyors found upon questioning that about one-third feel Christianity commits the nation to economic growth in the name of and as part of the essence of faith and another third feel the faith calls them to a simpler life-style. Years may have to pass before we see, in differing economic circumstances, which view of growth or stewardship will prevail. The one that does will no doubt be certified because of its success in helping Christians meet circumstances of change, not because denominational task forces have compelling interpretations.

The pattern is fairly consistent. People begin to get restless with institutional religion and find the "electronic church" on television appealing to them, until 47% of the people surveyed—higher, I believe, than the national average of churchgoers—find television church an attractive supplement and profess to listen to and watch it with some regularity. Meanwhile the number of people who see worship as integral to Christian expression, meaning by this the gathering for formal worship in churches, keeps declining and is already very low. Given the social and integral character of worship in Judaism and through most of Christian history, this is a belief-innovation. People have often been laggards and slugabeds, and Christian cultures may have had fewer churchgoers than does pluralist-minded American Christianity. Yet in our time rationales for staying away are developing, based on electronic intrusions into the home and the surrogation for common worship they can produce.

We have not suggested here that social behavior influences belief uniquely in America. Historians are aware of the constant interplay of religion and culture. We are saying that America sees this interplay in fresh ways, and thanks chiefly to pluralism and mass media of communications, modernity calls for and produces new Christian rationales. There is no doubt they will find such justifications. That part of the pattern *is* set.

14

Development

The social behavioral theme which undergirds all the other aspects of belief in Faith and Ferment needed only suggestive, by no means exhaustive, development. We can leave it formally aside now, since it will continue to be in the background of the major three themes of development, faithfulness and continuity, and toleration of ambiguity. The developmental issues, in other words, often result from changed behavioral circumstances. We need here only remind that to locate "doctrinal development" and change in a section following "social behavior" is not to downplay the cognitive elements of faith. In religion it is not only *Who* you know and trust (faith), but *that* you know (belief in) and *what* you know (belief that) that matters to practitioners. Similarly, to say "social behavior" is not to be committed to some biosocial theory of "behaviorism." Further, this approach is not to understress the ways in which "ideas have consequences," but also to notice the ways that "consequences spawn ideas." In short, the developmental themes are cognitive and intellectual and consequential. We shall trace them through almost all the chapters of the study.

The Problem of Suffering

Chapter 2, "Suffering and Crisis," contains an illuminating passage and speculation. Readers of the Psalms in the Bible and of most Christian literature on pain, illness, suffering, and the "art of dying" would lead one to expect 100% consistency in support of the idea that suffering includes in its purposes the reminder that we are dependent upon God. In the Psalms suffering and death are measurements of what constitutes creatureliness and the human, and of existence by God's design almost as if apart from human responsibility and sin. (We do recall, of course, that in the Pauline writings, death is the wages of sin, but while this theme is found elsewhere in Scripture it is not the only biblical description of sin. The Psalms also know this idea, but they have concepts of suffering and death that go beyond those based in human responsibility, and they do illustrate dependence upon God.)

In place of that 100% affirmation, only 45% agree that suffering includes strengthening of dependency of God. Even the denominations that tend to come through with orthodoxy, Catholics (57%) and Baptists (61%), do not score impressively high. This is not to charge the remaining 43% or 39% of the Catholic and Baptist populations with heterodoxy or heresy, but only to note that in this complex case something has happened to cause them to let go of one major consolatory theme in the history of Christian interpretations of suffering. Sister Joan speculates, and I tend to agree but would elaborate, that modern popular psychology is leading to this development of independency or nondependency and its role in the interpretation of suffering.

Neither all of America nor Minnesota have monopolies on such therapies. But on the world spectrum, both of these relatively affluent "islands of gadgets suspended in hells of international insecurity" (Reinhold Niebuhr) make possible the intrusion of self-help devices and therapies. The world of positive thinking and possibility thinking fused with "I'll do it my way!" and "take charge" psychologies seems to be leading to a new development in theodicy and the explanation of evil and suffering.

Conservative religious psychologist Paul Vitz has spoken at book length of "psychology as religion." In his work he scorns the therapies for stressing so strongly the human initiative, both for suffering and for recovery, that psychology takes on a religious cast and theological explanation or divine dependency is diminished. Whether this trend is wholly accurately portrayed, whether it is humanistically good or bad, or whether it can be squared with core Christianity—these are all valid subjects for debate. The historian in me is reluctant to leap too soon to the Chittister hunch, but my sensing devices and instincts place me close to her on this theme. Thus some of the current therapists for cancer, evidently effective in their own way in many cases (the Simonton method, for instance), ask patients to take charge of their disease. Through mental processes they must deal with it, name it, and find it an alien and enemy that can be countered, understood, and perhaps outlasted. To reduce it to such a few themes is to caricature it and to fail to do justice to its subtleties and quite possible positive contributions. Let the caricature stand as a stereotype for the many therapies that seek to minimize mystery, to push back the borders of divine circumscription of suffering, disease, pain, and death, and to let individuals have an ever stronger sense of responsibility for their health and well-being.

What such a development will mean over the long pull for Christian theology, church life, and creatureliness is hard to guess. However, those who have custodianship of doctrine and values in preaching and teaching would do well to stay alert to the subtle and sometimes bold transformations of faith occurring in this direction. The smiling television preacher who comes into the living room and describes almost limitless possibilities, also in overcoming suffering and disease, is offering something quite different from the approach to understanding limits in most of Christian history.

Changing Relationships

Chapter 1, on relationships, is one of the richest and most revealing of all, so far as development is concerned. Since it deals with more humanly comprehensive matters than do issues of determinism or the divine plan in suffering, we may properly dwell on it at some length. The stakes, so far as theological explanation are concerned, are less high. So far as human behavior is concerned, they are far-reaching indeed. Relationships, especially those symbolized by sexuality, familiality, race, and congregational life, are among the most profound and intimate in day-to-day existence for all people, including Minnesota believers.

Here one wishes for a canon or code book in which all past teachings and practices were set forth in regular and normative order, so we could easily match what it is from what we moved with what today's sample is moving toward. We shall have to rely on hunches, suppositions, and informed sensibilities, though in many cases the documentation behind these is overwhelmingly rich.

Page one of the chapter is certainly right: a fundamental shift has been occurring during the development of relational theologies. Sister Joan is perhaps a bit hasty in dismissing the old heirarchicalisms. Bill Gothard can fill Twin Cities arenas and convention halls with tens of thousands of people who come for Basic Youth Conflict Seminars. There they hear perfectly well-established heirarchicalism in which an authoritarian God endows the patriarchal family father with lordship over a submissive wife who still has authority over the children, who hold fixed and unmovable lowest positions of response to the heirarchies above. Elizabeth Elliott and a cohort of evangelical teachers of submission draw their thousands in person and sell to hundreds of thousands. There must be a great market for such static views of relationships. Yet response must be ambiguous when the chips are down and the pencil for the questionnaire is poised, for this part of the population does not loom large.

The historian of American religion and economic life can with some ease chronicle an epochal shift in the understanding of stasis and heirarchy in the 19th century during the rise of the middle class. Thus early in the century a Protestant cleric like Lyman Beecher could join virtually all his colleagues in declaring that the wealthy were fated to be wealthy and the poor to be poor. The wealthy should know that their "state" had its own temptations, and that it was easier for a camel to go through the eye of a needle than for the rich to enter the kingdom. Yet the rich were blessed to be rich, and they, through alms, should be generous blessers to many. Meanwhile the poor had been destined to be poor. They should learn "godliness with contentment," find satisfaction in their status, and look for the comforts of heaven for compensation.

His son Henry Ward Beecher used the same symbols of God, Father, Son, Spirit, heaven, and stewardship, but now there was a vast change. In entrepreneurial America, wealth was a lure of all. The honest and inventive young person could aspire to pass up people of old wealth. "Godliness is in league with riches," said Bishop William Lawrence of Western Massachusetts, and "Get rich! Get rich!" became a religious injunction. Meanwhile poverty was a sign of vice. America had too many opportunities for anyone honestly to remain poor despite industry. Hierarchy was jeopardized in the economic order, more suddenly than in the family or elsewhere, but typically for all.

The Minnesota survey begins to show wavering on the family front in the case where one-third of the respondents held to "control and strong discipline" of children as a strong norm, while two-thirds did not. Self-discipline for children and adults and relationships of a more warm and equal sort replace the old child-obedience heirarchicalism. The study of the family in America, studies enhanced by the work of Philip Greven and Edmund Morgan, among others, have shown how in colonial New England the obedience motif differed vastly from what two-thirds of the Minnesotans now hold as a Christian norm. Philippe Aries in *Centuries of Childhood* has even shown that the kind of childhood that allows for more open relationalism is itself an invention of recent centuries. Earlier Christian thought and practice saw and even dressed the child as a miniature adult. Yet this miniature adult was definitely in the bottom end of the continuum of authority, obedience, and heirarchy.

We have already commented on both the large percentage of those who feel that sex education should prosper beyond the confines of home and the growing percentage of those who are nervous about such education in a "secular humanist" era apart from the Christian greenhouse of faith. This is a scene of great fluidity, whose flux underscores the theme of the "relational" chapter, but whose direction is too uncertain to admit good speculation.

When we turn to the discussion of marriage in Chapter 1, we come to one of the more developmental sections in Christian understandings as the Faith and Ferment respondents see it. Sister Joan Chittister wants to prepare us for the change with a yawn: "It is certainly not a discovery to point out that the indissolubility of marriage, once an accepted part of American life, has faded in practice." But this study begins to document how in a state where religious traditions are strong and supposedly conservative, changes in theology and understanding are also occurring. "Everybody knows this," too, in some senses, yet anyone with the long perspective of Christian history has to be aware here of a great shift occurring, with theology coming along to justify changes in behavior and secular interpretation as these increasingly affect the Christian community.

Older Americans who can remember national life in the 1930s and 1940s—before the pluralism occasioned by World War II, suburban living, mass higher education, and the media explosion—carry in their minds an earlier theological interpretation. Marriage of two people constituted a union of one flesh, to be broken only by adultery of one partner and not to be followed up with marriage again. Every Catholic family knew of a distant or close member whose life was changed and whose being was stigmatized by a divorce. Exclusion from the sacraments was but one sign of the limits of participation in full Christian life. Every evangelical, pentecostal, and fundamentalist of senior age recalls the utter taboo against divorce or condoning divorce, and many would have a hard time recalling a close relative or friend within the circle of faith who had divorced. A divorced cleric was all but automatically barred from ministerial functions. The line was massive, unbroken, and hardly challenged in the more moderate churches which were more exposed to the world. Divorce was sin and scandal. Period!

Today in this sample, where people go to church regularly (80%) and consider themselves close to God and hold to God in steady faith (98%), divorce can be "a reasonable solution," "a necessary provision," "a matter of personal decision" or "a recognized human right." While we cannot know whether 76%, 86% or 96% of Christians four decades ago would have considered divorce "always wrong or sinful," since it at least had to involve adultery, today only 16% of those sampled see it thus. When human problems are too numerous within marriage, 55% no longer see divorce as anything but "required."

The suddenness of this change may have inspired some of the conservative Christian reaction that seeks a "secular humanist conspiracy." *Someone* has to have produced these changes. In some respects, the humanist hunters have a point, though the conspiratorial tone and the secularist charge are both too strong. Without question the appearance of a television situation comedy which downgrades the seriousness of marriage, has never heard of "one flesh" religious sanctions, and makes a comedy of divorce, has made passage into the world of divorce easier than before Christian homes daily received such signals. Traditional assumptions about marriage, held by men and women, have not been able to withstand economic goals which drove women into the work force, or the needs of women to find their own destiny and its expression.

These changes occurred in conservative Catholic and evangelical families as they had occurred in mainline Protestantism slightly earlier and on a somewhat larger and less trauma-inducing scale. But they have occurred. One must think of the cognitive dissonance that occurs when young Catholic or evangelical women join the ten thousands in convention halls to hear Phyllis Schlafly, Marabel Morgan, Elizabeth Elliott, Anita Bryant, or any of a score of other heroines tout the values of domesticity. The message is clear: stay at home and tend to husband and children. Keep the hearth. Don't move from the zone of submission. Be submissive. Remain passively feminine. Yet where are the husbands in all these cases? Who is tending the children and the hearth? Whose submissiveness matches her injunctions to be submissive? Who is passive? Aren't these speakers gifted, capable, aggressive? How long, the observer asks, can cognitive dissonance of this sort be sustained? How soon will Catholic and evangelical young women make their move? The answer is that they already have, while paying nominal attention to submissiveness and hierarchicalism when it is convenient or suits their purposes.

Similarly, as for divorce, a corollary set of activities occurred. Strains came in evangelical marriages or among Catholics. Many Roman Catholics, their eyes open, publicly expressed resentment at the ease of annulment of the sacrament of marriage among the well-off, prominent, conveniently positioned Catholics. Sooner or later it occurred to them that annulment was becoming the Catholic equivalent of Protestant divorce, and that lesser Catholics were being discriminated against when their marriages went bad. Some of the evangelical leadership in relational theology found grounds to break up their marriages and to write descriptions and prescriptions for such circumstances. They all admitted that some measure of sin was present in all divorce, but the sin came out to be no worse than scores of others, and could be lived with under a forgiving God. What mattered now was Christian acceptance and new relationships, new beginnings for creative vocation. The number of books written by and beamed for evangelical singles who have been divorced has grown astonishingly in a few years. Such "how-to" books would have been as helpful before the revolution as they are useful after it.

Paradoxes abound. A clientele that a quarter century earlier shunned presidential candidate Adlai Stevenson, who was divorced from a woman who seemed to give public evidences of grounds, though these were other than adultery, produced a new generation that elected as defender of the family Ronald Reagan, who gave no evidence of grounds for his divorce and whose children were very publicly divorced or living with people of the opposite sex without marriage vows. Evangelicals and fundamentalists denied candidates in the Stevenson era and boosted them, despite divorce and without mentioning it, in the Reagan era. Those dates, both of which point to change without sudden trauma, may be as dramatic symbolically in the history of the family as the election of a first Roman Catholic president was for Catholic symbolism and reality in 1960.

To cite these changes is neither to judge them nor applaud them but only to notice how in two or three decades in the Minnesotas of America there has been more sudden change than in previous two millennia of Christian history. Expect a great deal more theological adjustment coming from Rome and evangelicaldom in the years ahead, even as Christians struggle for new meanings to the concepts of fidelity.

Change is not consistent on all fronts, and the creativeness or humaneness that adaptive Christians applaud as they see new possibilities for divorce are countered by attempts at firmness in supporting fidelity. I refer to the fact that 85% do still—fatal word, still, for what it gives away about the writer's hunches as to where history is going— find "extramarital sex 'always wrong or sinful.'" And Chittister notes a growth in responsibility and fidelity after divorce. Almost 60% think there should be a Christian responsibility to relatives of the past spouse. This is a notion that probably had not occurred to many in the past, when the scandal of divorce meant such a complete and hostile break. Here is a positive evidence of the new "relational" development in Christian lay theology.

Birth Control

Earlier we made reference to *Humanae Vitae* and the developmental consciousness. In this case, John Newman, who wrote on "consulting the faithful in matters of doctrine" would have to report that the faithful were not consulted. If they were, they did not find their views followed. The papal commission of scholars and lay couples, among others, appointed by Paul VI to advise him on artificial birth control, clearly advocated measuring change in church teaching. Paul VI, arguing more on the basis of immediate past precedents in papal teaching than with an appeal to Scripture or a long tradition, showed that he was more alert to a crisis of faith that might occur if doctrine changed than if he held the line on a practice that was no longer practiced and made it a subject of conscience and faith. He bet wrong, say his critics, who argue that his document *Humanae Vitae* was the great mistake of his career and perhaps of the modern papacy. They say it did not do justice to the biblical or traditional or modern theological and scientific data. What is more, the pope misunderstood: after Vatican II the church must persuade, not coerce—remember the decline in numbers of those who fear hell?—and they did not find the document persuasive at all. He may have therefore contributed to the crisis of faith and confidence by countering informed Catholic opinion and practice than he would have by changing the direction.

The survey, at any rate, shows that faithful Catholics who want to follow the church and the pope, and who do when persuaded (as in the case of higher percentages of assent in the matter of opposing abortion) were not at all persuaded. As so often in this study, the faithful seem to want to be faithful. But where the theological leadership is unempathic and unconvincing, as in the matter of Catholicism on birth control, the believers engage in what Yinger spoke of as religious change under the symbols of nonchange. They employ the language of relation and fidelity but apply it differently where they can find plausibilities.

In Protestantism the change came more easily, more gradually. When modern birth control devices and instrumentalities were invented in the late 19th century, Protestants in many states hurried to the law books to put anti-birth control laws on the list of statutes. They made enemies of advocates like Margaret Sanger and saw demonic purpose in her concept of Planned Parenthood. Birth control was usually seen, at least in the conservative manuals, as a shirking of the responsibility to fulfil marriage and replenish the race. Sex in marriage apart from procreative possibilities was a perversion.

All this changed by the middle of the 20th century in all but the most conservative Protestantism. Protestants tried to remove from the laws the strictures they had placed there, only to be met (in states like Massachusetts) by prolonged and massive Catholic opposition. Today the laws are largely gone and about 90% of all non-Catholics find nothing wrong with most forms of artificial birth control. About one-third of Catholics are still opposed, a figure that is somewhat higher than the national Catholic average, suggesting a measure of Minnesota conservatism on this point. Still, to have two-thirds of the Catholics departing from recently and firmly announced official church teaching suggests improvisation and development that will almost certainly have to be reckoned with by future councils or popes.

Abortion

Abortion is a far more complex pattern, one that cuts across Catholic, Jewish, agnostic, and Protestant samples in the polls. If this were a subject for interview and not for mere questionnaires, it is likely that even more ambiguity would be present. Birth control presents few ambiguities except in the case of "morning after" abortifacient types. The rest is clean and clear cut: may one use means other than the rhythm methods and indicators which assist these to prevent conception? In the case of abortion, the respondents have to think through the many scales and kinds: to save the life of a mother, the cases of rape and incest, the degrees of responsibility toward life in various potential mothers, the casualness of the demand for abortion, the militancy of advocacy. Everything is muddied. In that confusing picture, we note that one-third of the Catholic population and three-fourths of the Lutheran and Baptist populations, some of whose church bodies have taken antiabortion stands, join the population majority in envisioning circumstances wherein they could support abortion.

Here it is more difficult to know from what tradition the developers have departed. Some studies find ministers more open to abortion than were doctors in the 19th century. Father Richard McCormick says that Catholic opposition to abortion could be stated for many decades without reference to the term "murder," which falls so quickly from the lips or is mounted so readily on the the bumperstickers of the miltant antiabortionists. We have here a more fluid tradition in which people have not made up their minds. We may hypothesize that the direction is not all one-way, toward more open ideas of abortion. Some are having second thoughts and oppose it more than before. Still others seem disconcerted by tactics on both sides and are reluctant to side with antiabortionists in pursuit of constitutional amendments, preferring the route of persuasion. Here is development, but the trends are not clear. Suffice it also to say that here "doctrinal" issues will have a bearing, since the determination of what life is and when it begins, say many, is not a scientific matter so much as a theological judgment. What one believes about the meaning of life and its originating instances does have consequences on practice.

Racism

The American religious historian has no difficulty at all pointing to development on the issue of theological interpretations of race in American religion over the past century and a half. Most studies have dealt with the American South, but more recent ones explore the scientific and religious communities. Without question, until the recent past most white Americans believed in white genetic superiority and human inequality, and at least lip service to the old beliefs has now declined.

As for white superiority, Thomas F. Gossett, in *Race: The History of an Idea in America* (Dallas: Southern Methodist University Press, 1963) clearly shows how much theological support there was for this cultural idea particularly through the 19th and into the early 20th centuries.

Even generally benign movements like the liberal Protestant Social Gospel were consistently racist, by modern definitions. Most of these Social Gospellers were liberal evolutionists who saw white Anglo-Saxons as the peak of development, with none others in the offing as competitors. Bishop James Spalding and the Reverend Washington Gladden laid much at the door of genetics and heredity and were gloomy about the limits of the limited. Josiah Strong built on old ideas of an elect people and saw the Anglo-Saxons on the mountain top. Before them the greatest Protestant theologian of the period, Horace Bushnell, asked, "What if it should be God's plan to people the world with better and finer material?" He did not picture a new genetic strain but the spread of the white Anglo-Saxon one. Ultraliberal Theodore Parker noted that the Caucasians had always shown the most instinct for progress. Strong himself thought that "the extinction of inferior races before the advancing Anglo-Saxon . . . certainly appears probable." Yet he opposed race prejudice and did not want blacks to be mentioned pejoratively.

These expressions were mild compared to those of Southern churchmen, who drew their views from cultural observation and from the Bible. For their heirs, to change has definitely meant "development of doctrine" on conservative Protestant soil. In the book *In His Image, But . . . Racism in Southern Religion, 1780-1910* (Durham, North Carolina: Duke, 1972) H. Shelton Smith finds an unbroken link of theologically supported orthodoxy which found blacks to be inferior to whites. Henry Holcombe Tucker, Baptist president of Mercer University and the University of Georgia, wrote a "Confession of Faith" to defend himself against charges that he was soft on the question. "We do not believe that 'all men are created equal,' as the Declaration of Independence declares them to be; nor that they will ever become equal in this world. . . . We think that our own race is incomparably superior to any other." He added, "We think that we are orthodox. If we are not so, we should be glad for some one to point out the heresy." (This occurred in 1883.) There is no point in elaborating on this orthodoxy; Smith has hundreds of examples and cites other secondary sources of similar sorts. David Reimers in *White Protestantism and the Negro* (New York: Oxford, 1965) shows how the South "won Reconstruction" in this matter and how its values prevailed in the North, where they found congenial soil. I. A. Newby in *Jim Crow's Defense: Anti-Negro Thought in America, 1900-1930* (Baton Rouge: Louisiana State University Press, 1965) documents similar racism in anthropology, sociology, history, and other disciplines of the university in that period.

As abhorrent as the racism may have been, it is important for latter-day historians to judge past expression in the light of the context of possibilities then open to people. For millennia human slavery had been taken for granted. That it was abolished in the Anglo-Saxon world within the century after agitation first appeared seems almost miraculous to one who takes the long view of history. Racist attitudes in their modern form flowered from the Enlightenment through the Imperial Age into the period when evolutionary theories justified the ideas of racial superiority and inferiority and are now diminishing and dying but slowly. What is important to note is that these came barnacled to theological notions and rationales, and to change racial attitudes therefore amounts to what honestly has to be called "development of doctrine," though such a notion might be resisted by the conservative orthodox who do not admit to development. They would say that racist ideas were marginal, not essential—even if they were explicatory of the human pole in the divine-human relationship.

However mixed "progress" may be on this front, and however strong residual racism is, it is at least less respectable. Most respondents to polls like to think of themselves as less prejudiced or unprejudiced and their answers differ markedly from the opinions of the Bushnells and Strongs and Tuckers. In Minnesota 97% of the church member respondents "denounced with vigor" the notion that God created blacks inferior to whites, and 88% did not think it God's will that Indians be disadvantaged. For a partly urban state, Minnesota has an uncommonly low black population. It would be interesting to compare this prejudice factor with states where racial contacts and clashes are more frequent.

Sexism

The issue of sexism is far more complicated, in part because of the recency of change on the subject and in part because the races can be kept apart better than can the sexes. Issues of race and sex in secular worlds and in religion also differ, since some sacramental churches still have strictures against the ordination of women, claiming that this is not an expression of sexism but a bowing to theological norms. What is more astonishing and problematic in the current findings is that men are far more open to the idea and reality of women's equality in religion than are women. Chittister ponders this a bit and implies that it results from the fact that women have been theologically conditioned to be submissive, while men have been more psychologically mobile to adapt when cultural change came. They had not "heard" the submission message personally and had therefore been less convinced by the words as they shot past their ears or eyes.

The change is coming, and coming fast. Minnesotans in their churches, we must surmise, have changed more in the past decade and a half than in the previous century and a half. Inevitably, says Sister Joan, there are strains and tensions, but she, too, finds surprising the suddenness of gain in attitudes and opportunities. As with black-white relations, here, too, there is almost unanimous consent to the idea that God created men and women equal. How could this unanimity have come about if, as the author says, Aquinas and Luther (along with non-Christian worthies like Aristotle and Rousseau) had viewed women as created inferior? Men were, she says, "spiritually superior and intellectually ascendent."

What puzzles the analysts is that equality of men and women is easier to support outside the churches than in them. Here Chittister's own biases, which I share, show. She sees as purely sexist the theological strictures which some men and women have against, say, the ordination of women. Many of them would honestly examine their hearts and find themselves moved not by ideas of female inferiority but merely responsive to what they see as absolute prohibitions in the writings of St. Paul. Yet if they follow his mixed teachings literally, they will find some in which he does discuss female equality. Pope Paul VI's saying that only men could offer the Eucharist because only they had a "likeness to Christ" can also easily be seen as a belief in female inferiority. The subject is so volatile that it is hard to discuss in purely theological terms.

There are signs of change. Only 23% of all participants in the survey are firmly of the opinion that women must be excluded from ordained ministry, but the results are too confusing to see how many in the Catholic and other churches which do not ordain women (e.g., Missouri Synod Lutherans) have less firm views in support of their inclusion. However women gained their self-images, it seems that women's movements have the most work to do first among women. More men (48%) than women (36%) endorse the women's movement, and more men (57%) than women (49%) accept the place of women in ordained ministry.

However dispiriting these findings may be to Catholic advocates of women's ordination, they will have to admit that across the board in the churches attitudes now begin where they formerly left off. Lutherans, who had no ordained women in America in 1970, had by 1980 over 250, and this was a relatively low figure compared to some denominations. Pope John Paul II has been very firm against the ordination of women, but there is much speculation that one or two popes from now there will be a change, perhaps an easy transition, since in the meantime women will have been incorporated into many forms of ministry which border on the ordained and the offering of the Eucharist. In many cases, the pressure is so strong that we can fairly say that among the faithful there is "development of doctrine" and improvisation for change.

The Place of Jesus

In a more formally doctrinal area, a safe distance from touchy questions like race and sex, there is also innovation or special accenting. H. Richard Niebuhr once said that American evangelical Protestantism tended to be a "Unitarianism of the Second Person of the Trinity." He would find confirmation of this in Minnesota among the respondents, though I am not prepared to say that this is an utterly new development, if Niebuhr is right about the durability of this "Jesusism." In the spiritual development chapter we learn that four-fifths of the sample find Jesus to be "God the Son," not a remarkable finding. But 97% say that "they pray most to Jesus" and that their faith in Jesus as God the Son is nearly universal. In some classic formulae, one prays "through Jesus" more than "to Jesus," and very rare are the classic collects or prayers addressed to Jesus.

The finding by itself should not be overstressed, since discussion of the Trinity and internal relations in the Godhead has always been difficult. One can hardly expect theological precision in a survey of this sort. On the other hand, the status of Jesus as divine seems secure among the people in this whole sample. A century or so of modernism in theology has had little telling or lasting effect, and Jesus is cherished as central to faith. Development, then, is not away from Jesus toward the Godhead in general, but toward Jesus as the way of addressing and communing with the Godhead.

Sister Joan is troubled or confused by the fact that 25% are "inclined to think" and 18% more are "certain" that the resurrection of Christ had little or nothing to do with the relevance of Christian teaching for them. Here is not so much development of doctrine, she suggests, as a kind of falling away. At the same time, what is meant by resurrection is extremely complicated, and the survey may not help people out. Modern physics and understanding of process have led many away from medieval notions of resurrection as molecular reconstitution or resuscitation. If that is what respondents are referring to, give them credit for orthodoxy: the Bible does not speak of Jesus' resurrection in such terms either. His resurrection in *some* understanding or other, however, is integral to all other aspects of faith, and that 43% figure gives some pause and leads to questions about the coherence and consistency of people in the sample. Interestingly for the Catholic population, there is little praying through Mary or the saints. This is certainly a change from pre-Vatican II piety, and suggests that an evangelical focus on Jesus has taken over so strongly that appeals by conservative Catholics to a new Marian devotion have not yet caught on.

The Church

The understanding of the church has also seen some improvisation. "One thing is not essential to the faith life of churchgoing Christians and that is going to church." This is surprising, given the historic understandings that worship is the central act, integral to the Christian life. One could absent one's self because of personal inconvenience caused by sickness or travel. But if one was casual about attendance, as most Christians were, they found no justification in belief for this casualness. We are seeing a new development as faithful Christians adopt the modern cultural notion that congregational and liturgical participation is something that people can take or leave.

In *Daedalus* (Winter, 1982) anthropologist Mary Douglas does not want people to romanticize the integrality or coherence of premodern Christians or to make too much of the rise of choice among postmodern types. To some degree in the past people could choose whether or not to participate, and, as Delumeau has shown, they could smuggle in their own practices and meanings. Yet, before the Enlightenment it is harder to find the kind of "privatized" or "individualized" sense of Christianity that is developing today, also in the Faith and Ferment sample.

In ancient Israel people were saved as a people, through and with a people, in a social setting. The "New Israel," while that is not an encompassing or fully satisfying New Testament metaphor, is a very self-conscious replication of Israel, even to the point of twelve disciples to recall twelve tribes. The church as the body of Christ is seen as a form of integral bonding as well. Christendom knew no individualized Christianity. Absenting one's self from the congregation represented drift and coasting, not working at faith.

Today this has changed. The Enlightenment and the severing of church and state made some contribution. Thomas Jefferson was a startler when he announced that if he could not go to heaven except with a group, he would not go at all. His contemporary Thomas Paine similarly said, "My own mind is my temple." A century later in American philosophy William James was describing as religious only the incandescent moments of experience of the individual, and then

Alfred North Whitehead spoke of religion as what one does with his solitariness. Religion becomes a matter of personal choice, and the church is the sum total of human voluntary action more than it is the body of Christ. Liberal Protestants adapted to these ideas fairly early and the ideas swept Catholicism when Vatican II made participation a matter of voluntary or persuasive life. It may be that evangelicalism is coming to it because the electronic church and other instruments particularize and render private religious experience and choice.

Thomas Luckmann has spoken of "invisible religion" as the final consequence of this modern trend. No primary or secondary associations are supportive of one's quest. Catholic philosopher Louis Dupre in *Daedalus* summarized the private trend well: "The religious person [today] embraces only those doctrines which cast light upon his inner awareness, joins only those groups to which he or she feels moved from within, and performs only those acts which express his self-transcendence." The Minnesota survey bears this out. Robert N. Bellah has put it similarly: people today determine a certain spiritual trajectory. To the degree that the church as an institution meets it and supports it, to that degree do they meet and support the church. Otherwise they go their own way.

Few points in this survey or others like it have more bearing on the strategy of the church in the future than this one, and it is worth dwelling upon in any theological analysis. In the course of time it is becoming clear that the enemy of church life in America is not so much "secularity" as it is "do-it-yourself religiosity." The polls find few citizens who are wholly atheistic, agnostic, or secularized in outlook. Most are somehow responsive to stirrings of the Spirit. Well over 90% in Gallup and other polls say they believe in God, and their orthodoxy index on the authority of the Bible and the divinity of Jesus is impressively high. Where they depart substantially from the view of classic orthodoxies is in their understanding of the church and its integrality to Christian life. As Bishop Stephen Neill once said, everyone wants to like Jesus but few want to like his church.

One can look, and should look, at the positive aspects of this form of individualized religiosity. Note that it happens not against the background of apathy concerning church life but in the company of people who are generally supportive and faithful. Compared to most industrialized nations, America is still a society of churchgoers. To find four out of ten citizens claiming to have worshiped any previous week-end may be a demoralizing figure in the eyes of the clergy or those with short historical perspective. It is far higher than that of other complex Western societies, including even the near neighbor Canada. Without question it is higher than in most of earlier America, including colonial times. The postwar religious boom found the percentage reaching as high as 47%. Since then the greatest decline has been in Catholicism, which, as part of the reforms in the Second Vatican Council, made mass attendance a subject of individual conscience more than before. America remains a nation of church members and church-goers. Yet the ethos and ideology concerning the integrality of the church in the scheme of salvation and the living of personal life have changed.

The individualism of "pick-and-choose" Christianity has long served to keep leaders, especially clergy, on their toes, and this is another positive factor. It has allowed for a certain kind of "politics between the pulpit and the pew," one that serves to dispel illusions about the character, quality, and power of clerical or other leadership acts and proclamations. That is, the minister must work constantly to generate, satisfy, retain the loyalties of, and motivate a constituency. I put it in these crass market terms not to degrade the relation but to point to public perceptions of the power context. This means that congregations and denominations remain somehow responsive, on the leadership level, to what the followers are thinking and on what they are ready to act.

Similarly, because participation in the life of the church is seen as somehow arbitrary, accidental, and chosen, the leadership is constantly on notice to produce its best, or at least its better. One cannot permanently coast with slipshod worship, low quality fellowship, or pointless activities. There is always someplace else down the block where one can affiliate, or one can drop out entirely if the ministrations are too unexciting or unchallenging. The individualism breeds a healthy skepticism about many churchly claims. It assures that personal decision remains prime: if American Christians are not conscious of being saved as a people, they are conscious of being saved as persons. The personal appropriation of what I call "laic" Christianity is from almost every angle superior to the kind of faith that simply comes with the territory, as much European faith had done, or as earlier American religion when it was established by law had appeared to be. For all these reasons one is not impelled to overcriticize the individualized and privatized religious response.

Historical analysis suggests some reasons for this arbitrary approach to the body of Christ in American Christianity. For one thing, religious roots in the United States are largely Protestant. From the early 17th century until the middle or late 19th century Catholic Christianity was a distinct and often suspect minority presence. This meant that the Catholic concept of the body of Christ, of the corporate character of faith, and of worship which one must attend for the sake of being "in the presence" was not deeply stamped on the public mind. The Episcopal Church held to similar notions, but in colonial times the particular forms of Episcopalianism that were established in the Southern colonies bore the spirit of 18th century Anglicanism in general: it was a part of the way of life, often casually apprehended. Church attendance was low, and respect for the clergy lower. A few "high-church" movements like the Mercerburg forces in Pennsylvania German Reformed churches tried to stress the integrity of the church and tradition, but these were minority voices.

The dominant forms of public Protestantism, then, derived frequently from congregationalist, independent, and separatist Puritanism. While the high Puritanism of Massachusetts Bay sustained a convenantal view that in every respect was corporate, hypercongregationalism and the rise of the Baptist presence served as counterforces. In the time of the Great Awakening religion was seen to be a voluntary force. One made a decision for Christ. One chose to be converted. The time came to choose between churches, or to choose whether to participate at all. Through the years such processes and mechanisms lead people to highly voluntaristic notions. They have seen congregations and eventually denominations form. They have recognized them as human projects, gatherings of like-minded individuals who for practical purposes or for reasons of praise decided to get together. As denominations divided and competed with each other, the idea of the church being a single body of Christ or the American Christians being "a people of God" inevitably was compromised. Meanwhile, the myth of American individualism prospered and was carried over into the life of the church.

Through the years, later Protestant innovations further assured the individualistic approach. Numbers of "primitive Christian" movements developed—the Disciples of Christ, the Churches of Christ, the Christian Church, the Christian Connexion, and similar groups. They all set out to restore the pristine character of the New Testament church as they perceived it. This meant a rejection of most Christian history. The Middle Ages was a time seen as the fall of the church from its original purity. Even the Reformation was part of a tradition that these Disciples could do without. To speak of organic growth and development of the church or of all the people formed in Christ as the body of Christ was a denial of what the primitive movements were about, however eager they were to promote Christian unity on their terms.

Still another force for developing individualized or "churchless" faith was a factor in the rise of modern fundamentalism. Fundamentalism as we know it today is not simply historic Christianity in its classic form, or even simple Protestantism. It was instead a reaction against liberal and modernist adaptations to modernity. The liberals tended to adopt doctrines of progress. They were at home with evolutionary theory. The scientific study of the Bible, as it was then called, or the higher critical approach to Scripture was not seen as a threat to faith but as a support for it.

The ancestors of the fundamentalists at the turn of the century would have none of this. They took selective elements of Protestant evangelical traditions and fused them with new forces and agencies to create, by the mid-1920s, the parties today typed as fundamentalist. One of the most prominent of these new directions was dispensationalism, a little-recognized form of Christianity around the world and one not often known by name in America. Yet it has been influential among those who do not know it. The dispensationalists thought that God dealt with the world and the Christian people in very different ways in the successive "dispensations" of history. In the most popular readings of these dispensations, the period between the apostolic age and the second coming of Christ finds the church in "a great parenthesis." In a sense, it does not exist. What remains in the intervening period is a company of individual Christians who voluntarily get together for common faithful purposes in institutions of their creation, institutions called the church.

All these conspired then to promote "churchless Christianity": separatism, empirical observation, voluntary practice, primitivism, dispensationalism, and individualism. Roman Catholics living in this Protestant ethos may well have clung to the doctrine of "the mystical body of Christ." In the Second Vatican Council their bishops came up with new accents on the church as "the people of God." The catechism kept the old orthodoxies, but the Protestant spirit and American individualism worked subtler effects. The airport newsstand had racks of books on all the religions the world had known. The Catholic as well as the Protestant could take it *a la carte*. After Vatican II many of the Catholic people, particularly the young, drifted from mass and church attendance, yet made clear that they thought of themselves as Catholic Christians.

Let us look again at the Faith and Ferment study. We shall have to lump together clergy and laity, men and women, rural and urban, Catholic and many kinds of Protestants. According to the Chittister findings, half of the people attend church weekly, and another third attend church functions even more frequently. A very high percentage, 92%, value the church as an institution. Now: "but, though church as church is important to them, only half are firmly convinced that they could not have a good relationship with God without belonging to a parish or local congregation." Almost half feel that "having Christian faith and belonging to a church" are not the same thing. In that case a certain imprecision in the question may have been a problem. No different things are ever quite the same thing, and classic Christian statements never claimed that having faith and belonging to a parish are "the same thing." Yet despite that confusion, there is no reason to suspect the respondents of failing to get their point across. Chittister is cheered to see that 59% did somehow see the church as an "incorporation into Christ," and did not see the church as purely instrumental. It would seem that church leadership should work through these three out of five Christians, to strengthen and vivify their view of "incorporation" and to diffuse this notion in the rest of the church and in society at large, if they wish the corporate character of "the people of God" to develop.

Less disconcerting to me than to Chittister is the finding that only one-third of the respondents accept all the teachings of the church as essential to their faith and almost two-thirds saw no reason why they could not reject some church teaching and continue to have a deep Christian faith. Why less disconcerting? For one thing, this has to do with cognition and intellectual assent to propositions about faith. For one schooled in Catholic orthodoxy, finding such assent was once assumed to have been easy, so Chittister sees the new as a departure. Readers of Delumeau, Groethuysen, and Bossy would be more likely to find that Catholics long engaged in creative footdragging or quiet withholding of consent from the presumed common body of doctrines. This meant that there was not such a great fall.

Another reason not to be overly concerned about the fact that two-thirds of the people feel free to deviate from church teachings is that it is hard to know exactly what is a church teaching. In Catholicism, papal infallibility has only been invoked twice—on two Marian teachings. Infallible proclamations have a different status than do encyclicals. Conciliar resolutions have still another kind of authority. Expressions of papal or episcopal opinion are of one more kind. Exactly what is and what is "in" the "magisterium"? The faithful are not sure, but they often hear teachings in homilies with which they disagree—and it may be that they are right and the homilist is wrong. Homilies often incorporate elements of folk Catholicism that do not agree with the official body of teaching.

If such wavering about degrees of authority is common in Catholicism, it is likely to be much more widespread in Protestantism. Take the case of Lutheranism, for instance. This is one of the more doctrinally intact bodies, one which has a body of teachings to which members can refer. The Book of Concord, a collection of 16th-century confessions, is a fundamental document, and many Lutheran pastors and teachers are ordained or commissioned to teach in faithful response to it. Yet the Lutheran confessions have many levels of "teaching" in them. They at one point call penance a sacrament and speak of Mary as "ever-Virgin." Should Lutherans feel bad departing from such statements? To bring it to a more trivial level, these confessions say that to rub garlic on a magnet will cause it to lose magnetic power. In some bodies Lutheran pastors swear to teach the confessions not only *insofar* as they are faithful in all details to Scripture but *because* they are thus faithful. Of course, orthodox Lutherans have figured out hermeneutical ways to cancel out embarrassments about garlic and magnets, but the laity are not likely to follow the arguments. More seriously, these Lutheran official teachings regularly spoke of the pope as the biblically prophesied Antichrist. When they did, or when Luther did, they departed from Luther's own hermeneutical principle, since he demanded that the Holy Spirit both set up a sign and seal it—and this, on Luther's grounds, could not happen after the canon was completed. One could read the signs of the times in the light of the Bible, but not be sure of them as one could when the New Testament mirror was held up to Old Testament types. Yet the pope is Antichrist in Lutheran teaching. Should the faithful who are unfaithful to that proposition feel guilty about belonging to the two-thirds who feel free to depart from official church teaching? Should the Lutheran bodies which still boldly insist that their members must believe that the office and persons of Pope John XXIII, Paul VI, and John Paul II are "the Antichrist" be congratulated for their faithfulness to Christian teaching?

For all these reasons, the two-thirds who have some intellectual problems with cognitive elements of church teaching are less significant than the one-third who see the church as an arbitrary and instrumental human construct. At the very least, this latter third helps form an agenda for Minnesotan and American Christian futures.

The Resurrection

One aspect of the doctrinal side of Christianity referred to in the previous chapter does deserve isolation at this point, especially since Sister Joan makes so much of it. It is one thing to be light about "ever-Virgin," garlic on magnets, or John Paul II as the very Antichrist. It is another to waver on the central theme of the resurrection. "Almost one-third of the church members sampled in Minnesota said that Christian teaching would be meaningful to them whether Christ had risen from the dead or not." In 1 Corinthians 15 Paul made the resurrection constitutive of faith. Without it there would not have been a Christian community or Christian hope. Without it, "we are of all men most to be pitied" (1 Cor. 15:19). How then can one-third of the Minnesotans make it an arbitrary aspect of teaching?

The data provide few means of speculating, so we shall have to use other materials of historical and theological analysis to locate reasons for Christian response without a firm belief in the integral character of the resurrection as the basis of faith. How can this be? Of course, in any complex body of people, there will be some who through ignorance or as mavericks will prevent 100% response. Yet these sampled folks come close to 100% on some other indicators, and the one-third deviation has to be taken seriously. A second response could be that there is a form of humanistic Christianity, particularly in the liberal Protestant churches. This quasi-Unitarian form of modern Christianity is impressed by what Thomas Jefferson called "the life and morals of Jesus of Nazareth." Its adherents welcome the ethics and social patterns of Christianity. For them the teachings have meaning whether or not the resurrection occurred. They make up a significant portion of that one-third who do not vote for the resurrection as necessary for their faith.

Earlier we have speculated on other reasons, among them the intrusion of modern scientific world views. In that case, people locate superstitious views of the resurrection with understandings of atom, molecule, and life process and reject them. We have also said that such rejecters are probably more faithful to the Bible than are those who have seen Christ's resurrection as some sort of molecular and corpuscular resuscitation or reconstitution. The Pauline writings do what they can to push people away from such concepts by speaking, for instance, of Christ's "spiritual body." In their simple but mysterious stories the synoptic Gospels also suggest that the resurrection presence of Christ had a different character than did his bodily presence before his death. The early Christians did not "prove" the resurrection by waving the Shroud of Turin in front of would-be converts. The book of Acts says instead that because a preacher like Barnabas was a person of good character, full of the Holy Spirit, many believed.

In our time numbers of scholars, notably Wolfhart Pannenberg, have set out to show by principles of historical reasoning, that the tomb was empty and that Christ was risen. Such reasoning is satisfying to Pannenbergians, to an elite of scholars who possess certain tools for philosophical and historical analysis, who have chosen to identify with the particular school of criticism associated with Pannenberg. Those who do not accept his terms for comprehending what is historical evidence may be totally unmoved but therefore not less totally trusting in the God who raised Jesus from the dead. These "proof" methods tend to make the church into a company of biblical, historical, or philosophical scholars of a particular school. The Barnabas approach has worked more widely and more compellingly.

Because the complexity of the questions having to do with "what do you mean by the resurrection?" is richer than those having to do with whether Christianity has a corporate character, we should not read too much into dissent. Individualizing Christianity is more likely a part of what we here see as "development" of doctrine, while refusing to make a particular view of resurrection integral no doubt belongs to classic inside-the-church skepticism or difficulty with a teaching that can mean so many things. The data can do no more than inspire speculation, not confidence in the result of the speculations. Therefore the flags Chittister places at this point deserve to be noticed by the custodians of Christian teaching in Minnesota and, presumably, elsewhere.

Development and Deviation

On these pages we are making a distinction between development and deviation. Deviation is a timeless pattern, born of ignorance, willful departure from the faith, casualness, obstreperousness, or creative enterprise. Development finds a body of Christian people adopting an outlook on a wide scale and over a longer period of time, an outlook that eventually shows up in the books of theology and even, in the case of Catholicism, of fresh doctrinal statement. The classic modern case of this is the shift on religious freedom as defined at the Vatican Council II. For two centuries American Catholics held civil views that error had rights; this was a departure from the views in the papal Syllabus of Errors in the 19th century and from many other formal and informal Catholic expressions. A "development" occurred and is now established.

Development does not mean that the eventual resolution has to be through formal doctrinal declaration. Many of the churches in Minnesota are not part of bodies that make much of doctrine or dogma; others have no mechanism for stating what the teachings of the church are, especially after the founding. Usually development issues in a new informal but deep consensus: the *creencias* of a church or of the church change.

Thus Christian views of the atonement, the central shaping activity of God in Jesus Christ, have not been subjects of extensive dogmatic treatment in ecumenical councils. The Bible has rich and sometimes conflicting imagery or symbolization for the events called the atonement. The Christian imagination seizes on different ones through the years. In the Middle Ages a "penal theory" had classic status. It is less proclaimed and held to today, though never officially rejected. The penal view—for whatever biblical warrant it has, and it has some—could easily be caricatured. In the modern sensibility it left God as a kind of petty tyrant who in outrage over the breaking of his laws demanded that someone be punished and a penalty be paid. Since no one on earth was appropriate, he sent his Son and had this Son killed. Such a condensation has more of a folk character than any precision or integrity, but the penal theory has come to that. Christians had difficulty squaring this trivial image of God as tyrant who kills his Son or accepts the Son's death—something that even mediocre earthly fathers find repulsive—with other biblical pictures of God. Through the centuries they have allowed other biblical symbolization to replace the penal theory, without formally repudiating it. This is what we mean by informal development.

The Minnesota sample suggests that more of this informal development has gone on in respect to what used to be called "the doctrine of man." No one expects an ecumenical council to be held in Minneapolis, Rome, or Geneva, with an end to canceling widely held views of "total depravity." But the concept is being shelved, is atrophied, not available for most faithful Christians. Why speak of development? If our reading is correct, Catholic and Protestant Christianity in colonial times had little difficulty with what that term implied. Today the connotations of the words are lost, irretrievably, and therefore the concept is no longer available or acceptable.

While Americans perpetrated near genocide on native Americans and engaged in unspeakable injustices against black slaves, they have not known an Auschwitz and have not seen their history as a tragic drama. Even the Civil War was soon turned into a kind of atoning central event in the American unfolding. Instead, people have found reason to develop somewhat more optimistic views of what it is to be human. When theologian Reinhold Niebuhr resurrected the concept of original sin and made efforts to have it culturally available, he scored many points for realism. But at the end of his life he had to admit that using the term was "a pedagogical mistake." Not only cultured despisers of the faith but many believers found it hard to use the term with understanding. The word "total depravity" was even more problematic. It was designed not to say how terribly depraved people were—depravity itself having a different context in Calvin's time than in our time—but that the depravity reached all aspects of the human being, including one's spiritual strivings. Even these were of no effect apart from God's initiative in rescuing humans.

The chapter on guilt gives many indications that an American sample has seen development, not deviation, of a sort that shows up in or reflects theological change. Thus we find that three-fourths of the people believe that if Christian principles were applied to international affairs war could be eliminated. Nothing in Christian history gives warrant to such an optimism. Some counterrealism appears when we hear that only 18% are unprepared to accept moral failure.

Then comes the stunner, over which Chittister passes more lightly than I would. "One explanation for human weakness is roundly dismissed by the greater body (83%) of the participants. In the minds of these Christians, whatever their persuasion, human nature is not totally depraved. In fact, some (28%) strongly believe that 'humans are inherently good, and unless they are brutalized by savagery will strive toward what is good.'" The 28% figure is not surprising, and belongs in the "deviation" class. The 83% figure suggests development. Colonial and early national period Calvinism joined Lutheranism and Roman Catholicism—and these three make up the ancestry of most of those sampled in Minnesota—to stress original sin and cognates for "total depravity." They all had profound and high views of what humans are, could be, or have become "in Christ." They look at humans not only "in Adam" but "in Christ" (Rom. 5). Martin Luther could even say that the Christian was to be more than "as Christ," but "a Christ."

The natural man, said 100% of the classic definers of doctrine and most earlier American Christians, was seen, in the light of God, to be "totally" removed from divine purposes. There were in Catholic views of the retained but obscured "image of God" some higher understandings of human potential. But the baptismal liturgy also showed how deeply "depraved" was the character of the human apart from God and the ministrations of Christ's church.

Calvin, Luther, and other reformers seemed to be in competition to see who could say most about the extent of the human fall. They did this not to degrade people or ruin their potential for self-esteem as new people in Christ but to emphasize and, some said, exaggerate the necessity of Christ's rescue and the power of the new creation. Luther's writings are replete with references to the ways in which it was precisely spiritual striving that frustrated the purposes of God. Those who thought they were naturally good enough to reason their way into Godhead, or who chose the mystical path of spiritual identity with the One, or who by their merits and works felt they could become good enough to please God were entirely wrong. The fall extended to piety, spirituality, good intentions, moral acts, and the like.

All through the 19th century the main line of Protestant theology in America kept adapting this theme, as H. Shelton Smith showed in *Changing Concepts of Original Sin.* "Total depravity" did not square with what Christians perceived in their children, was not good public relations, and, they felt, limited human self-confidence. The Minnesota survey shows that it was not only elite theologians who did the adapting. The faithful church people do not find the inherited symbols attractive or usable. Only 57% of the sample "consider themselves, without reservation, to be sinful or believe that it is of the essence of the Christian faith to believe that all people are sinful." This is a development. Christians have lived in the century of two World Wars, of genocide and holocaust. They have had political scandals in a "moral Christian" presidential administration, and have learned to be suspicious of all who hold power in politics, media, commerce, and even the church. They know of white-collar crime and spend billions protecting their possessions. Yet 57% in this sample qualify their notions of how the awareness of sin (which 98% believe in) affects their personal self-understanding.

In our time philosophers and preachers of self-esteem have risen to help implant in Christians a sense of their worth. Some do their preaching in the context of the new Adam or the new creation, where self-esteem is derived, a given and a gift. Others make it a general philosophy and apply it to what used to be called "the natural man." The Minnesota survey suggests that they start from a strong base. While the respondents are not satisfied with themselves, they do not see the divine rescue and restoration as a "starting from scratch."

A corollary of this view may be a development in the understanding of the source of evil. This is the century in which "the demonic" has been rediscovered and made culturally available. How else explain a Hitler? In the 1970s, after a number of films like *The Exorcist,* the Gallup poll found an impressive increase of belief in "the devil." Yet if we read this survey correctly, the free enterprise of Christian people has led to a decline of belief in Satan along with a decline in fear of hell. Satan remains a "personal being" for 29% in the sample or an "evil force" for 59%, so the symbol is not in danger of disappearing. Yet the Minnesota understanding is one in which Satan is less readily available as scapegoat or figure of blame; there is a growth in personal responsibility. Chittister rightly backs off from overinterpreting these findings; the method of gathering data does not provide enough material, and future surveys should pursue the issue. At the same time, it is safe to say that in this sample the radical character of human evil, limits, or tendencies to corruption is tempered, and there is considerable — understandable — confusion concerning the sources of evil in God's creation and the human heart.

More ambiguous is the testimony about conscience and the law of state and church. Here there may also be some development. In theory, Christians have always believed that one "ought to obey God rather than men." Christian history has numbers of saints, heroes, and martyrs who suffered for their response to conscience over against the laws of church and state. Yet on a church-wide basis there has been an instinct to suppress conscience. In Paul Tillich's terms, law has often been perceived "heteronomously." If it has been passed by external bodies of authorities, it demands assent. For this reason most of the churches have not until recently made room for "conscientious objection" to killing in war. Martin Luther might say that for a person to kill in a war he believes is unjust is murder—but then he turned around hawkishly and moved back into a tradition which almost always finds all Christians finding their side in all wars to be just.

In World War I there were only a very few conscientious objectors to military service among Catholics and all but "peace church" (Quaker, Mennonite, Brethren, etc.) Protestants. By World War II the numbers had grown to only a few hundred in each. After the Vietnamese War and the institution of "higher-law" theories during the Civil Rights movement of the 1960s, the idea of conscience superseding state and church law has become more widespread.

There is certification for this cultural development in the Faith and Ferment survey. About half the group (48%) believe that "without qualification" they must sometimes obey their consciences rather than church teaching. They were less ready to resist the state than the church, since 63% felt it wrong to withhold taxes for conscientious reasons. Is the state more likely to pass proper legislation than the church? Or are Christians more insecure about societal confusion than churchly confusion?

As a Roman Catholic, Chittister is more surprised by deviation from church law than most Protestants would be. Many of them reject the "law" approach to church life. Most of them are aware that in their Protestant traditions there was a fundamental rejection of the whole

Catholic canonical system. On those terms, there is less improvisation than she thinks, but she is right not to minimize the belief in conscientious objection in the face of state or church law. "Development" here is probably part of a long process of modern "autonomy," willingness to take responsibility for one's own action. In the Christian orbit, when this is seen against the background of divine law, it may be understood, in Paul Tillich's parallel term, "theonomously," which means in a way that is transparent to divine order. In any case, the laws of church and state are less frequently seen as untouchable external impositions of all of life. Only 15% defined their church as "an important source of moral and spiritual values." Chittister said that people do not go to church to be told what to do, and those who do, have low expectations for what they will hear.

Ecumenical Development

A final sample of documentable development, chosen from any number of possibilities, is the ecumenical understanding. Anyone who claims that Christian faith and life are static will have to revise the claim in the light of the astonishing growth of ecumenical sentiment in the Christian survey samples. We do not have exact statistics from polls before 1910, when the modern ecumenical movement began to take form at the great Edinburgh Missionary Conference. It may be that Christian people long felt drives for unity, but these were suppressed by their heirarchs. Yet the very ill-defined stirrings toward Christian unity expressed decades ago are no match for the growth of acceptance now. This cannot be called "development of doctrine," for Christians have always professed that the church, the *una sancta,* is somehow one. The ancient creeds assert this, and New Testament teaching is clear. Yet if it is not doctrine that is at stake, at least profound understandings and practices are.

In the early stages of ecumenism, some of the leaders seemed to move cautiously. They had known of interethnic and interreligious tensions and conflict. They assumed that the laity wanted to be at war with each other across the boundaries of church bodies. How could ecumenical committees convince Christian people to lay down their arms, bury their hatchets, and accept each other in Christ?

Like all others, this survey shows that this was a tremendous miscalculation. Christians are perfectly capable of warring with each other in the name of Christ, but they evidently prefer to do this within denominations, not between them. Baptists do not fight Methodists; they fight other Baptists. A two-party system in most church bodies allows for civil war. Between churches, however, it is another matter. The laity either has wearied of battle, never was really at war, or has caught the Holy Spirit. In this study 95% felt that the churches should cooperate with one another whenever possible. This may be lip service, since ecumenical events in local communities rarely draw as well as do separate denominational or congregational activities. Yet the 95% figure shows that sentiment for cooperation is high. Similarly, 77% of the sampled Minnesotans want to press beyond cooperation to more formal expressions of permanent unity. About two-thirds "argued that in every church the sacrament of Holy Communion should be open to members of other denominations." The ecumenical committees have to caution Christians constantly not to use all the unity they have, so far as the Lord's Supper is concerned.

In decades past there were more open efforts to proselytize people of other traditions. Cynics will say that apathy, secularism, or self-protection in the competitive market has set in. Hopeful believers say that the Holy Spirit is creating a new circumstance. All this adds up to the fact that while subtle and secret predatory activities may be going on through public relations activities and programs of the church—or maybe even some tract passing and high pressure witnessing from conservative evangelicals—78% felt that new converts should be given a choice and should not be pressured to join "my church." Over 40% had reservations about persuading members of other denominations to switch churches, and only 46% would use the language of "the true church" of Christ for their own. The denominational principle was established a couple of centuries ago to assure open competition and the integrity of one's hold on truth through one's own denomination. The statistics here suggest development beyond that original rationale for denominations.

It is interesting to lift out Catholic responses on this question. In this sample 83% strongly endorse church unity, but they remain less committed to "open communion," since only 33% were ready for it. For Lutherans the comparable figures are 76% and 58%, the latter perhaps kept low because one of the three large Lutheran bodies discourages and even forbids the practice. For Presbyterians the open communion figure is 89%; for Episcopalians, 83%; for Methodists, 87%;

and the like. The ecumenical movement may be in trouble, but the ecumenical spirit seems strong. In a state with fewer Catholics and Lutherans it is possible that the "open communion" figure would even be higher, but it is hard to see how support for the *idea* of ecumenism could be much higher. Given the Christian past, this is "development."

15

Faithfulness and Continuity

To speak of development and change is not to suggest that the Minnesota church people are radical innovators. They may be restless and uneasy with aspects of the tradition, but there is little sign that they wish to make great breaks. Here as so often, one is impressed by the relative contentment and conservatism of American churchgoers. For centuries the philosophers of history have predicted the demise of religion. Many have worked on a "secular" assumption in which there would be a progressive decline of myth, magic, mystery, meditation, mysticism, and metaphysics—to stay, for the moment, simply with the m's of the spiritual alphabet. In Bonhoeffer's vision, the world had "come of age," and was passing from adolescence to adulthood. Any form of Christianity that would have to survive would be "religionless." That vision coincided with the academic secular assumptions which pictured one level of rationality pervading the modern world.

Christians have known many assaults. Christendom—the fusing of church and state, Christ and culture, as it persisted from the fourth to the 15th century—was divided by the East-West schism in the 11th century and the Protestant-Catholic break in the 16th. Yet the faithful were not plagued by the problem of disunion and the clash of rival Christian symbol systems. They dug in where they were and remained faithful. The Renaissance implied a kind of paganization on Christian soil, right to the heart of the Vatican, yet Christian symbols survived. Humanists restored the pre-Christian classic motifs, but Christian humanists took over the classic world and used it to enhance biblical translation and Christian interpretation.

The 18th century Enlightenment turned out to be an assault on the particularity of Christian revelation and churchly institutions, but it was followed by a period of Christian revivals and renewals. In the 19th century on the soil of Western Europe what historian Robert Binkley called "the pitiless and persistent rivals" of the church took shape. The death of God and the rise of new individualisms or social forces on the soil of Christendom, alongside the religion of nationalism, made up part of the rivalry. Devastating world wars on Christian soil led to a questioning of centuries of Christian humanist tradition. The Jewish Holocaust occurred on Christian and post-Christian soil. Modern totalitarianisms set out to destroy the faith. Yet it persisted.

In some respects America seemed exempt from the more radical processes. There was religious change more than mere secularization. Religion did not go out of business; it relocated. Legally separate church and state? Fine, the churches said; let us help provide a rationale for doing so and give us freedom to operate. They did better on voluntary grounds.

To many, Christianity was a faith for farm and small town; how could it survive the impersonality of the modern city, the disruption of tradition occasioned by the move of rural people to the metropolis? Certainly industrialization and technology would take tolls; they did in Europe. Yet the percentage of Americans who joined churches and attended them increased; it did not decline in this period. Denominational division was nowhere more confusing than in American pluralism. Yet, far from distracting the people, it only inspired them to loyalty to their own and at least some dim affirmation of larger Christian purpose. Depressions should have depressed a prosperous people, yet the church survived. Affluence was supposed to distract them; who needed God in the suburbs? Yet it was in the suburbs of the 1950s that Americans built churches as never before. When the high-rise apartment and the long weekend were invented in affluent America and there were new reasons to be gone, churches adapted and somehow held members. When the baby boom that brought people to the churches ended, a new set of churches started to attract the teenagers lost from the older mainline churches.

I have presented these lines in bold terms, deliberately stereotypically. They can be read as bravado, whistling in the dark. Each of these modern trends and events has exacted a price, and there have been losses. Historic Christendom, Europe, is full of empty churches and monuments of a once vital faith. The Christian symbol systems belong to American subcultures more than to American culture as a whole. In a pluralist society it is hard to coerce assent to Christian norms—the Constitution opposes this, and Christian people are fortunately too divided to agree on which norms to impose and how to do it—and Christian people have not persuaded the larger society to accept its distinctives. The population of mainline churches is aging; the young have not been won back; efforts at converting new cohorts seem futile; apathy can be rampant; understandings of the faith—as this survey shows—can be vague and confused. The high-rise and the long weekend will remain as new social patterns that plague and bemuse the churches. The ghost of European Christianity, the decline of participation in Canada and the American North, the drift of black and Hispanic populations—all these portend great troubles for the churches. There is a balance sheet, and on balance no one should feel secure.

Despite all the reservations and strictures, however, one cannot help but be impressed by the way people in a state like Minnesota express their continuity with their national, state, and churchly traditions. They do go out of their way to support voluntary associations of a religious character. They wish to be faithful. I am often drawn to Solomon Schechter's address in 1903 when he dedicated the building of Jewish Theological Seminary in New York (Solomon Schechter, *Seminary Addresses and Other Papers*. Cincinnati: Ark Publishing Company, 1915). It depicts the character of American continuity, perhaps slightly overstressing the Bible for the Catholic population, but still properly describing the national spirit:

"If there is a feature in American religious life more prominent than any other, it is its conservative tendency. The history of the United States does not begin with the Red Indian, and the genesis of its spiritual life is not to be traced back to the vagaries of some peculiar sects. This country is, as everybody knows, a creation of the Bible, particularly the Old Testament, and the Bible is still holding its own, exercising enormous influence as a real spiritual power, in spite of all the destructive tendencies, mostly of foreign make. . . . The large bulk of the real American people have, in matters of religion, retained their sobriety and loyal adherence to the Scriptures, as their Puritan forefathers did." One might disagree with each line, but the capping line makes all the rest worth while: "America thus stands both for wideness of scope and for conservatism."

The developmental chapter underscored the "wideness of scope," while this one comments on the Faith and Ferment evidences of a kind of conservatism, of fidelity to inherited forms. From the beginning they project some note of confidence, one that hardly reveals marks of the nuclear threat or of moral decay. Apart from Baptists and evangelicals, where the language of the second coming of Christ and the attack on secular humanism are strongest, not many—only one-fourth including these conservatives—are firmly of the opinion that America is heading for moral disaster. They have a certain steady sense in the midst of crisis. Curiously, ironically, almost amusingly, the field study found that in the other three-fourths of the sample there were as many worriers about the worriers as there were worriers. That is, many feared the effect of doom-saying handwringers, since they might set out to upset the America that was. They did not like right-wing efforts to reestablish Christianity on legal terms. They feared anything that might limit cherished American pluralism.

Fidelity in the Family

In the chapter on relationships we see the surveyed people giving respect to the concepts of "fidelity, control, responsibility, and commitment" as central to the Christian ethos in the past, but much survived in transformed relations in our own time. The attack on extramarital relations in an era of divorce showed how selective Christian people could be about supporting fidelity. Support for family ritual to support fidelity to family and God is so strong that I am almost suspicious of it. Are Minnesotans more at home around the family altar than one pictures other Americans being, or do they cheat when they respond to a survey? I have a hard time picturing that over two-thirds pray at meals "most always." It is hard to conceive that "for most Baptists, Catholics, Lutherans and Evangelical groups in the sample, family worship is reportedly a daily exercise."

We have read so often of the disarray of home schedules and disintegration of mealtime gatherings that one wonders when such family worship occurs? And is not the family itself more "together" in this survey than one would expect in an American sample at large? Is this sample accurate? Do fathers with custody of children after divorce *daily* have devotions with their offspring? In a world of working women who come home late and join in "throwing a dinner together," are there time and energy left for spiritual ritual with the family? Unless they are in the United Church of Christ or Episcopal Church, the Minnesotans tend to say "yes." Whether or not they do thus engage in family worship, the fact that they claim to be doing so or perceive themselves as regulars provides a sort of stable base for future accenting.

As with family worship, so with sexual relations. We have already mentioned the shunning of extramarital sexual expression; 85% find it "always wrong or sinful." In premarital sex, where fidelity and continuity are not yet as strong, only 64% find it to be wrong. Especially when couples were engaged, those surveyed seemed to be less critical about such intimacy. Patterns designed to test or reject fidelity were themselves rejected. Only 3% were for "open marriage." This may not be surprising, since the best-selling authors of a book on the subject some years later repudiated it, saying that it did not work even for them. The world of the swingers exists in America, but does not show up statistically among Minnesota churchgoers. When some new stress comes along, as typified by the movement for women's rights, those surveyed show signs of struggling to integrate old values and new, and not to reject all of either.

Prayer

As with national and familial life, so in personal communication with God, the Faith and Ferment respondents claim to show more faith than ferment. Modern philosophy finds it problematic to talk about God, not finding ways to verify empirically the referent to that symbol. The theater of the absurd finds existence to be meaningless. We hear of the death of God, or the silence, absence, or eclipse of God. Theologians ponder the remoteness or impassivity of God and satirists deride those who claim easy commerce with the deity. Yet those surveyed show that their commerce with God is regular, consistent, fulfilling, and personal.

Recalling that this is a churchgoing sample, it is still impressive to find that 88% believe in prayers of supplication, since such an assumption suggests that God is available for the interventions of ordinary people in day-to-day affairs. In all, 83% "frequently" or "always" consider that God takes an active part in the direction and decision-making process of their lives. Many theologians advocate ways of speaking about God as having to do with the whole of life, but they discourage easy talk that identifies the supernatural with the natural, that too readily invokes "the Lord's will." The surveyed people do not seem to have trouble with this issue. Prayer changes things. No detail is too small for troubling God.

The Bible

Equally firm is their faith in the Bible. Schechter may have underdone the influence of nonbiblical religion, whether from "the Red Indian" or the innovative sects, or the traditional Catholicism that he did not mention. Yet he was correct about the overall influence of the Bible and the regard in which it is held. Almost all (95%) say that somehow the Bible is "the authoritative" Word of God, and 77% feel that reading the Bible helps them develop their spiritual lives. Again, 92% said that the Bible was a great contributor to their spirituality; "even 59% of the Roman Catholics" said something of this sort.

While a survey of this sort cannot get into the niceties of interpretation, it did reveal that, close to the national sample, 41% believe in biblical inerrancy. Those advocates of inerrancy in fundamentalism or conservative evangelicalism who believe that this construct is necessary for the future of faith run into considerable countertestimony here. The traditionalists in Protestantism, who want to make inerrancy the touchstone, would have a relatively small church in Minnesota: most Christians, three out of five, do not need "inerrancy" to support the notion of the Bible's being "the authoritative Word of God." The majority found that there were "errors," as a result of copying (29%) or because of the human dimensions of the Bible (25%). It is hard to certify exactly how one comes to a sense of authority, at least in the shorthand and with the brevity that polls demand. The evidence is clear, however, that without usually seeing the Bible as inerrant the respondents still cherish it and its role in their spiritual life. Solomon Schechter, 80 years later, might beam, but he would not be surprised.

The God Who Intervenes

The assumption that God will welcome supplication and will intervene in personal life tells much about the concepts of God cherished by people who responded to this survey. In the Enlightenment era when America was born, the thoughtful statesmen tended to be deists more than theists, nominal members of Christian churches. Either their churches were in deist phases, or they drew their religious sentiments from places other than their churches. In the slightly overdrawn type, the deist God was like a watchmaker who set a watch in motion after creating it and then absented himself. God had set up natural laws, and one did not need Bible or church to interpret the divine way, nor could one expect to have easy traffic with this rather impersonal God. The deists were sure that theirs was the faith of the future.

Not so, or at least not in the Faith and Ferment samples, where theism has triumphed over deism. In the Faith and Ferment samples there was strong belief in miracles, in supernaturalism, in the intervention of the divine power in daily life. While the most interesting expressions of belief in providence came from interviews, a statistic is important: 73% believe that God intervenes in supernatural ways in personal life—though, curiously, only 63% saw this intervention with the same clarity in society. This may result not from a loss of faith in providence and supernatural so much as from an awareness of the complexity of interpreting the social world, where there are more than two wills, God's and mine, and where answers cannot be as clear. I take this 10% statistical disparity as a sign of the "smarts" of the laity. They may very well not waver in their faith in God's involvement in society's affairs, but are properly modest about interpreting the meaning and character of that involvement.

Life After Life

The God who intervenes in the midst of life continues to have power over the faithful after life. Here again most modern prophecy was wrong. The main strand of secular thought has been to take mechanistic views of the body, which, when run down or when life is snuffed out, ends its story. Here and there idealistic philosophers kept alive a faith in human immortality, and large subcultures devoted to the occult have stressed reincarnation or other views of perpetuated life. Yet "life after life" was to disappear: so said the Marxists, who found it a distraction or opium; so said the Nietzscheans who wanted superman now; so said the Darwinians who confined human purpose to this-worldly evolution; so said the Freudians who found hopes for immortality to be illusions or projections. Such one line cryptic summaries of complex positions do not do justice to them; they only erect a few billboards of reminder that major shapers of the thought of millions did not reckon with continuing faith in afterlife.

The Minnesota survey shows how strong this faith is in the church-going communities. Over 90% claimed not to be indifferent about the question or their fate. Almost two-thirds have rather vivid expectations of a restored life in community with loved ones who have also died. Beyond this, it is hard to get agreement, probably because of the limits of human imagination, the complexity of biblical evidence, the contradictions in Christian tradition, and the growth of folk piety. Most respondents (60%, not an overpoweringly impressive number, given the biblical strictures) do not believe that anyone can communicate with the spirits of those who have already died. Chittister is justifiably surprised to find that despite Bible, technology, and science, 32% of church people will not take "a firm position against the possibility."

Law and Order

Again in the mundane sphere, the survey shows the essential sense of continuity and conservatism in the Minnesota support for law and order. "Anarchy is not a Christian virtue in Minnesota," says Sister Joan of the least surprising finding in the survey. In all, 82% of the people in all churches insist that it is a Christian moral duty to obey the laws of the country. What would we expect most to say: to disobey them? After that initial response, however, there were variations that allowed for Christian conscience when it clashes with the law of the land; we have already commented on these.

Where it is not a threat to law and order, as much effort for justice in the world must be, the surveyed people were for support of the poor (93% say they should not be neglected) and for churchly mission of mercy and charity among them (85%). Meanwhile, because the human record shows that such mission can soon move beyond mercy and charity to inconveniencing those in power, there is some backing off (out of fear of anarchy?). At any rate, only 76% are for churchly support of the causes of justice for the poor and oppressed, a figure substantially but not awesomely lower than the 85% who would have the church engage in mercy and charity. We shall reserve comment on the ambiguities over support of the cause of justice for the chapter on ambiguity. Suffice it to say now that in the minds of respondents "mercy" is a more conservative cause than justice, and "charity" expresses more continuity with the world they have known than would "siding with the oppressed."

Daily Work

A final choice for observing the continuity in life has to do with daily work. Here, as so often, one gets the impression that church people for the most part are a solid, stolid, not easily moved set of middle Americans who do find meaning in their daily lives. This shows up in a chapter on occupations, where we learn that two-thirds of the people feel that God called them to their work. If this is a legacy of the Protestant Reformation, which wanted such daily secular life to be seen sacrally as if it were the contemplative life previously valued in the monastery, then the Reformation has made its point. One does not need to be at prayer or pursuing spiritual ends to live under God or be of divine service. At the same time there is among many a sense of autonomy in vocation: 46% were not conscious of employing their faith to choose calling or job.

The people also want to connect Sunday with the other six days of the week. In all, 83% connect the Sunday life of the teaching, counseling, praying, and celebrating church with their daily work. It may be that the churches have gotten more of their message home than many think. While clerical and other leaders often hear expressions about the gap between church life and worldly expectations, a huge proportion of their members must find help in making connections.

Minnesota is usually listed as a progressive state. The Faith and Ferment sample suggests that it would make progress without rocking too many boats, inconveniencing anyone too much, and by choosing to see the hand of God in worship and work alike. The solid, durable character of life as revealed in this survey does not, however, mean that people are not thoughtful about their faith. When they express themselves, their thoughts do not always seem to be fully consistent with each other. Paradox, contradiction, ambiguity are present as the Minnesota church people try to deal with urgent issues of life in the light of their belief in God and their membership in Christian community. To their ambiguities we now turn.

16

Tolerance for Ambiguity

F. Scott Fitzgerald once wrote that it is a mark of a first rate intelligence to hold two contradictory ideas in the mind at the same time and still function. One critic of the line pointed out that it occurred in his novel *The Crack-Up*. Yet not all people who live with contradiction, paradox, or ambiguity are victims of "crack-up," and many preserve their ability to function. Such dealing with complexity is appropriate in any understanding of the Christian life. Two fundamental sets show up in the Faith and Ferment survey, and they are of quite different characters.

Evil and a Good God

The first family of difficulties arises from the presence of evil in a world supposedly created and ruled by a good God. How reconcile the two? How account for the presence of evil, especially in the lives of those who experience themselves as faithful and trusting in that God? The second family is less intellectually but more morally complex. If the message and mission of God are to spread justice in the world, why is it so easy for Christians to see how this operates in individual lives and so difficult for them to apply it to the corporate life of the church and the structures of justice? The two themes course through the chapters, and we shall run variations on them, seeking to provide historical and theological analysis.

On one issue all respondents were unanimous: they were involved with the issue of suffering in God's good world. "Not one of the interviewees in this study claimed to be free of suffering, and those who spoke of it spoke feelingly." Starting from a 100% basis is wonderfully clarifying for the mind. However fortunate Americans have been in the perspective of world history, they all lose loved ones and they all die. They all have hopes denied and have to defer dreams. They all know frustrations and lack of fulfilment. If they experience loss without belief in God, they may be comfortless, but they have no problem reconciling this loss with faith in the divine. If they do believe, they must somehow explain the difficulties to themselves and others. Sometimes they must welcome the Zorba-like response, "I spit on your explanations." With pagan Walt Whitman they might envy the animals who do not have the problems, who do not whine over their condition. But they are given no choice except to ponder.

One has the impression that, however respresentative the sample may be, as a whole the respondents belong to comfortable America. Churchgoers by nature tend to be somewhat more familial, more located in contexts of care, than is the general population. Minnesota has been one of the more prosperous states. Even in a state with a substantial Native American population, there would be room for only a few Indian families in this mixture. Therefore we do not hear of Christian Indians who have to make sense of two conflicting symbol systems, two contradictory sets of expectations imposed on them—in one case by invaders, exploiters, conquerors, and killers. If the questions were sharply poised, what sense would they make of their kind of suffering and oppression? Was it caused not by the Great Spirit of their ways, or by people acting in the name of the Christian God? Do any of the individualized sufferings behind the voices in this survey speak out of such a context?

Similarly, the black population of Minnesota is relatively low. If this were a scientific sampling of Mississippians, where great numbers of blacks live on in hard-scrabble situations, in little leftover sharecropper shacks or urban shanties, what explanation of suffering would there be? These people have a long history of oppression caused by other Christians. These Christians passed on selective elements of the faith, denying the literacy that Protestants considered all-important, stressing the duties of obedience to masters, not permitting application of the Moses story to a people in search of a promised land. We know that blacks on the plantations pondered whether "God is a fair man" for permitting them to be "fo'ordained" for servitude. Where was God when the whip was present, when the dogs chased, when the family was broken up?

Minnesota has its Hispanics who entered America illegally (and some who entered legally) and its substantial Asian community. How do the Christians among them make sense of their uprootedness, the hatred they have felt, the days of persecution, the existing economic insecurity among Latin peoples even now? What would their voices add?

I raise these questions early in this chapter in order to suggest that the issues would be even sharper if we had more of a population that connected the questions of evil under a good God with oppression at the hands of a supposedly good nation. It occurred to me after reading all the responses that throughout I kept picturing the answers coming from well-established middle-class families in the Twin Cities, in Brainerd or Bemidji, on farms in range of steeples. We may well trust those who set up the survey to have included many classes and ethnic groups, but the Minnesota mix is different from the Mississippi or New York City mixes, and this allows both for some domestication of the "evil" or suffering story and for its separation from the "justice" and oppression story.

God is good, say the people who respond, and 68% are sure that somehow that goodness can be reconciled with evil and suffering in the world. They are orthodox. Eighty-eight percent of them do not believe that God creates evil. Faith in Jesus as the model of one who lives out the paradigm of suffering is the greatest aid for them (83%). Through all this, there is conventionality and strength in the faith confessed.

The history of theology reveals many futile attempts to prove the existence of God and to provide philosophically satisfying answers to the problem of evil. Before one derides Minnesotans who are given a few lines in a survey to ponder the imponderables of the ages, it is well to be reminded of that futility. Whatever it might be that the philosopher wheels out on stage as a provenly existent God cannot *be* God, because God is boundless, not confined by definition. Similarly, almost no one is content with someone else's philosophical explanation of the origin of evil or the secret of its power. A person may sit spellbound by the logic of an ontologist. Such a philosopher can show how we would not know what evil is were there not good, and vice versa. None of the verbal fireworks dazzle, however, when that philosopher suddenly has to make sense of a malignant tumor or the loss of a loved one. "I spit on your explanations."

That is why many Christian theologians propound views similar to those which 83% of these surveyed Minnesotans have stumbled upon, deduced, or come to by church participation (maybe some of those sermons do produce an effect!). Jürgen Moltmann in *The Crucified God* (New York: Harper and Row, 1973) takes up the theme, connecting in a rare and creative way suffering under God and oppression caused by humans. While his treatment cannot be fully satisfying, given the nature of the subject, it does at least provide a framework for inquiry and for viewing the Minnesota findings. For Christians the cross is the center of any concentration on suffering.

Moltmann says that the cross "contains the element of abandonment by God, expressed in Mark 15:34. [Jesus' cross] includes acceptance of rejection, by the Father's Father, in which, in the context of Jesus' resurrection, election and atonement are revealed. We must ask whether this cross of absolute abandonment by God is not exclusively his cross alone, and is endured in the cross of those who share in his sufferings only in a watered-down form. The cross of Christ cannot be reduced to an example for the cross of those who follow him. His suffering from abandonment by God is not merely a blueprint for Christian existence in the abandonment by God of a world which is passing away." There is no question of Christian suffering being on the same level as the suffering of Christ, as is shown by the story of Gethsemane. "Jesus suffered and died alone. But those who follow him suffer and die in fellowship with him. For all that they have in common, there is a difference."

Then Moltmann quotes Dietrich Bonhoeffer: "Hence while it is still true that suffering means being cut off from God, yet within the fellowship of Christ's suffering, suffering is overcome by suffering, and becomes the way to communion with God. . . . And therefore to follow Jesus is joyful." Could it be that the 83% sample which identifies with Jesus in the mystery of suffering has caught something of what the theologian Moltmann has read into the situation? Or, perhaps, that

Moltmann has been gifted enough to intuit what simpler Christians have read in the texts and heard in the Jesus story? (It is another virtue of the Moltmann book, by the way, that he keeps before us the need to see human justice as part of the mission which places Christians under the cross and in fellowship with Christ.)

When she comes upon a very wide disparity between denominations on this point, Chittister raises some questions that I cannot answer. While 85% of the Baptists were able to reconcile the existence of overwhelming iniquity with the concept of a God of love and goodness, only about half of the Methodists could. For them, the presence of a world of awful evil might just preclude the notion of an all-loving God. "What special insight does each denomination bring to their understanding of the problem of evil?" she asks.

It may be that the Calvinist and Arminian lineages of these two churches, with roots that go back two centuries, still help provide some explanation. Of course, "Calvinist" and "Arminian" are code words for complex realities. The Calvinist interpretation overall stressed the sovereignty, will, and foreknowledge of God and the nothingness of human response. God was inscrutable, but had somehow broken through to care for his elect. The Arminian deviation from Calvinism, in the Netherlands, then in England, and through Wesley in one form in America, began with much more stress on the accessibility or availability of a benevolent deity who in love wishes nothing but good for all. The corollary of this version of Arminianism was also a more benevolent view of humans, a higher faith in their capacity to transcend circumstance and evil, and even a complex and qualified concept of Christian perfection. The Calvinists, and hence many Baptists, begin with a theology that prepares them for mystery and leads them to be surprised by joy. The Arminians, and hence many Methodists, begin with a theology that prepares one for love and joy and then leaves one stumbling in the face of the pervasive aspects of the demonic in the created order, the nonmalleability of intransigent humans, the mystery of evil.

If this hunch would prove to be correct, it would be a compliment to the genetic programing in the theology behind each tradition and to those who impart the tradition in word and act two centuries later. (One might also need to know what percentage of these Baptists are Southern Baptist or members of any number of small conservative northern Baptist groups, some of which are reasonably well represented in Minnesota. The more liberal Baptists in the American Baptist Convention, I would guess, would be set apart from the more rigorous Calvinists in this Baptist sample.)

Methodists and Baptists, Catholics and Protestants all unite evidently in their belief that when suffering comes "it is not taken as a sign of God's hate or personal vindictiveness." We mention this because of its bearing on the greatest issue of suffering in modern times, the experience of Jews when the Nazis set out to exterminate them. Many theodicies or explanations of suffering under God melted in the face of the death of six million. At first some wanted to say that here was an expression of divine hatred. That died early, or the God who might express it soon disappeared. Jews came to reject the idea that they were being punished for unfaithfulness or that God was trying to teach them a lesson. As the death camps lived on, there were almost no European Jews left to take any lessons! The Jews came either to reject the God of Israel, as did Richard Rubenstein in *After Auschwitz* (Indianapolis: Bobbs-Merrill, 1960), to fall silent in the face of mystery, or to affirm the presence of God in spite of Auschwitz—and to resolve not to permit another Hitler to arise. There are Christian corollaries to all these interpretations, but those that express divine hatred are certainly disappearing from the scene.

I have not often paused to isolate the clergy in these samples, feeling that in the limited space it was more important to talk about the whole survey or, because clergy voices are more frequently heard in church affairs, to lump them with laity or leave them aside. Yet in the demographic section of the chapter on suffering we learn that the clergy could "far more easily absorb the idea that evil can take place in a world in which a loving God exists." Clergy also "far more than the laity" (51% to 29%) could see an obligation to connect suffering with service to the suffering. In the latter case, were more compassionate people called to be clergy, or did the professional role of the cleric inspire the impulse to make the connection? The data do not help us.

We can speculate, however, why clergy have more ease in dealing with the idea of suffering under a good God than do laity. For one thing, the sensitive and busy priest or pastor is in daily contact with many sufferers. He or she is called in at the times of crises, and sees some rhythm and pattern in them. While the lay families may have to deal only with puzzles and mysteries when their more limited circles are hit, the cleric must cope daily. This does not mean that the minister develops a spiritual callus, a psychic cuticle, a professional distance. It may simply imply that by having to be on the scene so frequently when people ask the question "Why?" the minister develops a broader range or richer repertory of partial explanations.

The theology school is at least a place where the many apologies and theodicies are taken up as part of preparation. In a sense this equips the minister to be a bit like those who view hurricanes from airplanes or radar stations. They can speak of directions of wind and force of hurricane, from a little distance. They are not in the huts. When ministers are themselves victim of the catastrophes of suffering, many of them testify that they fall mute and benumbed alongside their members. In the silence both of them find some strength by identification with Christ. If theology school helps the ministers to some extent, they may be able to do more through homilies and teaching in parishes to help people anticipate suffering and crisis. If the message is always sugarcoated, are people prepared for when the bitterness is exposed?

Wherever clergy and laity, men and women, or other demographic slices of people stand, they again unite around the figure of Jesus as the compassionate understander of moral failure in the world and thus help separate moral failing from personal suffering. Alfred North Whitehead's picture of God as "the fellow-sufferer who understands" takes on flesh and lives in the figure of Jesus. The counsel to look at the wounds of Christ when the ways of God seem inscrutable, a constant theme in medieval and Reformation-era pastoral care, is here evident and evidently satisfying. At the same time, it is so consistent in the survey that again one wonders whether American churchdom is not characterized by a tendency toward a "unitarianism of the second person of the Trinity." God gets us into trouble or lets us get into trouble, and then his son Jesus shows compassion and gets us out of it. He is the overcomer of contradiction and ambiguity: so say formal theologians and Minnesota church people. Is that all that is to be said? Is enough attention paid to what "Father" and "Holy Spirit" symbolize in the Christian economy?

The Church and Social Action

If the problem of suffering led to ambiguity or paradox which had to be tolerated, the issue of humanly induced suffering—including suffering because humans permit it when they could prevent it—introduces a somewhat different range of apparent contradictions. Most of these have to do with a gap in perceptions between what God calls the church to in respect to promoting justice, equality, and care, on the one hand, and what church people perceive as their responsibility for carrying out that mission on the other. In some cases the hesitations, confusions, or possible blindness of the sampled people remain a problem—a sign of weak faith, perhaps. At other times the presumed double-mindedness may result from more complicating factors. Under analysis, some of these may be partially explained, and the Minnesotans will seem to be less obviously victims or articulators of "bad faith." To state that part of the case or to offer my speculation by way of analysis may mean showing some differences between Joan Chittister's interpretations and mine. If so, may the differences contribute to the readers' alertness and further inquiry.

The trouble begins to show up in the chapter on relationships, both in the findings and in the comment upon them. We have already noted that on the subject of race, 97% of the sample were for equality as a given for Christians as they viewed the touchiest American subject, black-white relations. Given this, they should pass all subsequent tests, one would think. Yet the surveyors were disconcerted to find that only 66% agree strongly that it is part of the mission of the churches to help act upon the knowledge of and mandates about such views of equal human rights and dignity. (Though another 23% agree at least "slightly" that this is part of the church's mission.) Optimistically one can say that 89% were ready for some participation in seeing realized the equality of races and classes. Yet this support progressively dwindles as the questions become more difficult.

What seems shocking is that 67% feel that other agencies are better equipped than the church to undertake the task; let others do the dirty work to improve matters of racial justice, they seem to say. Who are these others? Those who uphold American laws? Why are they better poised, given the relative character of human law, than those who believe in the inclusive power of divine law? The survey does not help us hear answers, but the questions remain vital. Could it be that Christians find their congregational and denominational fellowships so frail that they cannot discuss touchy subjects or test difficult ones in the specifically Christian context? Could it be that political structures and secular town meetings allow for more give and take without disruption of civil ways? Again, no answers can be provided here; they have to be pursued in countless local fellowships.

The issue comes clear as Joan Chittister focuses on "liberation movements" and gets concrete and specific. In a chapter on spiritual movements she sets out to connect spiritual life with commitment to liberation causes. That this connection can be made is evident from the Bible. Charles Peguy put it into shorthand when he said "Everything begins in mysticism and ends in politics." Dag Hammarskjöld argued that today the path to holiness is necessarily through action. Yet this fusion is not part of common parlance in church life, where piety and activism are kept more separate. The people do not see how Martin Luther King or Dorothy Day sustained themselves spiritually in order to be active in the world. They gain impressions of Christian activism from the media when communicators concentrate on street demonstrations or other visible pushes into the world.

Given that atrophy so far as making connections between spirituality and activism is concerned, it may be that Chittister is a bit hard on people whose survey instruments do not allow for all the subtleties. She notes that 52% have come to a greater consciousness of the dignity of all people as children of God because of the struggles of disadvantaged groups for their rights. There has been gain. Another 30% have known some growth through these struggles. In all, 82% of the sample have profited from the liberation movements.

Name the two most prominent, however, and there is a falling off. Only three-fourths, not 82%, were touched by black power; only about half were moved by the women's movement. "This communal dimension of the spiritual life does not seem to come alive in either of the two great liberation movements in the United States." Why is there a breach, a failing, here?

Similarly, the chapter on justice raises the question of liberation movements. Almost all respondents were for the poor, and many saw their issues as part of the mission of the church. What happens when we drop in the phrase, "True Christianity requires that the poor and oppressed be liberated"? Now only 43% are sure of the idea, though another 30% have some inclination to agree slightly. Chittister found this total of 73% low; it strikes me as being high. The words "oppression" and "liberation" have now become so politicized that few Christians can hear them Christianly any longer without filtering them through the slogans and images of liberation on the mass media.

"Liberation" by now includes a collage of confusing impressions: the Palestine Liberation Organization, wars of national liberation, women's liberation, liberation theology, San Salvador, Korea, Chile, Harlem, la Causa. When 59% say that the affirmation "Jesus is Lord" extends to all of life, social as well as individual, this leaves 41% behind. Why can they not make the affirmation? Can they really believe that lordship stops in the social sphere? Then is it lordship, or is Christ limited? These are the questions that come to mind so long as a purely theological context is prime. They change, however, when the political filter comes on. Now people grow suspicious: does the affirmation of the lordship of Jesus commit me to support of socialism, the welfare state, affirmative action? It may; hence, they are wary.

One of the touchier subjects in the 1980s is the character of the economy. America is divided. On one side are those who feel, with the Reagan administration that came to power at the turn of the decade, that one must support "supply-side" or "monetarist" economics. Thus through trickle-down theories, prosperity will spread and people will have security. The private sector can engage in leftover welfare operations. On the other side are those who feel that the immediacy of needs does not permit long-term economic policies which may or may not allow for trickling down. The demands and needs of the poor must be met at once. Somehow through governmental planning and economic stimuli, the economy will prosper enough that the welfare programs can continue. It is a delusion to throw all welfare into the diminished private sector.

In the Minnesota survey, 30% said that Christianity implies commitment to economic growth of the United States, but this is countered by a nearly equal figure, 25% who want to see a Christian-based reduction of the material standard of living in the nation. And 44% are bystanders. Chittister sees the church thus divided into three economic camps. One may safely surmise that the breakdown would not be too different on many social and political issues.

When it comes to the local scene, the divisions become lively, even intense. Only 10% say, in the abstract, that their churches locally may or may not participate in discussing social issues; they don't care. A surprising 85% are ready for their churches to take up the questions, and 72% see their parishes doing it. But again consensus breaks down in the concrete, since only 57% are sure their churches should be "involved" in social justice and 45% feel that the denomination nationally should be involved. That hardly represents a consensus base, if all the states are like Minnesota so far as religious opinion is concerned. Why more trust locally than nationally? One suspects that Christians feel that the local entity is and has to be responsive, while the modern bureaucratic forms of church life breed a remoteness that makes the national spokespersons unrepresentative. Such national agencies have grown to be very controversial in recent decades.

The clergy are more ready than the laity to see "liberation of the poor and oppressed as a gospel mandate" by a 90% to 75% margin, and 41% of the clergy but only 33% of the laity, would foresee working for a change in the American economic system as a necessary outgrowth of Christian principles. By a 74% to 46% margin the clergy outstrip the laity in wanting to see the church provide social justice leadership. Here there may be an analogy to the issue of interpretation: the clergy had a richer repertory of explanations as they viewed the hurricane, while those in the huts in its path had few options. The clergy have a vantage point from which they can more convincingly seek societal relevance through social involvement. While they may not be economic experts, they are occupational gatekeepers to a world society and should be more sensitized than are many laity to keep social justice issues in front of all.

Of all the plaguing issues of the day, that of war in a nuclear age, when civilians are in no way protected, has become the most difficult. In the Minnesota survey 69% were very clearly not pacifist and were unable to see how Christianity must commit them to keep themselves from war "under any circumstance." At the same time, only 29% believe that the Bible and Christian tradition are clear and consistent on the issue of support of war. On few issues was there as much diffidence about expressing Christian commitment and conviction as there was on war and peace. About 46% would not take a firm position for or against the idea that church or Scripture give precise and predictable guidance on the morality of war. Chittister calls this "troublesome," but, in defense of Minnesota, I would say that the trouble begins in the Scriptures themselves.

Bible-reading respondents cannot duck the fact that the Old Testament portrays God the warrior. In the Book of Judges genocide is commanded and commended. Yet in the New Testament Jesus seems to be issuing absolute prohibitions against taking life; can these all be reduced to one-on-one personal relations and seen in no way as addressing killing in war? That ambiguity results from a reading of these two traditions is understandable. In the Christian tradition, "just war" theories theoretically put some boundaries on the savagery of war, but how do Christians relate "just war" to nuclear circumstance? And how useful is a doctrine that has been used by both Christian sides in almost all wars in which Christian nations have engaged? Again, ambiguity seems to be a natural expression.

When foreign relations break down, 94% do not find in their religion barriers against war. One can deduce that about 6% might be pacifist. The scale of percentages of Christian citizens who would support various sorts of war does not need replication here; it does serve to point out the texture of complexity and the fact that the people have given discriminating thought to a subject that admits of no easy answers.

In all this, my analysis is a bit softer than Chittister's, though her political views and mine may well coincide. Many church people in the 1980s are still reacting to the patterns of church participation in the political order in the 1960s and have not yet been caught up in new ways of responding. This means that when one mentions "activism," they think of street demonstrations (generally ineffective on most causes now) or pronouncements by denominational and ecumenical agencies. These, the respondents seem to be saying, are not representative and are less trustworthy than are congregational matters.

Meanwhile some of the words used to describe causes, words like "oppression" and "liberation," connote to them radical movements for which they are not ready. North American enemies of liberation theology in South America have reinforced the suspicion that Marxian analysis and momentum play a disproportionate share in shaping such theology. The new conservatism of the late 1970s and early 1980s conditions people to suspect all sorts of progressive movements. It may also be that there is a growing recognition of the complexity of issues. The Vietnamese War issue was relatively simple: stay in or get out. The civil rights voting issue was also rather clean: assure constitutional rights or do not.

The causes of the 1980s produce much more sense of and need for ambiguity. The nuclear issue seems clear cut for pure hawks or pure pacifists. Others have to make complex determinations: are they for a nuclear freeze, for unilateral nuclear disarmament, or for reliance on conventional weapons? Under what circumstances would they be ready for wars? The ecological causes, as noted earlier in this comment, are not easy to face. Not to use a pesticide means loss of crop, and thus too little food. To use a pesticide may mean to spread cancer. Where should the church stand?

To ask what will be necessary if church people are to act upon their awareness that the Christian faith commits them to the spread of equality, the promotion of justice, and the diminishing of poverty, is a fresh way of expressing Christian concern in these fields. Many of the Minnesotans are not ready to be as concrete about social issues as the Bible is. A rereading of Isaiah 58:1-10 or any of a hundred similar prophetic passages shows that in the prophetic writings Yahweh did link integrally and permanently the acts of worship and the spread of justice and sharing of wealth. On the other hand, they do not want to draw their models only from secular politics, which frames issues on partisan lines that divide the fellowship. The church is involved in the public world, but it did not gather its people for a particular form of address to its partisan political causes.

Not to take a stand is to take a stand. The Minnesota majority is aware that the Christian faith calls for commitments but is hesitant to give "the church"—seen somehow as congregation or denomination— too much power to speak for it in the complexities of politics. At an initial stage of reformulation there is a set of questions: who knows what the issues are? Who knows that they are being well phrased and poised? Should the church take stands? Should not the church be on the move? What is the church? Is it the bureaucracies, the congregations, the individual Christian citizens, the movements?

Why should the church be involved at all? It is interesting to see how many of the respondents restrict the lordship of Christ to the personal or individual sphere, abandoning the social to "the powers." Can the churches seek to change this situation, to help Christians be discontent with this sense of limits?

Another question: what good does it do if Christian people do study the issues of equality, justice, and poverty, and then disagree with each other? There are some answers; we do not have to be simply mute in front of the question. Debate on specific issues at least impels all sides to become involved, to become aware of what is at stake. Positions do get changed in the light of dialog and debate, even if not all Christians come to agreement. The church learns to subject all viewpoints to biblical and theological norms. After the privatism of religion in the 1970s there are signs that the 1980s will have a more public side. The entrance of right-wing Christian groups into politics and the presence of antinuclear forces are harbingers. The Minnesotans are telling us that they and all of us have to put new energies into framing and addressing the issues in a new day.

17

Two Church Clusters

The Faith and Ferment survey makes it possible for readers to break the sample apart in several conventional demographic ways. We can learn what men and women, rural and urban people, young and old, clergy and laity have thought. The rest of the time the pattern is largely denominational. This is both illuminating and frustrating.

The denominational model has its limits. Designed to make fighting meaningful across the lines of division, the denominational pattern has lived on into the ecumenical age when it is no longer customary for denominations to fight denominations. Today there are more important or enjoyable conflicts within than between the churches. Informal coalescences have formed between wings of several denominations. Liberal Presbyterians and Catholics have more in common with each other on many of these questions than they do with another style of member or faction in their own churches. Presbyterian and Lutheran women will have sympathy for each other over against Presbyterian and Lutheran men on another set of causes. What can we learn then from the denominational model as here employed?

Whoever rereads the pages of my comment will find gleanings illustrating different styles at many points. Thus most other churches were more ready for "open communion" than were Catholics and Lutherans, for reasons deriving from their peculiar history and doctrines. On other issues Catholics may be closer to Baptists, and Lutherans to Episcopalians. There is a rather consistent pattern of agreement between Baptists and Evangelical Covenant members on the one hand, and the United Church of Christ, Episcopalians, Presbyterians, and Methodists on the other. How do we account for some rather predictable responses?

Separate Clusters

We might do well to trace a few illustrations of the separate clusters through the pages. Thus on suffering we find an issue that does not separate liturgical from nonliturgical, or evangelical from mainline. The Baptists were far more ready than the Methodists to cope with the ways a good God permits human suffering: we began to account for this by reference to an ancient theological point dividing Calvinists and Arminians. That distinction may not show up again with any consistency in the findings. In general the mainline, members of the Episcopal and United Church of Christ, found their faith taxed by the struggles of life, with Episcopalians by far the largest part of this respondent population. It may be that these mainline groups, more open as they are to secular impulses, are less reliant on church tradition and biblical explanation and thus are also open to some problems that those with more enclosed and authoritarian views of church and Bible may avoid.

The openness to secular worlds and norms is present also in the relational chapter, where the United Church of Christ and Episcopal churches experience less family worship than do Catholics and Evangelical Covenant respondents. Have mainline families broken down, or does devotional life mean less? On ordination of women there are significant differences. Seventy-nine percent of the Presbyterians, 77% of the Methodists, 79% of the United Church of Christ, and 68% of the Episcopalians favor it—low figures in all four cases, it seems to me. Meanwhile only 30% of the Catholics, 32% of the Baptists, and 53% of the Lutherans favor such ordination. That is a strange mix of high-church sacramental and biblical literalist reasons for reluctance.

In the chapter on spirituality there are signs that the mainline— the Episcopal, United Church of Christ, Presbyterian, and Catholic— groups are less conditioned or trained to "witness" for their faith. The

Baptists and Covenant Church members find that sort of talk coming naturally.

One of the most significant differences is over the sphere of Christian activism. The liberal Christians favored "housing, health care, human rights programs, education for social change, economic development and the peace movement." Conservatives went for more domestic issues, those that derive from old causes over which an individual had control: sexual expression, sex education, the teaching or following of evolutionary science, and the like. Liberals are at ease with broad social emphases, sometimes overlooking the role of personal responsibility in intimate life. Conservatives are expert at addressing individual control issues but are wary of talking about "structures." This is a fissure running through American religious life for a long period.

The New Right

The recent reintrusion of right-wing and fundamentalist Christians into the political order was occurring at about the time this survey was made. It may be that in the course of time there will be some change in responses. Some conservatives in the Catholic camp, under the leadership of men like Philadelphia's John Cardinal Krol or evangelist Billy Graham, have become outspoken in opposition to nuclear armament. To be effective, they must deal with the larger structures of society. The rightists are linking up with moderates to bring about constitutional change toward prohibiting abortion. For a long time we have been used to speaking of a "public" and a "private" party in politics. Is that day over?

Yes and no. Insofar as one equates "public" and "politics," the once-private group has made a move. Recognizing that a dozen years before it was calling such political involvement un- and even anti-biblical and sub-Christian, its leadership now justifies the move because the crisis has become so bad. Southern Baptists, once guardians of a voluntary spirit that abhorred governmental custodianship of religion, at their convention in 1982 by a three-to-one majority came out in favor of school prayer amendments. The justification? Things had grown so bad, and secular humanism was so powerful that the Baptist children of God had to do an about-face and deny their most ancient and treasured principle.

The goal of the Christian right is to find ways to legislate their particular social positions and theology, to give them a privileged place in American society. The moderates and rightists, of course, have often tried to legislate on the basis of their theological convictions: the race and peace causes were thus justified. In a sense, then, more and more parties are playing the same game.

What keeps the new right-wing political group in religion from being thought of as distinctly "public" is that it does not share or wish to share meanings with those who are not part of their faith. Only by a kind of theocratic interpretation, in which the Bible and the Christian faith are privileged in society, can moral laws and respect for God be reinstituted in national life, they would argue. A true public theology has to find room for a theological interpretation of those who do not share the faith, who do not "know Christ." Traditions as old as the Pauline, which could live under uncongenial regimes and among the pagans, had this public dimension. So did concepts of "common grace" and "civil righteousness" in Augustinian, Aquinian, Calvinist, Lutheran, and Anglican theology. The Lord of history was Lord also of those who did not recognize the name, but who could serve divine purposes by supporting justice. The political Christians of the right have not yet come up with ways to legitimate non-Christian and even nontheist public participants.

Yet for all the upheaval and inconvenience they bring to moderate or liberal Christians, their presence on the political scene does demonstrate once more the "ferment" in American religion, and it will show up in future polls.

Two Styles of Church

Are there "two churches" in Minnesota, two styles of being church people? While there are exceptions on specific issues, it would seem as if there are. On the one hand, there are the very intact bodies. They stress intense religious experience, very high views of biblical authority, the shunning of the secular order, the intactness of the elect church as conservative Catholics and Covenant Church members must if they are faithful to their doctrinal traditions. But they can also understand each other and coalesce over issues like abortion.

The other style, often called "mainline" Protestant and incorporating liberal Catholic, is less bounded. The members are encouraged to serve Christ not by keeping the church lights on but by carrying Christian witness and interests into the public forum and marketplace. The mainline is less put off by the secular and may form alliances with "people of good will who do not know God." It seeks to be an interpreter of the pluralist culture by drawing on both Christian tradition and the best in secular thought. It pays a price for this openness to the secular, in that rewards for membership are smaller in groups which cultivate less distance from the surrounding environment.

If faith is to remain in ferment in Minnesota or anywhere else in America, each cluster has its gift to bring. Without conservative Catholic, evangelical, Baptist, and fundamentalist churches, it is not likely that there would be as much rich experience. There would certainly be fewer efforts to enlarge the Christian community through conversion. Without mainline Catholic and Protestant churches there would be no "middle force" interpreting church and world to each other in positive ways. The risks of self-enclosure plague the first; the risks of expending the self and losing identity, boundary, and mission, plague the second.

The mainline churches were "born sectarian," and for the most part took root in standoffish, high experience enclaves. The experience of the years in which they found the American environment congenial led them to become open to the larger world. The void they left was filled by new groups—Methodist and Baptist two centuries ago, evangelical and fundamentalist in this century. As these move to the mainstream, they leave a vacuum which is likely to be filled by other self-replenishing groups. These are likely to begin extravagantly and effervescently and then also gradually move to the mainline.

Both styles, coded under denominational names, have left their mark in this survey of Faith and Ferment in Minnesota. Yet if these styles are separate, it is also interesting to see how often they merge. On numbers of issues there is almost unanimity.

Open Questions

A host of questions remain. How would these findings compare with questions addressed to an equally scientific sampling of nonchurch members? The Gallup poll suggests that on many issues the differences might not be too great—especially since church people have started to see church membership as rather arbitrary, and nonchurched people show so much respect for God, Jesus, and Bible. How honest are people with themselves when responding to opinion polls? It is not hard to answer "Do you intend to vote for the Republican or Democratic candidate?" It is much more difficult to express complex opinions through the sharp decisions demanded by this kind of survey. How would American opinion at large compare with Minnesota opinion, or with Christianity in other countries?

While those questions remain, I find it easy to close this essay with an expression of gratitude to the people who inspired it, participated in it, and collated findings from it. Late in the second Christian millennium we have learned that for all the elemental unity in the human story, the religious world, or the Christian church, people live by and die for their particularities. Sometimes these take ugly forms. New tribalisms are behind most wars in the world today, and they often breed unproductive domestic conflicts. Yet the place in which one lives, the influences of those up close—the friendship circle, the family, the neighborhood, the club, the parish—all these can be "little platoons," as Edmund Burke called them, against an impersonal outer world.

One's own parish is not, of course, the world. The decade in which this survey appears is probably the first one in Christian history in which the majority of Christians will live in the southern hemisphere. Is Minnesota Christianity the tail end of northern European Christendom, part of a new religious ice age coming down from Canada and stalled in the American Northland? Or is the vitality of religion in Faith and Ferment country a countersign? No one pretends that Minnesota is the world. But it is a world, with political boundaries, common economic concerns, an ethos, a set of peoples who have had a history together and a story to tell. Of them, 1017 used pencils to add an important chapter to their accounting of religious and Christian history. We welcome what they have come up with as part of a mosaic of a larger world, or a prism with which to see a greater Christian universe. One hopes that the Minnesotans will find imitators, so there can be more comparison, more parts of the mosaic, and additional prisms. There is still so much in that larger world, that greater Christian universe, about which we remain curious, so much we still have to see.

PART THREE

Essays in Response to the Data

I

Betty Wahl Powers

I, too, am a Minnesotan, from the county which once prided itself on having a greater percentage of Catholics than any other in the U.S. In those days our priests and sisters spoke with ill-tempered and inflexible authority on matters secular and religious to complaisant laymen. But in that same county I received from Benedictine sisters a college education in the gentle spirit of Virgil Michel, and though I graduated in the year of Hiroshima, I had been introduced to most of the ideas which were to attain currency in Vatican II.

In the early 1960s I moved away with husband and children to Ireland and returned in the bicentennial year to find an unfamiliar church. The authoritarians had been routed. Freedom, I thought—and then, anarchy. For the first time in my life I felt that I didn't know what people around me were thinking (a disaster for a writer of fiction); I had become a foreigner on my native ground. Through this Faith and Ferment study I had at last a chance to get inside a great many heads, to find out what they think and also, as it turned out, what they think they think.

Betty Wahl Powers is a novelist and member of the Roman Catholic Church, and a resident of Collegeville, Minnesota.

My first impression of the data was of contradiction and confusion, and after much rereading I find that the more I straighten out the thoughts and line up the ideas of us Minnesota Christians, the clearer become their contradictions.

Two key contradictions stand out. The first is all but incredible: 43% of us find that the resurrection of Christ has little or nothing to do with the relevance of Christian teaching for us.

It is hard not to go on in dithering disbelief at the figures or to draw out the fearsome implications of such a mass profession of insanity. Paul says it all: "If Christ has not been raised, . . . your faith is in vain" (1 Cor. 15:14).

The second contradiction is a more familiar one. We are agreed that Christianity means helping the poor and the disadvantaged, but in sizeable percentages—varying with how the question is asked—we are unwilling to touch our own standard of living so that others may have shares in the bounty of our planet.

The gap between theory and practice is as old as mankind, but I sense something less than universal in our attitudes to that failure. We don't seem to be shamefaced about it, nor, for the most part, to brazen it out with a what-the-hell-I-worked-my-butt-off attitude. There *is* a whiff of freewheeling casuistry, a suggestion that living well is an appropriate thanksgiving for such abundant natural wealth. But the dominant tone of our responses, the voice we adopt for our explanations, suggests something stranger: that we have been justified by our belief in our own goodness.

Again and again in the study we strike the same plangent note and give a recurring answer to a question not asked: we Minnesota Christians think of ourselves as a righteous people, a warmhearted people, above all, a *good* people. Only connect the dots in the right fashion and you will see our self-image: a Viking perhaps, clean-limbed, independent, but without the overtones of cruelty in that image, a warm, furry Viking, a *nice* Disney Viking.

Consider the man moved to tears by a Johnny Cash Christmas special, by a poem telling of an innkeeper who, unaware, received God three times with kindness. "I thought it was so nice," said the man in the sample. And it is, the nice half of a diptych, ripped off at the hinges from that picture of the innkeeper and his NO VACANCY, which used to feature so prominently in Christmas stories. It is the nice half of the Last Judgment scene, all sheep and no goats to disturb us. Our man continued: "That's the sum and substance of my beliefs. It's not what you believe about God, or what I believe, it's what comes from the heart."

That "heart" worries me. In the past few years I've heard a number of homilies on the theme of love, and only one of them was calculated to disturb, to call us to true *caritas,* that abiding love tinged with sorrow and pity with which our Lord again and again greeted the suffering, the hungry, the sheep without a shepherd. The others seemed more concerned with *amor,* a warm glowing feeling, a welling emotion which was to reach a pitch a few minutes later in the hugging and glad-handing of the sign of peace.

Before relating his heartwarming experience at the hands of Johnny Cash, our man mentioned that "as far as my religion is concerned . . . I have thrown out a lot of picky detail." I wonder *what* picky detail. The resurrection? Elsewhere a woman said, "I feel that in religious training . . . you are taught the basics. From those basics then, you sort out what you want, or pick it apart as you see fit." The figures suggest that she is not an extreme case, that a do-it-yourself theology is quite acceptable here. You might conclude that we think for ourselves—or that we are a stiff-necked people.

Consider prayer. We Minnesota Christians pray, 82% of us every day, and we prefer to speak directly to God without intermediary and in our own spontaneous words. This may mean that we feel close to him, or it may be simply a facet of our populist arrogance which wants to speak directly to the man in charge and without ceremony. The prayer of supplication is our Minnesota favorite, and we are not above petitioning God exactly as if he were a congressman, right down to keeping tab on the results (with its implied *or else*). We, Catholics at least, do come from a tradition rich in supplication—our litanies, novenas, rogation days—but always, I think, made with the understanding that "though the fig tree do not blossom, nor fruit be in the vines, . . . yet I will rejoice in the Lord, I will joy in the God of my salvation" (Hab. 3:17-18).

But the most disturbing thing about the study is, as Sister Joan points out, the way it discloses everywhere a division that cuts across denominational lines and leaves us in two opposing camps with a gray third in the middle, neither hot nor cold, but lukewarm. (The Son of God himself has spoken the last unmincing word on that condition.) From the two camps the reflected light of Christ shines forth in opposing stages of eclipse, as the shadow of the world falls between us and him, for, to change the metaphor, what we have is not so much two opposing versions of Christianity as a disagreement about the baggage that the two sides have brought in from their secular counterparts.

We conservatives don't object to clothing the naked or feeding the hungry. We do object to a careless theology that confuses psychiatry with ethics and acceptance with compassion, that inclines to champion the hard cases at the expense of society and install the deviant as an "alternative role model," to an unthinking acceptance of science and a rejection of the unproven, a refusal to countenance the leap in the dark that faith demands and embrace the foolishness of God that is wiser than the wisdom of man. We object to having a strict parallel drawn between race and sex and to a strident feminism which erodes our institutions and threatens the very language we speak.

(May I say a word here as a writer? Let no one think that language may be safely tinkered with. Pause first to consider whether sexism might be in the eye of the beholder, an eye so bombarded with images that it has lost the power of abstraction. English-speaking women, a traditionally spirited group, have never considered themselves excluded from "mankind." What male grammarians codified was no more than what had been passed on to them at their mothers' knees. To replace the delicate interconnections of grammar with fuzzy circuitry [as in: "let everyone take their pick"], to confine ourselves to unisex words, nonjudgmental terminology, and other grayness is to impair our ability to think with precision. To banish the noble words from the language is to cut us off—root, stock and branch—from the undeniably great literature of the English-speaking nations—including our two incomparable Bibles—and to commit a genocide, not of blood and bone, but of the very spirit of a people.)

On the other side of the coin, we don't object to an aching desire for Jesus or a deep reverence for the Word. We object to an obscene materialism, an unparalleled show of consumption and comfort, an idolatrous nationalism, a proud ignorance of science, a desire to keep women in "their place."

From neither side can we see each other as Christians. We see only smart-assed know-it-alls or Neanderthals. Deafened by the noise of our separate secular ideologies, we can't hear each other's words. As conservatives we summon our charity toward a word of deviant and disruptive life-styles to say we are prepared to forgive, and the liberals snap back: "*You* forgive? *You* are the guilty ones." As liberals we beg: "Open your eyes; civilization as we know it cannot survive a single nuclear exchange," and the conservatives cut us off: "Try living in Russia and see how far you get with that kind of talk." And the schism grows.

I am left with the feeling that we Minnesota Christians are not quite grown up. We are spoiled brats, whining "Gimme" to God, protesting "Mine" when asked to share, picking through the banquet of faith, afraid of missing the party (however unsuitable the time, place, or company), terrified of being the odd man out, the one not chosen by either team and left to languish on the sidelines.

The study finds our clergy more knowing, more ready to act on that knowledge, than the laity. But I suspect that the clergy, too, have carried populism into religion, have become leaders behind their flocks. They are careful of their own popularity and also, with true charity, fear to quench the smoldering wick. Thus they become Jonahs, silent prophets, refusing their mission and leaving us in baleful ignorance. (Concern for the lost sheep need not be absolute; Jesus might have saved Judas if he had let the people make him king.) They have shied away from pronouncements and counted on some instinct or innate knowledge to guide us, while the world relentlessly educates and instills a doctrine of consumption and adjustment.

Most of us think the parochial school is unnecessary. We seem to count instead on a few Sunday school classes, youth groups, and, of course, parents—whose treasure house of woolly knowledge this study has so fully explored. On the other hand, almost monthly the press features a new Christian school and shows us the young zealots standing for Veneration of the Flag or learning that God created the world, right down to the vermiform appendix, in 144 hours. And so the schism grows.

If there is one thing that emerges clearly from the study it is that we Minnesota Christians want to be on the side of the angels. We cherish our finer feelings. We would be compassionate; we would stand for an orderly society. We want God—and ourselves—to think well of us.

A merciful God may well find us worthy of personal salvation, but that is not enough in a world on the brink of nuclear holocaust, a world where whole continents of deprived peoples, driven by envy of our all-too-visible affluence, throw their few resources into an obsolete technology that presupposes an endless supply of everything and threatens global pollution beyond our worst dreams. (Ironically, the very survival of the earth depends on these mostly non-Christian people to show greater Christian virtue than we have so far been able to muster.)

There *is* a problem. We've known it in our hearts, and now we have the facts and figures, the proofs so dear to our age. We live in a corrupt society, and that society has begun our corruption.

But it is possible to live in a world and not be of that world. Consider how the Jews in Babylon, with an overwhelming sense of exile and separation ("If I forget thee, O Jerusalem, let my right hand forget her cunning." Ps. 137:5 KJV), retained their identity. Consider the Christian communities to which Paul wrote and his twin themes of separation and identity, the world within the world: "one Lord, one faith, one baptism." There were indeed two opposing camps, and when Paul drew the line, he drew it firmly and for all time, between the people of God and the people of the world.

2

Willmar L. Thorkelson

"Monumental" is the word that journalists would use to describe the Faith and Ferment study, which took researchers five years to complete and cost $200,000.

Never before has so much information been gathered on what Minnesota Christians believe and practice. What was learned will certainly have implications not only for churches of the state, but possibly for those of the nation. Enough material has been provided to last local church adult study classes for a decade or more. Clergy may find sermon ideas from the study. Theological seminaries should have a field day with the research.

Karl Menninger's book *Whatever Happened to Sin?* prepared us for the study's finding that there is tremendous tension in churches of the state about what sin is and what causes it. Only slightly more than half of Minnesota's Christians consider themselves sinful or hold to the belief that all people are sinful. Uncertainty was found about how to deal with guilt and whether God permits evil and suffering.

It was startling to learn that almost a third of Minnesota's church

Willmar L. Thorkelson is a journalist associated with Religious News Service and the Sun Papers in Minnesota. He is a member of the American Lutheran Church.

members do not realize the key role of the resurrection in Christian faith, saying that Christian teaching would be meaningful to them whether Christ had risen from the dead or not.

Clearly there has been some erosion in the traditional Christian teachings concerning not only theology but on such issues as marriage and divorce, birth control, abortion, homosexuality, and premarital sex.

Only a third of the church members accept all of their church's teachings as essential to their faith, and almost two-thirds say they see no reason why they can't reject some church teachings and continue to have a deep Christian faith.

The fact that many Minnesota Christians say they would obey their consciences rather than the laws of the church raises the question, as the study report points out, whether the church is losing influence in the area of conscience formation or ethical definition. This writer thinks it has.

But in many other respects, Minnesotans were found more traditional and/or positive in their views. For example, nearly all Minnesota Christians accept the Bible as the Word of God, although they are divided on whether the Bible is errorless. Nearly all believe that Jesus Christ is the Son of God whose gospel is necessary for the salvation of all people in the world.

Half report that they go to church at least once a week, with another third attending more often. More than four-fifths say they pray every day, and it is to Jesus that they pray most. About two-thirds say it is common for them to discuss their spiritual life with others.

More than 90% of Minnesota Christians believe in life after death, and 63% expect to be reunited with loved ones after death. Despite the feelings that the church's belief about life after death is a consolation, almost half would like to hear more in church about life here and now rather than about life hereafter. Incidentally, more than half those surveyed were in agreement that it is not unchristian to cremate the dead.

It is clear from the study that tension exists among Minnesota Christians over the private and public mission of the church. Half of Minnesota's Christians want their churches to exert influence on public policy —as a mission of the church—and half do not.

While more than two-thirds believe that the church should seek to better conditions for the elderly who are poor and discriminated against, less than half are willing to see the church take leadership in other social justice issues such as racism, sexism, and economic concerns.

As the study report notes, more Minnesota Christians seem likely to believe that giving food to the hungry is of the essence of Christianity than would believe that taking a position on food stamp legislation is also required of the committed Christian.

Less than half of those surveyed (48%) are agreed that their church or denomination should make a special effort to ensure that women have equal opportunity and rights with men in all aspects of church life and ministry. Fewer still (40%) would have the church work to insure equal rights for women in society.

A disturbing finding of the study is that Christians see very little relationship between the life and teachings of Jesus and the morality of war. Sixty-nine percent of the respondents believe that it cannot be clearly determined from the teachings of Christ that Christians should not support or participate in war under any circumstances. At the same time, strong support was found for the idea that Christian viewpoints and values relating to U.S. foreign policy should be expressed to the government by both individual Christians and their churches.

Minnesota Christians also are divided on the relationship of Christianity to economics, with one-third feeling a commitment to economic growth to be of the essence of their faith, while another third feels compelled by it to adopt a simpler life-style.

· Although most church members seem convinced that the proper management of the environment is a moral obligation, some question the propriety of the church's public involvement in ecological issues.

In another area the study found that the desire for ecumenism is strong in Minnesota. Ninety-five percent of those surveyed say their churches should cooperate with other churches wherever possible. Seventy-seven percent say churches should move beyond cooperation and try to achieve greater unity than they now have. Almost two-thirds of all Minnesota Christians (but a lesser proportion of Roman Catholics) are ready to open celebrations of Holy Communion in their churches to members of other denominations. So strong is the desire for unity, the study found, that conversion and proselytism have become uncertain values.

As might be expected, the study found differences among denominations on various issues. There also were differences within the denominations themselves. And there were differences on some questions between men and women, between the young and the elderly.

But to this lay person, the most significant differences uncovered may well be between the clergy and the laity. For example, 74% of the clergy want to see the church provide leadership on social justice issues, compared with 46% of the laity. Many more clergy (76%) believe that churches should express themselves on foreign policy than do the laity (43%). Similarly, more clergy (75%) approve of détente and negotiations with the U.S.S.R. than do lay persons (67%). Almost half the clergy say the U.S. does not have to have military supremacy in the world, while less than one-fourth of the laity agree.

More lay persons (40%) than clergy (25%) are convinced that the church should give "full support" to a war if the cause is "morally right." Fifty-eight percent of the clergy say economic aid is a Christian obligation, compared with 27% of the laity. Clergy were found more likely than laity to relate such issues as ecology, pollution, use of natural resources, and global interdependence to morality.

The differences between clergy and laity also carry over to ecclesiastical and theological issues, with the laity generally taking the more conservative position on each issue. For example, clergy were found more likely than lay people to regard the Bible as the product of fallible human beings and thus subject to critical judgment. More clergy than laity question the practice of proselytizing, and fewer clergy than laity hold their church to be the only true church.

Almost all the clergy can more easily absorb the idea that evil can take place in a world in which a loving God exists, but only two-thirds of the laity are comfortable with that idea. The clergy (57%) more often than the laity (35%) reject the position that illness, calamity, and other forms of suffering and crisis are the result of sin.

Far fewer clergy than laity take the position that the first and most important obligation of their congregations is to meet the needs of their own members. The clergy (69%), much more than the laity (55%), look to the resurrection of Christ to make Christian teaching meaningful. For the laity, it is the thought of life after death, not the resurrection event, that makes churches necessary and important in their lives.

Seventy-one percent of the clergy and 67% of the laity favor guaranteeing women equal opportunities and rights with men in church ministry. However, while 81% of the clergy support church efforts to help women gain equal rights in society, only 62% of the laity support this idea. Also, the strongest support that abortion should be permitted, at least in extreme circumstances, comes from Protestant clergy.

Should a lay person be concerned with these clergy-laity gaps? This writer feels strongly that the clergy should exercise a prophetic role in their ministry. But they should remember that they are not infallible and that if controversial issues are to be discussed in the pulpit, some method of feedback must be found for the laity. Also, they should be reminded that they sometimes might be more effective in enunciating principles rather than offering specific solutions to pressing social problems.

The study report does raise an interesting question about whether the gaps exist "because the church is not teaching what its clergy believe, or because the laity is resisting since prophecy disturbs, or because the clergy are wrong."

The recent experience of a visiting priest in a Minnesota resort community points up the problem. His homily dealt with the Christian's obligation to be knowledgeable and active in political affairs when moral issues like nuclear warfare and the nuclear arms race are involved. The priest called attention to the defeat of the nuclear arms freeze by two votes in the U.S. House of Representatives as evidence of Christian indifference. He saw the renewal of test-bombing of nuclear weapons in Nevada and the anniversary of the bombing of Hiroshima as an occasion for admitting U.S. national guilt for that catastrophe.

About five minutes into the homily, a well-dressed, distinguished-looking, middle-aged couple—visitors at the service—got up from their pews and left. The man told an usher as they were leaving, "We don't have to come to a Catholic church to hear Communist propaganda." Said the woman: "We are not going to give our money to a church that tolerates this radical teaching."

Reflecting later on the incident, the priest said he was saddened that the teachings of the church, including pronouncements of popes and bishops, "do not pierce the minds and hearts of many Catholics on social issues. They seem to prefer a priest to be a 'sacristy priest' and the church to teach a comfortable, middle-class, pie-in-the-sky doctrine. We have a long way to go."

3

Herbert W. Chilstrom

In Sinclair Lewis' *Main Street* young Carol Kennicott has just arrived in Gopher Prairie. She is a cultured and well-educated young woman from the big city of St. Paul. One of her first encounters is with the high school French and English teacher, Miss Vida Sherwin. As they talk about Carol's acclimation to this small village in central Minnesota, Vida thinks that it would be good for her to get involved in one of the churches.

"It would be lovely if we could get you to teach Sunday school," suggests Vida.

"Oh, yes," says Carol. "But I'm afraid I wouldn't be much good at that. My religion is so foggy."

To which Vida replies, "I know. So is mine. I don't care for dogma. Though I do stick firmly to the belief in the fatherhood of God and the brotherhood of man and the leadership of Jesus. As you do, of course. And that's all you need teach in Sunday school. It's the personal influence."

After reading Sister Joan Chittister's analysis of the Faith and Fer-

---

Herbert W. Chilstrom, Ed.D., is bishop of the Minnesota Synod of the Lutheran Church in America.

ment research data, one is tempted to conclude that not much has changed in Minnesota since Lewis penned those lines more than 60 years ago. For most Minnesotans religion is still as foggy.

But before we rush to hasty conclusions, a word about this writer. I have served in Minnesota for 16 of my 24 years of ordained ministry; for 10 years as a parish pastor in communities of 150, 1800, and 10,000 population, and for the past six years as bishop of 325 churches ranging in membership from a dozen in some small open-country churches to more than 11,000 in a major metropolitan congregation. In my role as bishop I travel the length and breadth of the state, worshiping and dialoguing with clergy and laity in every imaginable kind of community.

Three initial comments about the Faith and Ferment study are in order. First, it is of necessity an inexact survey. It is a measure of opinions based on an adequate but very limited number of responses. This being the case, the results of the study must be regarded with a degree of tentativeness.

Secondly, surveys of this kind are often skewed by the nature of the questions asked. No matter how objectively one tries to design a questionnaire or conduct an interview, it is inevitable that the framer of the query will have some degree of influence on the response.

Thirdly, there is the important question of differences *within* denominations as well as *between* them. It may be, for example, that Episcopalians are a relatively autonomous denomination in Minnesota. That is to say, the range of differences in religious conviction and opinion may not be very broad. The same cannot be said, however, about certain other denominations. A survey of Lutherans or Baptists, for example, would show as great a difference within their denominations as between them. All of which is to simply state that when Chittister makes a comment that "Lutherans believe . . ." or "Baptists tend to think . . ." it represents a statistical common ground, but may in fact be far from where the majority of Lutherans or Baptists actually find themselves. Unlike roses, a Baptist is not a Baptist is not a Baptist.

In spite of these limitations, one can still ask what the findings of the survey mean for parish ministry.

A fundamental question is raised by Chittister at several points. Given the technological progress we have seen over the past several decades, why is there so little evidence in the survey that we have made concomitant progress in the realm of ethics and morality? Why have our efforts in catechetics borne so little apparent fruit? Why is religion still so foggy for so many? Have the churches in Minnesota failed in their endeavor?

The answer to this question will be determined, among other things, by one's theology. If one belongs to a tradition which believes that the primary purpose of the church is to improve the quality of life, then the survey will indeed prove discouraging. But if one belongs to a tradition which sees creation and fall as symbols of humanity at any given point in time, then the survey results will come as no surprise.

Let us put it another way: if the one purpose of the church, above all other purposes, is to improve humanity ethically and morally, the study would judge the churches' efforts as a failure. But if one believes that the churches' purpose is to acknowledge the brokenness and the limitation of humanity and proclaim God's love for humankind in spite of that brokenness and limitation—then the "success" or "failure" of the churches takes on an entirely different perspective.

The survey does, of course, raise some serious questions about the effectiveness of the church in getting any message across to its constituency. This is most disturbingly borne out in two sections of the study. First, there is the repeated statement of a majority of people that while they value the church as an institution, they feel it is not essential to their relationship with God.

What does this say for the ministry? It is not easy to draw conclusions. On the one hand, we may see it as our failure to make preaching and teaching relevant to the daily experience of the people. Are those who preach the gospel and lead the church in its teaching ministry too far removed from the weekday world of the members of the congregation? Is the theology taught at our seminaries too distant from the work-a-day world of those to whom the graduates are called to minister? Is there a problem with the way we do ministry? Is the traditional Sunday morning setting, with the preacher at center stage, a good way to communicate the gospel? We could argue that the findings of this research call for a radical change in ministry for the church.

On the other hand, is it not legitimate to ask if we may expect too much of the church? Or, even more so, why *should* we expect the church to be the sole resource for people's faith and spiritual development? Respondents say the church is not essential to their faith, yet they continue to come to it for worship and learning. The fault may be in the nature of the question. It may be that they are saying that they *could* survive without the church, but are glad they do not need to. Rather than characterizing the church as a failure in its ministry, it may be that we should celebrate the fact that God is actively involved in the lives of people both through the church as well as outside of the formal organization.

Even if one accepts this more optimistic possibility, it does not erase the other disturbing finding of the survey, namely, that 43% of church members in Minnesota do not see the resurrection of Jesus Christ as central to the faith of the individual or the church. This ought to shake us to the core because of the utterly distinct character resurrection gives to Christianity. The teachings of Christ are not all that unique. Other great religious leaders have espoused ethical standards not unlike those of Christ. Other religions have had a strong sacrificial motif. Claims for miracles are not unusual in other non-Christian faiths. But resurrection stands as the keystone for Christianity. If, then, Christians in Minnesota do not see it as central and crucial, we can only conclude that we have failed at the very heart of our religious task.

Perhaps we should not be so surprised by this finding. Most sermons —regardless of the liberal, conservative, or middle-of-the-road theology of the preacher—tend to be moralistic. A look at Sunday church school curricula evidences the same tendency, namely, a strong accent on "how to be a good Christian."

What is at the root of all this? Has the resurrection been "demythologized" in the theology of so many clergy that they are relieved to give it scant attention on a single Sunday of the year? Or is the nature of resurrection so radical that we find it easier to ignore it, for the most part, while we focus on the more comfortable realm of ethics and morals? What can we do to change this obvious deficiency in our churches?

The answer may be in the responses to the survey. What little attention people do give to resurrection is related almost exclusively with death. Little wonder that it is seen as irrelevant for daily *living!* The mandate for ministry is to construct a much more dynamic theology of resurrection—a theology that relates the resurrection of Jesus Christ to all of life. So long as resurrection is limited to Easter and funerals, we can expect church members to see little relationship between resurrection and life.

If these are the most disturbing findings of the study, there are other laments which are only a trifle less distressing. The inability of church members to join Sunday faith with Monday practice is not new. But it speaks to an ongoing need for ministry that is not reluctant to apply resurrection theology to weekday experience. It is unfortunate, for example, that the survey did not probe more deeply and deliberately into the attitude of Minnesota church members toward the American Indian. Had it done so, it would have documented what we see almost everywhere in the state. Church members are quite content to invest multimillions of dollars in the starting of new churches and in mission work abroad, but little or nothing in work among American Indians.

This is only illustrative of the general unwillingness of church members to tackle justice issues. The study reinforces what we observe in nearly every facet of the work of the church. Christians are quite willing to speak about *individual* conviction, *individual* commitment, *individual* generosity, *individual* involvement. But when it comes to the *collective* voice of the church—either denominationally or ecumenically —there is great reluctance to give support to justice issues.

Again, the fault may be with the leadership of the church itself. Have we allowed the members of our churches to go unchallenged in their superficial devotion to rugged individualism? Have we laid so much stress on the need for individuals to be "born again" that we have left almost untouched the nature of the church as the "body of Christ"? Have we led members of our churches to believe that they do not even *need* the church so long as they can claim personal salvation? And in the process, have we given them reason to believe that their identity with the larger church is an option?

Furthermore, have we allowed individualism to extend to our denominational structures? That is to say, have we as denominations regarded ecumenical involvement as optional? Indeed we have! And little wonder that members of our churches have such a shallow conviction about the church as church. Obviously, a more comprehensive understanding of the theology of the church is of highest priority for us in Minnesota.

Much more could be said about the findings of this study that should disturb and dismay us. But this chapter would not be complete without a strong and positive word of affirmation for the churches of Minnesota.

Only 15 years ago we found ourselves wondering if congregationally based Christianity would survive—to say nothing of Christianity itself. It was popular to talk about the "post-Christian" age that was about to dawn. It was thought that whatever survived of Christianity would find its identity in small cells that would abandon traditional congregational forms and practices.

In the early 1980s we see that congregational life has not only survived but is as vibrant as ever. While it is true that so-called evangelical and conservative churches have shown the strongest rebound in the past decade, we ought not to write off too quickly the more traditional mainline denominations. Declining growth rates and budgetary problems are not unique to the churches. This seeming loss of vitality has been common to all of the major institutions in our society. Given the fact that mainline Protestant and Roman Catholic churches are located in areas that have experienced the most radical changes in population, it is surprising that they have not declined even more sharply. There are also those who believe that the mainline churches have "bottomed out" and will experience slow but certain growth in the years ahead.

And what about the influence of our churches in Minnesota? While we might deplore the seeming lack of impact on many facets of our common life, there is also a positive side to the picture. If we acknowledge, for example, that only 30%-35% of the members of a congregation are in attendance on a given Sunday, it is quite remarkable that the influence of the church is as broad as it is. Instead of bemoaning the influence of the churches, we ought to reflect on what would happen if we were to suddenly close our congregations and to think about how impoverished our life in Minnesota would be without them.

At the end of his monumental book on the religious history of our country, Sydney E. Ahlstrom, a native of small-town Minnesota, reflects on the difficulty of assessing the meaning of the era in which one is living. We may be at a loss to explain, says Ahlstrom, what is happening, even with the most comprehensive materials at hand. So it must be said of the findings of the Faith and Ferment survey. We must be humble and tentative about the conclusions we draw. But, like Ahlstrom, we can at least hope that the evidence will show that a few less church members in Minnesota are "foggy" about their religion, and a few more are "drawing on the profounder elements of their traditions, finding new sources of strength and confidence, and thus vindicating the idealism which has been so fundamental an element in the country's past" (Sydney E. Ahlstrom, *A Religious History of the American People*, New Haven: Yale University Press, 1972).

4

J. Timothy Power

There was a time when Jeremiah was directed to go down to a potter's house and watch the man at his work. He noticed that whenever the object of clay turned out badly he tried again, making of the clay another object of whatever sort he pleased. Then the message came from God to Jeremiah: "Behold, like clay in the potter's hand, so are you in my hand, O house of Israel" (Jer. 18:6). That is a rather upbeat image to keep in mind when looking at the shape of believers at any one point in history. It allows rejoicing at the good shaping and hope for the reshaping of that which might be deformed. It is the image we might keep in mind as we look at the shape of the pot we have become, we Minnesota Christians in the early 1980s, knowing that the potter may have to try again before he is pleased with the object. The following are the observations of one pastor as he looks at the shape of Minnesota believers as described in this study and thinks about the pastoral implications. Five areas seem to beg for this reflection.

J. Timothy Power is a priest of the Roman Catholic Church, and pastor of Pax Christi Catholic Community, Eden Prairie, Minnesota.

Whispers of the Risen Christ

Perhaps one notices the flaws before the beauty. The fact that "almost one-third of the church members sampled in Minnesota said that Christian teaching would be meaningful to them whether Christ had risen from the dead or not" jumps out for me as one of the most glaring portions that begs to be reshaped. We have been described as "Easter People," and the Christian parish has been described as "whispers of the risen Christ," yet almost a third of us do not hold the resurrection of Jesus as essential for the believer. This has tremendous pastoral implications, especially for the concepts of sin and salvation and practices such as Baptism and burial and our gathering together as "the body of Christ," to say nothing about how we face evil or are invited into the death and resurrection of Jesus.

I do not propose that we need to develop a new theology of resurrection but to be more creative with the one we already possess. Morton Kelsey suggests that many have become immune to the mere repeating of the gospel story. For many years he taught a graduate course at the University of Notre Dame on death and suffering. After assigning Menninger's *Man Against Himself* and Elie Wiesel's *Night*, he would assign C. S. Lewis' *The Lion, the Witch and the Wardrobe* to counteract the ugliness which the other two books conveyed. It is a fairy tale that talks of a deep magic from beyond the dawn of time which states that those who give their lives for others, expecting nothing in return, cannot really die. The hero who goes through this suffering, death, resurrection cycle is the lion, Aslan. Kelsey reports how the story of Aslan and his sacrificial love opened the doors of belief for students, the portals of which had been closed for years. One student provided him with a stained glass representation of Aslan, and Kelsey recounts how "the meaning of Easter and Christ touches me as well in a new way each time I see the sun streaming through the glass medallion into my living room."

When Peter preached at the first Pentecost, the people were "cut to the heart" (Acts 2:37). Scripture scholars suggest that they were shaken not so much by what Peter said but by the fact that they had a resurrection experience by actually encountering the risen Lord in the preaching of Peter. This has been the basic meaning of preaching all through the centuries. Shaken by this experience, people choose to join Christ in his new way of living. They choose to die and rise with Jesus. As Eugene LaVerdiere has said: "This is the most basic theology of all Christian belief, the very root of Christian life. It is the whole context of the beginning of the church—dying with Christ for the sake of others and their salvation. This is what the early Christians affirmed in their preaching, witnessed in their lives of conversion, proclaimed in their liturgies and hymns."

It would seem from the data of this study that there is a tremendous challenge present to be creative with the resurrection story and to invite believers, if they cannot preach like Peter, to be at least a whisper of the risen Christ. If we are not creative with the implications of the resurrection, we might have to face the fact that we actually shield people from making an act of Christian faith, that we make it easier to settle for less than God.

One Hand or Two

In Herman Melville's *Moby Dick* a minister preaches in a seaside chapel to the seamen who are going out to search for the great white whale. One of the lines he speaks, perhaps to enhance his own position, is: "Shipmates, God has laid but one hand upon you. Both His hands press upon me." There seems to be evidence in this study that people believe that God places one hand upon all but both only upon a few—specifically, that there is a difference between clergy and laity both in what is expected of them and where they stand on issues.

I believe this rift between laity and clergy must be challenged if faith is to be well shaped. When clergy and laity differ on issues such as whether humans can change God's plans, whether liberation of the poor and oppressed is a gospel mandate, whether Christian faith has implications for foreign policy, and the place and purpose of suffering in life, then important questions must be asked. Are the differences the result of theological training, a form of spirituality, a life-style, an image of self, or some such other accidental element, or are they the result of something more essential? I would suggest that they are accidentals that often have been denied laity and must be restored to them, such as a sense of ownership of the faith of the church and open access to theological resources.

I find this especially important in my own Roman Catholic tradition as we face several important factors in the next few decades. One is the decrease in the number of clergy. A study by University of Wisconsin sociologist Richard Schoenherr shows that even as the percentage of Americans identifying themselves as Catholic continues to grow—up from 25% in 1966 to nearly 30% in 1981—there will be a 50% loss of priests by the year 2000. This obviously means that our tradition cannot rely on clergy to be sole, or even more important proclaimers and livers of faith. It means, as Edward Schillebeeckx suggests, locating the essence of priesthood less in a special personal power to consecrate the Eucharist and relocating it more within the local community. Movements such as the Rite of Christian Initiation of Adults, base communities, and lay evangelism all point the way. Allowing the fact that God places both hands on all baptized seems to be a reality that must more and more be woven into the fabric of church life.

Orthopraxis

We are very familiar with the idea of orthodoxy (right teaching). In fact, we have all sorts of measures for, and a long tradition of preserving orthodoxy. We have developed great skill in passing on orthodox beliefs from one generation to another. The present study seems to indicate the success of such efforts in favor of orthodox beliefs. For example, almost all believe that Jesus is the Son of God, or that all people are equal before God. But there is a new word emerging called "orthopraxis" (right acting). It is the counterbalance to orthodoxy. The goal is not only to think right but to act right. The present study gives abundant evidence that we have not been as successful in evaluating our acting as we have our thinking. The challenge this presents for ministry is overwhelming and reminds us that in the converted life one enters into the death and resurrection of Jesus.

The evidence indicates that one of the hindrances to our present-day orthopraxis is something known in modern industry as "golden handcuffs." Many companies lure highly skilled technicians and executives into jobs by "making them an offer which they can't refuse." These offers consist of lucrative benefits like stock options, company shares, profit-sharing plans, or mortgages financed at subsidized rates. But the key ingredient of these offers is that they are available only to those who stay with the job over an extended period of time. These "golden handcuffs" can be more painful than brass ones, because the person is controlled by his own choices rather than by circumstances. It seems as if the phenomenon is not reserved to industry but imprisons believers in this prosperous state of a prosperous nation. The present study states that "the data reflect the struggle of a generation that is trying to come to grips with its own best ideals by making those ideals possible for everyone. The problem is that they are reluctant to give up their own standard of living for the sake of another people's growth." This seems to indicate that one very large object of pastoral ministry in Minnesota is the forging of keys that will free us from our "golden handcuffs" so that we might be free not only for orthodoxy but also for orthopraxis; or to put it in the words of a rabbi: "It is not so important how often you have been through the Torah—but how often the Torah has been through you."

Fighting Off Mosquitoes

Minnesotans pride themselves on their ability to cope with the abundant presence of pesty little mosquitoes. In spite of them Minnesotans continue to camp in the woods, barbeque, go on picnics, and listen to outdoor concerts. To borrow an image from Theophane the Recluse, a 19th-century monk, this study seems to indicate the Minnesotans are just as adept at warding off the jostling of distractions that might interrupt the quality of their prayer life. Theophane says: "Thoughts continue to jostle in your head like mosquitoes. To stop this jostling, you must bind the mind with one thought, or the thought of One only. An aid to this is a short prayer, which helps the mind to become simple and united . . . together with the short prayer, you must keep your thought and attention turned towards God."

A most encouraging find in this study is the high percentage of Minnesota churchgoers who pray every day, who pray as families, who find prayer not just the repeating of traditional words but the being in the presence of God, and who find it a common event to discuss their spiritual life with others. If there is any strength that parishes and parish leaders might draw on, it is this comfortableness with prayer. Perhaps it is an activity that believers would welcome opportunities to expand.

Perhaps we could become an even stronger people of prayer by taking advantage of the renewed awareness of ancient prayer styles—centering prayer, journaling, praying with Scripture, and forms of meditation. Perhaps the time is ripe, as Fr. Edward Hays suggests, to turn our strength at prayer into a subversive activity by using types of prayer that go against the grain of the common culture. This may help us go beyond letting God intervene only in our private lives to affecting the society around us. Some of the suggestions he offers are the "prayer of being alone," which challenges the conspiracy against solitude in American life; the "prayer of rest" (sabbath prayer), which challenges the work ethic; the "prayer of doing what you're doing," which challenges a culture that rewards those who can do more than one thing at a time; the "prayer of tears," which challenges a society that does not allow true emotion in public; and the "prayer of forgiveness" for a country which doesn't forgive the draft resisters any easier than it forgives its presidents. In our comfortableness with prayer is a great opportunity to make an impact on the world around us.

And What of the Church?

One closing thought regarding the image of "church" that emerged in the study. St. Augustine of Hippo said: "Some people who belong to God do not belong to the church; and some who belong to the church do not belong to God." Those of us who are officially identified with the church might not always be comfortable with the reality of Augustine's words, but the study seems to indicate that church members in Minnesota are. I find it encouraging that people are willing to question and even challenge the church and that they place conscience above authority. This may make it difficult for us who are church professionals, but it surely will keep us more honest. And honesty is something that the Potter of Jeremiah will find very beneficial in the shaping and reshaping that must take place.

5

Richard J. Mouw

As a teacher I sometimes find it depressing to read my students' examinations. There is often a significant gap between what I wanted my students to learn and what they did in fact learn, between what I thought they were hearing me say in my lectures and what they did in fact hear.

The Christians of Minnesota have been given an examination of sorts. They have been asked to give an account of the faith-traditions which have shaped them, to explain what the Christian faith means to them in a variety of contexts. And it would not be surprising to me if their "teachers"—catechists, preachers, counselors, lay readers in the parishes—are not a little depressed by the results. Is *this* what they have been hearing from us? Have they been listening at all? Do they really care about what we have been trying to teach them?

I must admit at the outset that I read the results of this survey through the lenses of a "conservative evangelical" perspective. But I don't think that my own stubborn affection for "orthodoxy" has made it impossible for me to empathize with church leaders who might oper-

Richard J. Mouw, Ph.D., is professor of philosophy at Calvin College, Grand Rapids, Michigan, and a member of the Christian Reformed Church.

ate with a somewhat different theology from mine. We can all be bothered by the results of this study, whether we are low-church Episcopalians, mainstream Presbyterians, traditional Roman Catholics, broad-minded Congregationalists, hard-shell Baptists, or crusading Moral Majoritarians. This report is truly ecumenical: it gives all of us reasons to be disturbed.

This is not to criticize those who have formulated the questions, collected the data, and sifted and interpreted the results. They have done us a significant service. To be sure, they have in many cases also whetted our appetites for more information. I for one would like to know how all of those Minnesota Swedes in Baptist General Conference congregations compare with their American Baptist counterparts; how the attitudes of Salvation Army troops fit into all of this; how Missouri Synod Lutherans compare with those in the ALC or LCA; or how Native American Pentecostals differ from Native American Catholics. But we now have an instrument and a framework for pursuing those kinds of issues. So the persons who are responsible for this survey deserve our gratitude.

The results of this survey are ecumenically disturbing, but it is also possible for all of us to find signs of encouragement in these results. As I studied this report, my evangelical heart was warmed a number of times. "When the Son of man returns, will he find *some* healthy faith in Minnesota?" The answer to this question must surely be an affirmative one, even on the most narrow and parochial accounts of what "healthy faith" amounts to.

The evangelical can take comfort in some statistics, and in some of the firsthand testimonies quoted. And so can pre-Vatican II Catholics and post-Vatican II Catholics, conservative Lutherans and liberated Lutherans, Methodists who still read Wesley and Methodists who refuse to read Wesley. We can all find some sign of hope from the point of view of the causes which we cherish and promote. We can all recognize in this survey the existence of people who are loyal to one or another of the traditional and not-so-traditional schools of thought that are familiar to those who study the theological and ecclesiastical landscape.

To return, however, to my original observation: this survey also demonstrates beyond question that there is much confusion in the Christian ranks today. As an evangelical Calvinist I may not agree with a Roman Catholic who believes that her church is the one and

only true church, who cherishes papal authority, and who understands
the Mass along the lines proposed by the Council of Trent. I may not
agree with such a person, but I do understand the patterns of thought
being defended. There is a coherence and plausibility to this pattern
of thinking which I can appreciate and be challenged by.

But I am baffled by many of the Christians whose profiles emerge
out of this study. There are, for example, many Episcopalians who
express the strong conviction that "women are equal to men," and who
claim sympathies for the women's movement. But they are not convinced that the church should "take leadership" in the fight against
sexism, nor do they believe "that women should have equal place with
men in church ministry." I find that very difficult to understand.

Or, how are we to understand the majority of Methodists who believe that the resurrection of Christ is not "basic to the meaningfulness
of Christian teaching"? The question that was put to them did not
require a commitment on their part to a "literal, physical" resurrection.
All they were asked was whether in some sense or another a belief in
the resurrection of Christ is important to their faith. Yet less than half
of them could say that it is. I am at a loss to know what their pattern of
thinking is on this subject.

And there is the puzzle noted in the text of this report. What is going
on in people's minds when they say that "the gospel of Christ is necessary for the salvation of all people," but also are opposed to Christian
attempts "to convert all peoples to Christ"? How do people hold these
two emphases together? What could be the pattern of thinking at
work here?

Of course, there may *be* coherent patterns of thinking here. My com-
plaints, if legitimate, merely demonstrate that the patterns are not ones
that are familiar to those of us who think in terms of the standard
theological and ecclesiastical categories. But it may be that this report
is revealing the existence of new and coherent patterns of thought
which we must decode and label, inventing new classification schemes
in the process. From the point of view of the older set of labels, these
new patterns may appear highly eclectic: bits and pieces from traditional Christian sources, borrowings from "civil religion," themes
adapted from politicians and electronic preachers, ideas imported
from the cults and from the classical "world religions," and so on. Yet
there may be new syntheses and configurations emerging here, which
can stand on their own as *patterns* of religious thought.

This investigation—the attempt to ascertain the patterns of thought operating among these data—is an important project to undertake. Indeed, I am convinced that it is an important first step in a proper response to this survey by the Christian "teachers"—catechists, preachers, counselors, lay leaders, and the like—of Minnesota. The results of this survey must be digested, reflected upon, discussed, argued about, and further sorted and interpreted. Helpful hints for doing all of this are given in the body of the report.

A second step might be to check out initial hunches and analyses (which might emerge from the process just mentioned) by talking with people like the ones from whom the data were collected. For example, 72% of the Lutherans surveyed view themselves as sinful; yet 57% of the Lutherans apparently do not think they have an "innate tendency" to sin. These data suggest that somewhere among the first five or ten Lutherans that one talks to there will be at least one person who views herself as a sinner, but not as an "innate" sinner. Christian professionals should engage such a person in a probing conversation, attempting to get some kind of explicit account of her general view of human sin.

These two steps would provide a procedure for better understanding whatever patterns of thinking there are in the views unearthed by this survey. But then there is another process that must be entered into: asking ourselves what we can do about the situation. How serious is it? What pedagogical and homiletical problems are we being presented with?

Here, I think, those of us who have been called to serve the Christian community in a variety of preaching, teaching, counseling, and administering positions must engage in some soul searching of our own. What do we really think about these matters? What is, after all, important to the faith of the Minnesota Christian community? What do we want the Son to find when he returns to our churches? We have found out what Minnesota thinks about God; now perhaps we must ask, admittedly with proper humility and caution: What does God think of Minnesota?

My own suspicion is that these kinds of questions, formulated against the backdrop of this Faith and Ferment study, could introduce interesting new dimensions to ecumenical dialog among the leaders of the Christian communities. This report certainly makes it clear that a gap exists between the official churchly theologies and the functioning theologies of the people in the pews. We—the professional leaders of the Christian community—exhibit a common failure to pass on our understandings of our traditions to significant portions of the laity. We might enjoy debating the question of which economic strategies best comport with biblical teachings regarding the poor and the oppressed, or whether a Platonistic view of immortality is compatible with a Hebraic understanding of bodiliness. But many of our fellow church members are oblivious to these discussions: they learn their economic theologies at the Rotary Club and their eschatology from the Phil Donohue Show. If we were to begin to talk more about these latter influences, while admitting our common inadequacies in countering them, would this not alter both the tone and the substance of our ecumenical dialog? Even if we hold to different theological traditions, do we not at least have a common problem with regard to the communication of our traditions?

And all of this must lead to an enterprise that is an urgent one for the Minnesota Christian community: new patterns of theological education for the laity. Those of us who have been active in recent manifestations of "the laity movement" have been pleading for innovations in this area. This report makes our pleadings even more poignant. Laity theological education must not be viewed as a watered-down version of seminary education. It must be a properly contextualized theology that is fitted to the areas of ministry—vocation, familial, political, recreational—in which the laity are involved. The present study points to many areas in which innovative programs in laity education can be directed. It tells us much about where people are hurting, where they are confused, where they are asking their questions. In that sense it provides us with an intriguing agenda for the formulation of pedagogical strategies.

We cannot develop programs for theological education for today's laity without first of all developing pastoral sensitivities to the complex problems faced by the laity. This report goes a long way toward providing us with a sensitizing instrument for that task. I hope that it will be given wide use, both as a mirror in which the "ordinary" people of the churches can examine themselves and as a window through which church leaders can study the patterns of discipleship which characterize the lives of their constituents.

I am no fan of the "positive thinkers" and "possibility thinkers." But I occasionally have to remind myself that a selective and discerning use of their methods and attitudes can be a useful strategy. It might be helpful for all of us to read through this report once or twice for the sole purpose of giving the most positive and hopeful formulations to these data. I have already observed that there were some items in this study which immediately elicited hopeful responses from me. But what of those other data—the ones which I found puzzling and disheartening? Are there legitimate challenges being presented here to our traditional formulations? Is there a yearning here—perhaps a very complex yearning—for new modes of service and stewardship? Is it possible that there are nuances in these answers that can easily be missed if we read them defensively? Could it be that many of these answers are in fact disguised requests—so that people are not really saying, "I'm a heretic, and I'm proud of it," but are instead asking for empathetic guidance in getting out of very real dilemmas which they face in their attempts to relate their Christian commitments to their cultural involvement?

I believe that we must proceed as if these are the challenges being presented by this survey.

"When the Son of man comes, will he find faith on earth?" This question of our Lord's is raised at several points in the report of these data. It is a good question. But it is important to note that, in Luke's report, this question is one with which Jesus concludes a parable. And in introducing that parable, Luke also tells us in very implicit terms what the point of Jesus' story is: "And he told them a parable, to the effect that they ought always to pray and not lose heart" (Luke 18:1).

This too is a word from the Lord for the state of Minnesota: "We ought always to pray and not lose heart." We have never adequately reported the data about "the way things are in the world" until we have taken note of the data of the gospel. The present survey shows us that there is much faith and much ferment in the Minnesota Christian community. The gospel tells us that God has not abandoned the good work of creation and redemption. We cannot be "realistic" Christians without taking that fact into account. The commitment "to pray and not lose heart" need not be a despairing one. Wherever we look, there are signs of hope to be seen.

6

Jerome P. Theisen

My response to the Faith and Ferment study is a theological reflection on the data provided by Minnesota Christians. It is a reflection that stems from my position as a Roman Catholic, a monk, and a theologian.

What is particularly striking in the data is the high incidence of the practice of prayer and of the remembrance of God. The monastic tradition to which I belong places a premium on "continuous prayer" and nonforgetfulness of God. It is both surprising and consoling to know that Minnesota Christians approximate this monastic—really gospel—mandate.

The Christians of this study pray to God often, some every day. God is extremely close to them, entering into their daily life. God is not so remote from life as to be found only in a world to come or only in an ornate sanctuary. Accessible at any time, in any place, and through everything, God is addressed in formal prayer but also in spontaneous prayer. These Christians foster an inner life of the Spirit in such a way that they turn easily to God in spontaneous prayer.

Jerome P. Theisen, O.S.B., S.T.D., is abbot of St. John's Abbey, Collegeville, Minnesota, and a priest of the Roman Catholic Church.

In this day of rapid transportation, immediate communication, pronounced freedom, and complex technology, God is not pushed to the edges of life. God is not served only in the breach, to avoid punish--ment—though probably some persons are "good" in order to avoid eternal death. God is active in the very midst of work and leisure, love and anxiety, decisions and problems. It would seem that the churches of Minnesota have communicated well the prayer aspect of Christianity, at least individual and family prayer. But it is significant, too, that a large proportion of Minnesota Christians attend worship services once a week or a few times a month. Public worship and private prayer bulk large in the faith and practice of the respondents of this study even when most do not view worship as the primary function of the church.

The image of God is also positive. God is not vindictive, but may test people by sending suffering. A large majority hold that a loving God and the existence of evil in the world are not incompatible; the clergy especially are almost unanimous in this position. Some hold, it is true, that God creates both good and evil; but most find that evil has causes other than God and that God is a source of support in the midst of suffering; in fact, God tests faith in the presence of suffering.

It is very encouraging to note the generally positive image of God and the widespread practice of prayer. While they need continual improvement, especially in the area of solemn liturgy and in the approach to a majestic God, these ideas are the basis of a mature and solid Christian faith.

The Christians of Minnesota realize that evil characterizes human life. There is a measure of suffering and calamity that touches everyone, and most of the people in the survey hold that evil can be present even without the personal moral failure that is called sin.

But sin is a problematic area for Minnesota Christians. On the one hand, they maintain in an overwhelming fashion that a person's spiritual development requires an awareness of sin, and yet a good number can maintain that they are not sinful in spite of mistakes in their moral and spiritual life. Is sin an outdated concept in the minds of a significant number of these Christians? Do modern psychological studies that distinguish between actual guilt and guilty feelings cause some to reject the notion of sin? While most clergy will not want to deliver the fire-and-brimstone sermons of the past, they will have to reflect on the way in which they teach the dimension of moral failure in human lives; for it is a traditional and basic teaching of Christianity that Jesus the Savior forgives sins and reconciles sinners with the Father.

What is the source of sin and evil? The respondents to this survey list four basic sources: external social circumstances, an innate tendency, Satan, and personal freedom. Twice as many persons see Satan as an evil force as those who view him as a person. It is significant that the causes of evil are often assigned to society (social circumstances) and to personal freedom. Many of these Christians reflect the conclusions of social psychology and sociology by maintaining and even emphasizing that humans are influenced by circumstances. They also stress the aspect of freedom; persons have responsibility for their lives and can cause good and evil for themselves and others.

What is still evident in the data, however, is that most Christians regard humans as being personally and inherently sinful. Personal responsibility for sin and evil must still do battle with a position that regards humans as inherently corrupt. The trend, however, is in the direction of personal responsibility and freedom. Christians today are less willing than they might have been in the past to view humans as corrupt; they are much more willing to see that humans are called to responsible freedom. This is manifested especially in their willingness to disobey civil and church authority or teaching if their conscience so dictates. Freedom is a primary value.

The survey reveals that Christians generally have a great respect for the church without worshiping it, and over half do not mind deviating from its official teaching. They view the church as anchored in the lives and concerns of people, not as floating in a heavenly realm. They look to it as a place of worship and mutual prayer. They look to it for many personal services, and they expect it to perform tasks in society. They want the church to get involved in their lives, especially when they are suffering, ill, or in need of direction. They want church members, especially the clergy, to support them in their loneliness and failures. Generally they also want the church to involve itself in social concerns of society: ecology, poverty, discrimination, sex education, and economic oppression.

It is significant that Christians on the right and on the left wish to be involved in social issues as a way of carrying out their commitment to the gospel message. The measure of personal involvement in social issues varies from Christian to Christian; so does denominational involvement. But one fact is clear: the Christians of Minnesota want and expect to be involved in matters that extend beyond the walls of the church building. Some, it is true, wish to hear more about the world to come, but generally they expect the church to say something about the present world, and they expect some involvement in the pressing issues of the day, including war and nuclear disarmament.

As viewed by Minnesota Christians, the church is not a private club, neatly separated from the public forum of the state. Their definition of church includes a reference to action in the public sphere and a concern for issues of the day. It is no angelic or hidden church that the Christians espouse. It is a very concrete group of people engaged as believers in crucial issues of politics and society. Such a definition departs both from the identification of church and state and from the world-denying isolation of the church. The church in the last 100 years, especially in the United States, has manifested increasing involvement in social issues; the Christians of Minnesota reflect this involvement in their concept of church and its activities.

Denominational ties are still firm, so that a majority of Christians believe that their tradition is the true church of Jesus Christ. The firmness, however, does not prevent most from desiring cooperation with Christians from other traditions; some even desire a thrust for unity. The firmness does not mean clean distinctions between the churches. Positions of involvement or noninvolvement in social issues are crossdenominational. Worship concerns, too, are crossdenominational.

The firmness of denominations does not prevent Christians of one tradition from seeing the gospel values in traditions other than their own. Proselytizing is still a significant phenomenon, but there is a wide acceptance of the Christian character of all denominations. It is significant that for Minnesota Christians the ecumenical age does not mean an easy movement from one denomination to another, but ecumenism does point out the wideness of the church of Jesus Christ and the Christian inspiration of the many traditions.

A commitment to the centrality of Jesus Christ remains firm. He is still the way of salvation, and his gospel must be preached to the end of the world in order to bring people into a salvific relationship to God. But it is encouraging to note that there is a measure of understanding of other religious traditions, even to the point of seeing them as vehicles of salvation.

The laity generally lags behind the clergy in most areas of social involvement of the church and in an understanding of Christian values of diverse denominations. Is this because the laity traditionally left study and action to the clergy in a clergy-dominated church? Religious education needs to close the gap between the clergy and the laity, and perhaps the clergy must prove their leadership by a teaching that leads to both understanding and action.

The major denominations of Minnesota will continue to exist in the foreseeable future, but they will not exist in isolation from one another. There will be a wide acceptance of the Christian values of all denominations, even while individuals view their own tradition as authentic. The lines of demarcation will be less clear in the future, and the bonds of unity and common actions will be strengthened.

The survey does not focus on the nature of salvation, but what Jesus effected through his life and message is certainly expressed often. The forgiveness of sins, life in the body of Christ, a peaceful relationship with God and eternal life are features of salvation mentioned by the Christians of Minnesota.

How much is the church involved in the salvation of individuals? The majority of Christians maintain that the gospel of Jesus Christ is necessary for the salvation of all peoples. This could mean that salvation, especially salvation in a world to come, really depends on an acceptance of Jesus and the Christian Scriptures, and indeed this opinion is well represented among the Christians in Minnesota.

It is not surprising that almost two-thirds of the Roman Catholic community still link the church and salvation. Many of them were educated to believe that adherence to the Roman Catholic Church was necessary for salvation. What is significant, however, is that a third of the Roman Catholics and more than half of the other traditions no longer see the church as a necessary link to the realm of salvation. Belonging to a certain denomination is important for many reasons, but nonattachment to a particular Christian tradition does not mean automatic exclusion from the benefits of salvation. The survey indicates, therefore, that the Minnesota Christians are not particularly willing to judge people of other religions or of no religion and to exclude them from a salvific relationship to God.

Significant, too, is the extremely high rejection of the idea that God determines the salvation or rejection of peoples before any regard for their life and works. The people of Minnesota overwhelmingly reject predestinationism because it is not compatible with ideas of freedom and their notion of a loving God.

It is apparent, moreover, that reward theology is strong in the belief of Minnesota Christians. Christian belief has some self-interest; it leads to a better life now, a greater acceptance of life's struggles, and a personal afterlife with God. But there are some Christians who adhere to the Christian gospel without the hope of a reward in a life to come; they are satisfied with the benefits of Christianity in the present world.

Minnesota Christians are overwhelmingly in favor of ecumenical cooperation between the various denominations and the vast majority want more unity; well over half want open communion. Ecumenism is a significant factor in the life of the Minnesota churches.

It seems that Minnesota Christians will seek new ways to bring the churches together. Their experience of living side by side in one state has given them respect for each other to the point where they generally do not wish to proselytize and to lure other Christians into their denomination. A little more than half of the Roman Catholics, however, approve of the practice of proselytism; perhaps the remembrance of the pre-Vatican II catechetical instructions on "outside the church, no salvation" urges them to continue this practice.

What is significant, however, and this is the trend of a different form of ecumenism, is that Christians of different theological and liturgical traditions are cooperating in their approach to politics, education, family, and race. Positions on the left and on the right are drawing Christians together to oppose or to support certain social issues. Today social action seems to be the locus of ecumenical cooperation. Christians who act together, often in prayer, will seek further unity.

The pluriform ways of understanding and practicing Christianity are evident in the study, but even more evident are the broad lines of unity that pervade all the traditions. Similar notions of God, evil, church, salvation, and Christ are crossdenominational. This likeness should be stressed, even as the differences are brought into relief. The churches have done a commendable job of communicating a broad spectrum of commitments and practices that stem from the gospel of Jesus Christ.

The identity of Jesus Christ as Lord and Son of God is not a problem for virtually all the Christians of Minnesota; they believe that he comes from the Father and teaches the gospel of salvation. But the identity of the church of Jesus Christ and a specification of its tasks in the world are problems. Jesus stands at the center of belief—in fact, most hold that the church is the body of Christ—but what his gospel demands of Christians is not uniformly proclaimed.

The survey contains a number of questions that concern the future life, but only one question mentions the resurrection of Jesus: "If Christ had not risen from the dead, Christian teaching would mean very little to me." The question does not deal directly with belief in the resurrection of Jesus; its point of reference is the significance of the resurrection of Christ for the meaning of Christian doctrine. It is true, and many responders acknowledge the fact, that the gospel contains some wisdom even if Christ had not risen from the dead. It would have been enlightening to probe deeper the way in which the Christians of Minnesota interpret the resurrection of Jesus.

In closing, it is important to underscore two significant dimensions of the survey: the increasing ecumenical character of the churches of Minnesota and the profound manner in which Christians remember a loving God in prayer and in daily life.

7

Don E. Saliers

What the church professes in creeds, liturgical action, preaching and official teachings is not always what individual believers actually experience and confess with their lives. The relation between what various churches claim we ought to believe and what we do believe and manifest in our lives is complex. At times the gap is enormous; at other times there is a remarkable coherence. What puzzles any sincere Christian, however, is why there are so many divisions among believers, even within the same denomination, who profess "one Lord, one faith, one Baptism, one God and Father of all."

Our present age is, by any measure, an age of pluralism, change, and shifting moral and religious perceptions of the world. On the one hand, the shocks and collisions of the social, economic, and political orders of 20th-century life in America and the world have generated unprecedented questions and pressures upon the inherited doctrines and images of the Christian gospel and of what it means to be faithful in our age. For many the older, comfortable pieties have been forever

Don E. Saliers, Ph.D., is professor of theology and liturgics, Candler School of Theology, Emory University, Atlanta, Georgia, and a minister of the United Methodist Church.

discredited. "God's in his heaven and all's right with the world" seems hopelessly naive for many, as the conflicting data of this study concerning the relation of God to sin, suffering, and social responsibility indicate. In this respect the Christian people of Minnesota seem no different from those living elsewhere.

At the same time, our century has witnessed widespread ecumenical recognition and searching as well as evangelical renewal across old denominational and theological lines. During the past two decades in America we have witnessed a series of renewal movements affecting both laity and clergy across the whole spectrum of communions. Ecumenical sharing, interfaith dialog, the reform and renewal of worship and prayer, renewed concern for biblical study, a new interest in the mission and ministry of the laity—all these have contributed to a positive ferment of faith and practice. Thus we should not be too disappointed with the wide differences in belief and practice reported in this study. It is indeed a time when *both* the uncertainties generated by new demands and images of power in the society and the new rediscovered images of the Christian faith contribute to the ferment of belief and practice. Whatever else emerges, we cannot fall back upon some happy obliviousness to these facts. Once we confront the nature of our pluralism and even inconsistencies in faith and practice, we cannot go home again theologically and religiously. It may be good news rather than bad that we are called to reexamine the essentials of the Christian gospel in its implications for our lives in light of these findings.

This study of Christian believers in Minnesota illustrates well both the impact of social-cultural reality and the impact of ecumenical and various crossdenominational renewal movements upon the lived faith of ordinary believers. Apart from the basic doctrine of God's existence and relatedness to the world, there are clear indications here that fundamental issues in theology have been called into question for many. At the same time there are clear indications of preserved lines of denominational identity, particularly among Roman Catholics and Baptists, on specific issues: abortion, the nature of the church, and biblical authority, for example.

Yet this study confirms in the main what many theologians and clergy have long suspected—that underneath a seemingly common vocabulary of terms such as "God," "sin," "salvation," "the will of God," and so on, Christians mean many different things. People may understand basic theological concepts very differently—and not simply along denominational lines. The social, economic, and political environments of Minnesota also shape how Christians actually understand and live their faith in daily life. What the study lacks, of course, is any comparison with the general non-Christian population on some of the critical ethical and moral issues. Nevertheless, we can detect in the extended quotations from the interviews cited just how matters of social responsibility and images of the self and community reflect tensions between the official teachings of a church and the images offered by the society.

Nowhere is this last point more clearly displayed than in the area of the social teachings of the various churches. All traditions agree that Christians are to love God and neighbor. The implications of such a claim for specific courses of action and involvement in the political and social arena are far from clear. Something of the deep American and frontier respect for the autonomy of individual conscience shows up throughout. So, too, does the older notion of the separation of church and civil state, which reinforce various conservative stances with regard to the church's engagement in changing American society. One cannot help but sense beneath the data that the relation between the church's preaching and teaching and national defense or the attitudes of Christians toward welfare is very mixed and ambiguous. The differences between clergy and laity on these specific matters, especially foreign policy, bears much further scrutiny. I suspect that differences in education and exposure to the issues have made a large difference in the reported attitudes.

There are certainly no straight-line inferences from Christian faith to the articulation of specific economic and social policies. In fact, the whole relation between personal faith and corporate ethical responsibility among Christians in Minnesota is unclear. Yet certain fundamental virtues stand out: hard and honest work, a sense of justice, and personal interest in family and community. These combine fairly well with a venerable way of construing the gospel.

The question generated for the church and theology from the data, however, is: what are the actual ways in which the churches of Minnesota are publicly wrestling with the inferences from the gospel to the pressing social and political issues confronting the region and the world? Diversity of conviction and practice should not, in itself, dismay us. But unreflective, conventionalized attitudes and practices should.

At the same time, shunning the substantial orthodoxies of doctrine—whether of God, christology, sin, the Bible or of social ethics—can itself be a cultural convenience. This latter point is precisely what some of the new conservative movements have in mind, though their polemical targets often make symbolic issues of "right-to-life," freedom from handgun or snowmobile control, school prayer, antiwelfare, or the like. When this happens, and the single-issue "religious" candidates emerge, the churches must be called to a healthy reflection on the essentials of the gospel and its implications for social ethics.

The conservative elements of theological belief and social attitude reflected in this study sometimes have a polemical target. When they do, it is most likely the omnibus enemy "secular humanism." I find this polemical spirit intriguing, for it invariably contains a mixture of religious and secular elements within itself. Having a definite, well-defined Christian point of view on everything has often, in the history of Christianity (and especially in the West), been founded upon a passionate protest of what *other* Christians have believed and practiced. This is characteristic of the Reformation and Counter-Reformation churches, and it has been played out with a vengeance in American Protestantism, especially in the sectarian wing. Perhaps it is time once again to ask whether Christians have a nonpolemical foundational view of the world which can yet offer an alternative to conventional religion and to various popular religions currently parading as "truly spiritual"—that is, unsullied by such worldly matters as money and politics. Can Christians articulate a view of the world, faithful to Scripture and the central church tradition, which can also be an alternative to a merely technological, one-dimensional humanism?

Such an articulation would require further discussion and study. The heart of this discussion would focus upon what baptized Christians ought to believe and practice about God, society, human responsibility, and how the Christian life is best lived. If nothing else, the Faith and Ferment study provides the generalized statistical profile which can provoke all of us to reexamine the relationships between Christ and culture more seriously than ever before. Such a reexamination, like that concerning basic belief, may best take place at the level of local churches, where laity are close to their work, where the joys and sufferings, and the hundred human pressures which impact their religious needs and wants affect the practice of their faith. Some of the interviews provide important case studies that could well be the stimulus for local parishes to begin to think together. The needed intensive discussion should never merely concern policy or simple denominational pronouncements, lest these become an ideology and not a genuine dialog between laity and clergy and the inherited traditions. Yet the theological temper—and even the social and theological teachings—of a whole denomination can be constructively affected by such serious inquiry concerning the essentials of Christian faith and practice among believers who must live with each other over time in light of their responsibilities as families, and as citizens in state, nation, and world.

Heightened awareness of these questions will not automatically produce a uniform conservatism or progressivism. Critical self-awareness is indeed painful to people who have not thought about their faith in God and its role in their whole life. But the Faith and Ferment study indicates that Christians in Minnesota *want* their faith to be informed and faithful, even when "being faithful" means a departure from inherited doctrines or conventional piety. It would be interesting along the way to note and perhaps discover why the clergy often hold views significantly different from the laity on certain issues and doctrines. Does the difference result from theological education, and is the latter detrimental or positive?

I suspect also on the basis of this study that significant numbers of professing Christians have not grasped the inner connections between worship and ethics. Questions concerning Christian ethics and the shape of the moral life cannot be adequately understood apart from discovering how and why persons internalize their faith through worship and preaching. Communal praise, thanksgiving, remembrances, repentance, being forgiven, and communing with Christ in sacraments and prayer are part of the very matrix of action which forms the character and disposition of Christians. How we truly pray and participate in the liturgy is linked to how we live. What goes on in worship both challenges and gives sanction to how Christians regard the neighbor and the world, and how their images of God "take hold" on life. My impression is that the realm of instruction and formation in faith, both for children and adults, especially as it focuses upon the relation between worship and the Christian life in the world, has yet to receive the time and attention it deserves.

There are and will continue to be differences in theological interpretation of the essentials of which we have spoken here. There will always be differences in styles or ways of being Christian. We can

never fully escape our denominational and cultural histories. The
Christian faith necessarily takes on cultural embodiment. It must always speak a language and manifest itself in particular social, political,
and economic contexts. A limited question—for instance, gun control
or abortion—may become symbolic of a large number of Christians.
When that happens, it is likely to be a reflection of the particular
society and culture in which these Christians live, rather than primarily
a response to Christian norms and principles. Developing a critical
awareness of the specific ways in which faith assumes the general
cultural and social attitudes toward war, nuclear weaponry, political
responsibility, abortion, human rights, and other such matters is
essential to an authentic Christian conscience. It is also central to a
more adequate grasp of the kind of quality of authority Christian
teachings and symbols should have.

Mine is no simple call to neoorthodoxy, with its sharp distinction
between God's will and revelation and "cultured religion." Rather, I
find this study issuing a compelling call for us to seek after the essentials once again. But now we must seek in light of the powerful ecumenical vision of faith given to us in the 20th century. Ultimately
this call to critical self-awareness as men and women of faith in a
particular time and culture is rooted in the prophets and in the gospel
of Jesus Christ. It will be carried out wherever the church seeks to be
truly catholic, truly evangelical, and truly reforming.

As it has been wisely observed, when the church marries the spirit
of the age, she will be left a widow in the next generation. By the
same token, the Christian faith remains empty unless, by grace, it is
incarnated in forms which address the suffering and God-yearning
world in this time and this place.

Appendices

I

Denominational Differences on Critical Issues

In the course of this study, though a number of respondents indicated that it did not make any difference what religion other people professed, none said that it did not make any difference what religion they themselves professed. Half the population took the position that their church was the only true church of Christ. On the other hand, almost all the Christians in the study wanted greater cooperation, even unity, among the churches in the Christian community. The question rises: what differences are there in the interpretation of the Christian tradition from church to church. Are there multiple charisms and insights variously reflected? Or, is one church no different from another but simply the inheritor of the schisms or revelations of another people and time? Do the Christian churches complement or counter one another's vision of the gospel?

The data collected in this research effort were analyzed in several ways. First, we set out to report what all the church members together, regardless of their denominational affiliations, felt about the demands of faith on some separate dimensions of contemporary life. Then, in each section, we pointed up in a special way those items which showed significant statistical differences among the responses across the denominations or sectors of the population. In these sections we pointed up those responses that departed from the average answer, either by most embracing that position or by most rejecting it. So, for instance, though few (16%) of the respondents in general considered church schools the ideal form of education for Christians, Roman Catholics (36%) were more committed to the position than any of the other groups represented, and Methodists (10%) were least supportive of the need for parochial education. Between those two extremes, however, are multiple variations on the Christian theme.

The purpose of this section is to trace through each of the denominations (all Lutherans figure as a denominational unity, as do all Baptists) some of the major issues in the study around which many other issues clustered. It is an attempt to look at each church separately, asking what positions most of its members might be expected to take on key issues if the sample were extrapolated to that church as a whole. The chapter is a profile of faith-life among Christians of different traditions.

Roman Catholics

Suffering and Crisis

The Catholics canvassed in this study accept suffering as a part of life that tests the depth of their faith but does not determine it. For the most part (66%), they do not feel that the presence of evil in the world is incompatible with the notion of a loving God. Very few (26%) see illness, calamity, and other forms of suffering and crisis as a result of sin. Most (95%) do not expect less suffering in life simply because they have attempted to lead faithful religious lives, but many (56%) do believe that suffering is a way we are reminded of our dependence on God.

Relationships

Most (57%) assumed that divorce is a necessary provision to alleviate insurmountable human problems. One-third of the Catholic population surveyed said that artificial methods of birth control and family planning are immoral, but two-thirds of the same found abortion "always wrong or sinful." Extramarital sex is unacceptable to most Catholics (88%) as is premarital sex, though to a lesser degree (70%). On the matter of homosexuality, the gap narrows even more. Only 61% of the group consider homosexuality totally immoral. Finally, less than half

(43%) of the group feel that every pupil should have a course in sex education in school.

In terms of human rights, Minnesota Catholics agreed almost unanimously (97%) that racial discrimination is anti-Christian, but far fewer (68%) felt that helping to improve the status of minority peoples was part of the mission of the church. Furthermore, though they are concerted (98%) in their understanding that men and women are created equal in God's sight, a considerable number of them (41%) are generally unsympathetic toward the women's movement. At the same time, almost a third of the group (30%) feel that women should have an equal place with men in the ministry of the church.

Personal Spiritual Development

By and large, Catholics believe that God plays an active part in guiding their lives and helping them to make decisions (81%). A large portion (88%) consider the Bible the authoritative Word of God, and over half (59%) consider the reading of Scripture important for the development of their spiritual lives. Most, though, (62%) are not prepared to say the Bible contains no errors or that it is a verbal report of the message of God. Many (41%) say they accept all of the teachings of the church as essential to their faith. The remainder (59%) make a distinction between the teachings of the church and the quality of their faith lives, believing that there is no reason why they cannot reject some church teaching and continue to have a deep Christian faith. Nevertheless, most (75%) say that their church is "the true church" of Christ.

Control of Life

In matters of providence and free will, Catholics believe that God intervenes in the daily circumstances of people's lives (70%), but seem less sure (54%) whether or not God also intervenes in the affairs of society. Predestination, or the role of God in individual salvation, however, is an issue that divides the group. Almost one-third (30%) believe that some people are simply predestined or marked by God to be saved; more (42%) think that is not so.

Death

Catholics say that when people who are close to them die, they do not feel inclined to despair, because they believe that they will meet again (74%). Nevertheless, there is no consensus in the group about whether they should hear more in church about life here (42%) or life hereafter (19%), though the trend is to want guidance in circum- stances now. Catholics oppose both mercy killing (84%) and suicide (94%) more than any of the other denominations represented in the study.

Sin, Guilt and Compassion

Catholics in general (98%) did not agree that human nature is ab- solutely and completely evil, totally depraved, with no good in it. In fact, a significant portion (38%) believe instead that humans are inherently good and strive toward the good. The group is not con- vinced that Christians must believe all people are sinful. Some (35%) think that to be the case, but just as many (37%) do not. In the same fashion 40% consider themselves sinful, while 36% say they know they fall short and make many mistakes but do not consider these situations culpable. They are inconclusive whether circumstances (32%) or an innate tendency to sin (28%) is responsible for the evil that people do.

Social Issues

Though the convinced majority is not great (59%), the general tendency among Catholics in the study was to favor the position that taking leadership in social justice issues such as racism, sexism, and economic concerns is a mission of the church. Consequently, about as many (55%) believe that true Christianity requires that the poor and oppressed be liberated. Fewer, however, (39%) believe that Christi- anity requires a far-reaching change in American society and its eco- nomic system or that it is necessary for Americans to develop simpler life-styles (41%).

Foreign Policy and War

The majority of Catholics (53%) who participated in the Faith and Ferment project felt that churches should express themselves on mat- ters of government and foreign policy. Yet many (32%) say that they do not find the teaching of Scripture or the church clear and consistent on the relationship of Christianity to war, and the remainder of the group is largely unsure what faith demands in these situations. That there is so little coalescence around any single response serves to confirm the confusion. Nevertheless, most of these Roman Catholics (58%) feel that no church should ever give unqualified support to any war. That the U.S. must be Number One in the military force it possesses is given limited (33%) clear support. On the contrary, Minnesota Catholics in this study are in strong favor (75%) of negotiations between the U.S. and the U.S.S.R. to eventually outlaw nuclear weapons, and they support (72%) relationships with communist nations as a general rule, a fact that seems to indicate that these Christians do not see the avoidance of communism as an essential of the faith.

Church

Catholics endorse the concept of church unity strongly (83%), but are not much committed to the practice of open communion (33%). Two-thirds of the respondents (67%) feel that new converts to Christ should be given freedom to join the church of their choice. Just over half (54%) feel that if Christ had not risen from the dead, Christian teaching would have very little value for them.

Lutherans

Suffering and Crisis

For most Lutherans (68%) the existence of evil in the world is no deterrence to the belief that God is a loving God. But there is no clear consensus in the group as to whether the calamities of life are or are not the result of sin. Almost half (44%) think that sufferings and crises are not the result of sin, while almost one-third think that is the case. At the same time, 48% agree that, whatever its source, suffering is a reminder of the human being's dependence on God.

Relationships

Artificial birth control and family planning are an accepted part of Lutheran morality (84%). Only 22% consider abortion always wrong or sinful, but they are firm in their rejection of extramarital sex (86%), and to a lesser but substantial degree, of premarital sex (64%). Homosexuality is regarded as immoral by most (64%), but many (35%) are inclined to say that homosexuality is either regrettable or permissible. Lutherans tend to believe (51%) that sex education in the schools should be mandated.

They oppose racial discrimination in any Christian church (96%) and think, in general (62%), that churches should be active in the attempt to improve the position of minority peoples in American life. The idea that women and men are created equal is accepted by most (90%). Most endorse and support the women's movement (59%) and, for the most part (52%), believe that women should have equal places with men in the ministry of the church.

Personal Spiritual Development

Lutherans (88%) have a high sense of the presence of God as active in guiding their personal lives. Almost all of the Lutherans who participated in the study (91%) recognize the Bible as the authoritative Word of God. They (86%) see the reading of Scripture as an important part of their own spiritual development. Many (49%) take the position that the Bible is an actual report of what God said and in the original text contained no errors. Some (36%) accept all of the teachings of the church as essential to faith, but the balance (64%) of these church members say that they can have a deep Christian faith whether they hold all the teachings of the church or not. About half of the group (53%) claim that theirs is "the true church" of Christ.

Control of Life

God does intervene in the daily circumstances of people's lives, most Lutherans (74%) say, though not as many (66%) are willing to argue that God intervenes in the affairs of society. The Lutheran community in this study divided in almost equal parts over the question of predestination. Some (28%) accept that position; some (36%) reject the idea; some (35%) declined to take a firm position on either side of the question.

Death

Most Lutherans (67%) believe that they will be united in an afterlife with people they have loved on earth, but they are divided over whether the church should deal more with life here (26%) or hereafter (22%). They are not inclined to accept mercy killing, even if its use is controlled by law (74%), and are even more rejecting of the concept that individuals have the right to end their own lives anytime they choose (93%).

Sin, Guilt, and Compassion

Though Lutherans do not widely believe (26%) that human nature is totally good, they do not generally believe (23%) that it is totally depraved either. They say, rather, that the essence of the human being, human nature, is not evil (43%). At the same time, they are more convinced that a Christian must believe that all people are sinful (78%), and do indeed think of themselves as sinful (72%). Nevertheless, not nearly as many of the group (43%) tend to believe that an innate tendency to sin, and not simply circumstances, is responsible for evil.

Social Issues

Less than half (45%) of the Lutherans asked were firm believers in the idea that part of the mission of the church is to exert leadership in social justice issues such as racism, sexism, and economic concerns, and even fewer (36%) think that true Christianity requires that the poor and oppressed be liberated or that Christianity requires a change in American society (29%). About half (49%) agreed that at the present time a Christian way of life implies the discriminating use of technology to make life better.

Foreign Policy and War

Consistent with their position on the relationship of the church to social issues, Lutherans are hesitant (43%) to say that the churches should express themselves on foreign policy. Few (22%) say that Scripture and the teachings of the church on war are clear and consistent, but a significant portion (39%) believe that no church should ever give unqualified support to any war, and their responses reflect the disparate attitudes: one-third call clearly for the U.S. to be second to none in military force, but another part (20%) are opposed to that proposition. Nonetheless, most (66%) prefer that Christians be strong advocates of nuclear disarmament, and they argue, too (77%), for interaction with the communist nations.

Church

Church unity (76%) and open communion (58%) are valued in the Lutheran tradition. Slightly over three-fourths (76%) of the respondents agree that new converts to Christ should be allowed to join the church of their choice. More than half of this group (62%) believe that if Christ had not risen from the dead, Christian teaching would mean very little to them.

Presbyterians

Suffering and Crisis

The fact that there is evil in the world does not presuade the Presbyterians in the sample that God is an unloving God (73%). On the other hand, they give much less credence (16%) to the idea that illness, calamity, and other forms of suffering and crisis are the result of sin or that suffering is to remind us of our dependence on God (39%).

Relationships

Family planning through artificial means is moral as far as Presbyterians are concerned (92%), and very few (7%) think that abortion is always wrong or sinful. Almost half (49%) consider abortion permissible in extreme cases, and a full third (34%) say it should be a matter of personal choice. In a manner similar to the other denominations, they are largely opposed (82%) to extramarital sexual relations but less firm (63%) in their opposition to premarital sex. Homosexuality, too, is somewhat more acceptable among the Presbyterians in the sample: barely more than half (55%) said it is always wrong or sinful; over a third (34%) feel that homosexual relations are permissible between consenting adults or ought to be a matter of personal choice. Over half of this population, too (55%), feel that sex education should be a required part of the public school curriculum.

Presbyterians reject the notion of racial discrimination in the churches (93%) and are promoters of church leadership for minority rights as a mission of the church (71%). Most of them (97%) said that men and women are created equal in God's sight, and most, though less (71%), supported or endorsed the women's movement and the place of women in the ministry of the church (79%).

Personal Spiritual Development

Presbyterians perceive God to be active in their personal lives (88%) and consider the Bible to be God's authoritative Word on earth (91%). They consider Scripture a necessary part of their spiritual lives (87%) but are rather equally divided over whether it is a verbal report of

God's Word and without error in the original (34%), or the Word of God that has come to us through fallible people and so must be judged by reason (31%), or the Word of God but marred by errors of communication as it has been passed down through the centuries (29%). They make a clear distinction between Christian faith and the acceptance of the teaching of the church and see no reason why they cannot reject some of the authority of the church and still remain faithful to God (81%). Few Presbyterians (22%) called their church "the true church" of Christ.

Control of Life

Presbyterians (79%) are relatively sure that God is present and active in their lives and more convinced than most (72%) that God acts in the affairs of society as well. For Presbyterians, too, the question of predestination is unclear. Some (36%) accept it; some (35%) just as firmly do not.

Sin, Guilt, and Compassion

Presbyterians were most comfortable with the thesis that the human being is not essentially evil (49%) but believe even more strongly (65%) that it is essential for a Christian to believe that all people are sinful. Most (59%) consider themselves sinful and are more inclined to see sin (36%) and not circumstance (24%) as the explanation of evil. Nevertheless, the concept is obviously not a settled one in the church, or at least in the people.

Social Issues

Presbyterians, more than any other church members in the study (57%), want the church to take leadership in social justice as part of its mission. They feel, too, that true Christianity requires the liberation of the oppressed (51%). Some (37%) have the sense that American society and its economic system must change if the culture is to be truly Christian. What is more, 47% assumed that at this moment in history a Christian way of life implies the development of simpler lifestyles.

Foreign Policy and War

The average Presbyterian in the study thinks that churches must speak to the foreign policy of the country (51%), but few (29%) are sure that the teachings of the church or the Scripture itself gives clear guidance about the place of Christians in war. Even so, they believe on balance (53%) that churches should not give total support to any war. Like the other Christian peoples observed in Minnesota, they are divided on whether or not the U.S. must achieve military supremacy. Only a portion (28%) are completely convinced that this is the case, but many more (76%) actually want the U.S. to negotiate with the U.S.S.R. for the elimination of nuclear weapons. On the other hand, they are well united (79%) in their opinion that the avoidance of communist nations is not a facet of faith.

Church

Presbyterians look forward both to church unity (81%) and open communion (89%), and the majority (85%) agree that new converts to Christ should be allowed to join the church of their choice. Most (59%) feel that had Christ not risen from the dead, Christian teaching would have little meaning for them.

Episcopalians

Suffering and Crisis

The presence of evil in the world is no proof that God is not a loving God, as far as most Episcopalians (69%) in the study are concerned. Few (12%) see suffering as a result of sin, and few (23%) agree that the function of suffering is to recall people to a sense of dependence on God.

Relationships

In the Episcopalian world view as it emerged in this study, artificial birth control is morally acceptable (89%), and abortion, too, is not sinful, at least under some circumstances (86%). Extramarital sex is never moral (78%) but in comparison premarital sex is considered sinful to relatively few (42%). Homosexuality is marked totally and absolutely wrong by an even smaller part of the sample (38%). Sex education in the schools is considered imperative by most (64%).

To the Episcopalian the church has a social mission to minority peoples (72%), and women are equal to men (98%). Almost no one (10%) claimed to oppose or be generally unsympathetic toward the women's movement, but only two-thirds (68%) of the group felt that women should have equal place with men in the ministry.

Personal Spiritual Development

Fewer Episcopalians (78%) than other Christians in the study claimed that God is actively present in their lives as guide or decision maker. They see the Bible as the Word of God and necessary to Christianity (84%), but do not see it as important to their own spiritual lives (65%), as most of the Christians from other denominations do. They are also more prone to feel (52%) that the Bible must be judged by reason. The teachings of the church are not a measure of faith for these people (81%), and only some (25%) call themselves "the true church" of Christ.

Control of Life

Most Episcopalians (67%) feel that God does intervene in tangible ways in the occurrences of personal life, but, like most of the other Christians surveyed, they are less sure (54%) that God intervenes on the level of social affairs as well. Most are unsure about God's role in salvation, but 46% do not accept the theology of predestination.

Death

Barely half of the Episcopalians questioned (51%) think that they will see their loved ones again after death, and 49% want to hear more about life on earth when they go to church than about life hereafter. They do not believe that suicide is a natural right (76%), nor do most believe that mercy killing can benefit society (62%), even if its use is controlled by law.

Sin, Guilt, and Compassion

More than any other denomination, Episcopalians were basically agreed (60%) that human nature is not essentially evil, and only a portion of them (38%) firmly believe that Christians must regard all people as sinful. Most of them, however (55%), do see themselves as sinful, but were divided over whether or not it is sin (30%) or circumstance (22%) that is responsible for the evil that people do.

Social Issues

Among Episcopalians there is a tendency to believe, but not a clear conviction in the group as a whole (42%), that it is a mission of the church to take leadership in liberation movements like racism, sexism, and economic concerns. Fewer than that (38%) accept the notion that liberation of the oppressed is a goal of true Christianity. Fewer still (29%) take as a matter of faith that Christianity requires change in American society and its economic system. Almost two-thirds (65%), however, take the position that technology should be used in a discriminating manner to make life better.

Foreign Policy and War

Episcopalians show limited (37%) firm support for the idea that churches should express themselves on matters of government foreign policy. The largest single group of them (41%) take the position that the Bible and historic Christian tradition are unclear guides on the question of whether or not Christians may support war, but the majority (67%) think that churches should not give wholehearted support to any war. Not many Episcopalians (27%) felt strongly that the U.S. must be second to none in the military force it possesses, and one-third were actually opposed to that idea. They do not believe that the churches should obstruct international relations with communist countries (91%), and they support Christian advocacy of negotiations to outlaw nuclear weapons (70%).

Church

More strongly than any other group, Episcopalians said that the various Christian denominations should try to achieve greater unity than they now have (88%). Open communion is a high priority (83%), and the vast majority (91%) believe that new converts to Christ should have freedom to join any church of their choice. Members of the Episcopal church are not strong (39%) in their belief that Christ's resurrection gives value to Christian teachings.

Methodists

Suffering and Crisis

Unlike the other denominational responses, only slightly more than half of the Methodists surveyed in the course of this research (55%) believed that evil can take place in a world in which there is a loving God. On the other hand, there is little support among them for the idea that suffering, illness, and human calamity are the result of sin (12%). Some Methodists (37%) believe that one of the purposes of suffering is to remind us of our need for God. Just as many (36%) felt that this was not so.

Relationships

Almost the entire Methodist sample (91%) rejected the position that artificial methods of birth control are immoral. Few (15%) feel that abortion is always wrong, and a good many considered it not only permissible in certain cases (36%) but simply a matter of personal choice (32%). A firm majority (74%) considered extramarital sex sinful, but here, too, more Methodists (18%) considered it a matter of personal choice than any of the other respondents. A slight majority (58%) regarded premarital sex sinful, but less than half (46%) held that homosexuality was totally immoral. Methodists were more supportive of sex education in the public school (69%) than were any of the other denominations involved.

Most of the Methodists (65%) expect the church to help improve the position of minority groups—Indians, blacks, and Latin Americans—as a proper part of its mission. They are firm, too (96%), in the position that women and men are equal, but far fewer (66%) say that they endorse or support the women's movement or believe that women and men should have an equal place in the ministry of the church (74%).

Personal Spiritual Development

The Methodists in the survey felt sure (79%), as did most of the other denominations, that God is at work in their lives, helping them to make determinations and giving direction. They accept the Bible as the authoritative Word of God (82%) and see it as an important part of their own spiritual development (75%). Nevertheless, most (65%) leave room for error in it, in one way or another, without ceasing to see it as the Word of God. Most (79%) do not feel that accepting all the teachings of the church is an essential part of the faith life. Few (27%) of the Methodists identified their church as "the true church."

Control of Life

Intervention by God in the daily affairs of life is taken for granted among the Methodist church members in this study (72%). Whether or not God intervenes in the affairs of society at large is another question, and fewer people (60%) are as convinced of that. Methodists do not take a concerted position on the issue of predestination, as is the case in most denominations. The largest proportion (38%) reject the teaching, but a substantial minority (26%) do feel that some people are predestined for salvation.

Death

The Methodist believers in the survey are not fully convinced (53%) that they will again see those close to them who have died, and the greatest number of respondents feel sure that the church should concentrate on life here (38%) more than it should emphasize life hereafter (13%). Methodists are strongly opposed to suicide (87%), but much less closed to mercy killing (57%).

Sin, Guilt, and Compassion

To the Methodist, apparently, human nature is not essentially evil (56%). Some (29%) assume, in fact, that humans are inherently good, and unless they are brutalized by savagery they will strive toward what is good. Yet half say, too, that a Christian must believe that all people are sinful, but are less inclined (42%) than church members from other groups to consider themselves sinful. The Methodists sort into thirds over whether or not circumstances or innate sinfulness accounts for the evil that people do: one-third agree; one-third disagree; one-third hold neither opinion entirely.

Social Issues

Many Methodists (46%) look to their church for leadership in such social areas as racism, sexism, and economic concerns, but only a minority (39%) believe that Christianity requires redress for the poor and oppressed. Few (35%) are convinced that Christianity itself requires a change in American society and economic system. Over half (55%) are convinced that in the present time a Christian way of life implies that technology should be used with discrimination to make life better.

Foreign Policy and War

Exactly half of the Methodists adopted the premise that the church should express itself on matters of foreign policy, but, like every other tradition, Methodists held widely differing opinions on whether or not the church and the Bible are clear and consistent on the subject of war. Some (27%) find the teaching apparent; others (18%) do not; the majority in between qualify their answers. Perhaps for that reason, other related data are uneven. More than half of the population (56%) are convinced that the church should not give unqualified support to any war. At the same time many Methodists (40%) thought that the U.S. should be second to none in its military force. But, then again, most Methodists (76%) reported also that Christians should advocate negotiations to limit and outlaw nuclear weapons and support relations with communist nations (80%) as the proper Christian approach.

Church

As a group, Methodists want church unity (71%), but they are considerably more hesitant about this than any of the other denominations. At the same time they appear to be highly committed (87%) to the quest for open communion in the Christian churches. A strong majority (88%) of the Methodist respondents favor giving new converts to Christ freedom to join a church of their choice. Less than half (46%) believe that the resurrection of Christ is basic to the meaningfulness of Christian teaching.

Baptists

Suffering and Crisis

Unlike other groups in the study, most Baptists (85%) are certain that the evil on earth is no reflection on the loving character of God. On the other hand, they are less convinced (17%) than others that it is the result of sin. For most Baptists (61%), suffering is believed to be a reminder of the human need for God.

Relationships

Artificial birth control is almost universally accepted (90%) by the Baptist Christians who participated in this study, and abortion is basically permissible (70%). But most of those who see abortion as morally permissible feel that, to justify abortion, the case must be extreme (48%). On the other hand, extramarital sex is roundly condemned (90%), as are premarital sexual relations (83%), a much higher rejection of premarital sex than in any of the other churches. Homosexuality is considered always wrong or sinful (90%) and again by a much higher percentage of these respondents than of those from the other denominations surveyed. Finally, fewer Baptists (32%) than other Christians believe that every pupil should have courses in sex education in the public schools, although many (46%) say that this may be a regrettable but necessary trend.

Baptists deplore discrimination in the churches but depart from the other denominations, too, in their more hesitant (49%) acceptance of the idea that helping to improve the position of minority groups is part of the mission of the church. They are convinced that men and women are created equal (98%), but much less supportive (51%) of the women's movement. Finally, Baptists are not largely (32%) accepting of the idea that women and men should be entitled to equal places in church ministry.

Personal Spiritual Development

Like the rest of the Christian community in the survey, 88% of the Baptists believe that God is guiding their lives in direct ways. In their opinion, the Bible is the actual Word of God and the authority on which their faith is based (90%). Reading the Bible is a more important part of their spirituality than it is for any of the other groups (95%), and most of them believe that the original text contains no errors (63%) and is to be seen as a verbatim message from God. Perhaps as a consequence of this intense focus on Scripture, most of them (73%) see no reason why they cannot reject some teaching of the church and continue to have a deep Christian faith. Some Baptists (33%) identified their church as "the true church," but an even larger number of them (43%) chose not to make that claim.

Control of Life

The Baptists in this survey are firmly convinced (81%) that the intervention of God is a real part of daily life. They feel to a greater extent (71%) than the other denominations that God's intervention in the affairs of society is also certain. Nevertheless, like many of the other churches, they are divided on the question of predestination. A fraction (29%) take the firm position that some people are destined to be saved, a large number accept that theology with reservations (39%), but a significant portion (22%) are firmly opposed to the idea.

Death

Most Baptists (61%) believe that there is an afterlife in which they will see again the people they have cared for on earth. Furthermore, only 34% look to the church to attend more to life here and now than to life hereafter. Life, they seem to believe, is in the hands of the Maker and not to be shortened either by suicide (85%) or by the controlled use of mercy killing (63%).

Sin, Guilt, and Compassion

Unlike any of the other groups, more than half of the Baptists represented (51%) declared that "human nature is absolutely and completely evil, totally depraved and has no good in it." They hold (78%) that Christians must believe that all people are sinful and that they themselves are sinful (71%). Of all the groups surveyed, they alone consider Satan a personal being rather than an evil force (65%). And they most of all (68%) reject the suggestion that circumstances are more responsible for the evil that people do than any innate tendency toward sin.

Social Issues

Though they tend to agree with the position "slightly" (42%), Baptists show little firm commitment (24%) to the thesis that it is a mission of the church to make God's love present by taking leadership in social justice issues such as racism, sexism, and economic concerns. Only one-fourth agree that true Christianity requires that the poor and oppressed be liberated (27%) or that American society and its economic system need to be changed if the U.S. is to be a Christian nation (28%). More than half (53%) believe that the discriminating use of technology to make life better ought to be the Christian posture at this time.

Foreign Policy and War

Baptists (29%) are less sure than other Christian groups that the churches should express themselves on matters of government foreign policy, but at the same time, these Baptists are more inclined (32%) than most of the other Christians in the study to feel that the Bible and the teaching tradition of the church is clear and consistent on the question of whether or not Christians may support war. Baptists (43%) hold to a greater percentage than other church members that the U.S.

must be second to none in the military force it possesses and are much less committed (42%) than other denominations to advocating negotiations between the U.S. and the U.S.S.R. for the limitation and eventual outlaw of nuclear weapons. At the same time they are clearly opposed (83%) to the position that we should avoid all relations with communist nations.

Church

Baptists are less intent (59%) about the question of church unity than others are, but they support the premise that the sacrament of Holy Communion should be open to members of other denominations (73%). Also, most Baptist respondents (83%) feel that new converts to Christ should be allowed to worship at a church of their own choice.

More than all other Christians asked, Baptists (83%) believe that if Christ had not risen from the dead, Christian teaching would have little importance in their lives.

United Church of Christ

Suffering and Crisis

The fact that evil exists in the world is not a major obstacle to faith in a loving God for most (62%) of the members of the United Church of Christ. However, unlike most of the other church members represented in our study, they are greatly opposed to the contention that suffering and crisis are the result of sin (76%). Few see it as a way by which we are reminded of our dependence on God (21%).

Relationships

UCC members accept artificial birth control without question (98%), and abortion to almost the same degree (93%), but with qualifications. Some (33%) contend that abortion, though not always wrong or sinful, should be permitted only in extreme cases. Some (30%) feel it should be permissible for those women who have received counseling and have come to a conscientious decision. Another 30% argue that abortion should simply be a matter of choice. Whatever the case, UCC members are the most accepting, of all the Christian respondents, of the practice of abortion. Like the others, though, they do not easily tolerate extramarital sex. A large majority (84%) find that "always wrong or sinful." At the same time, they are considerably more accepting of premarital sex than most other groups represented. Barely more than a third (37%) find it "always wrong or sinful." Not even that number (33%) take the position that homosexuality is also "always wrong or sinful." Most UCC members (61%) want sex education to be a required part of the public school curriculum.

Human rights are a major issue among the members of this denomination. They take a clear position (71%) that the church is obliged to promote the human welfare of minority groups. It is consistent, then, to find that they not only say that women and men were created equal by God (98%) but support and endorse the women's movement (79%) and believe (79%) that women and men should have equal place in the ministry of any denomination.

Personal Spiritual Development

These church members are convinced (68%), but to a lesser degree than the others surveyed, that God does take an active part in the daily direction of their lives. There is also less certainty among them about whether Christians must believe that the Bible is the authoritative Word of God (67%). It is not surprising, then, to see that fewer UCC members (58%) consider the reading of the Bible to be an extremely important element in the development of their spiritual lives. The greater portion of them (39%) feel that the Bible communicates the Word of God but that since God spoke through fallible people there are errors in it which must be judged by human reason. More UCC members (16%) than other participants in the study take the position that the Bible is the record of the early moral and religious progress of the Hebrews and Christians which contains much wisdom from great human beings but which we cannot be sure contains any divine element. They feel, as well, that there is no reason why they cannot reject some church teaching and continue to have a deep Christian faith (88%), and fewer of them (13%) than of any other denomination say that their church is "the true church" of Christ.

Control of Life

Few more than half (56%) of the group are firmly convinced that God intervenes in their daily lives. And almost the same number (52%) feel that God intervenes in the affairs of society also. They are more concerted than any other group in their rejection of predestination (50%).

Death

The UCC community (39%) has much less real expectation than others that they will meet in another life those whom they have loved on earth, and are more sure (59%) than others that they should hear more in church about life here and now than about life hereafter. But whatever happens in the next life, they oppose suicide (77%) and mercy killing (60%) as the proper end to life here.

Sin, Guilt, and Compassion

Most UCC members (66%) do not consider human nature evil, but they are unsure whether all people are sinful or not. Some (37%) consider that true; others (35%) disagree completely with a theology that maintains that people are inherently sinful, and they are as equally divided over the question of whether or not they themselves are sinful. They are inconclusive about whether circumstances (28%) or an innate tendency toward sin (25%) accounts for the evil that people do.

Social Issues

In the UCC 54% agree that the church should take a leadership position on social issues because the mission of the church demands it. They (49%) believe that true Christianity requires that the poor and oppressed be liberated, but are not sure (27% agree, 29% disagree) whether or not that implies a far-reaching change in American society and its economic system. A discriminating use of technology to make life better is considered to be a Christian imperative by over half (56%) of the UCC members sampled.

Foreign Policy and War

The trend in this church (43%) is to expect churches to express themselves on matters of foreign policy but at the same time to declare the teaching of the church unclear and inconsistent in regard to war (38%). The members (44%) tend to feel that no church should give unqualified support to any war. As is the case with most of the groups, not many (32%) are willing to contend without qualification that the country must have military supremacy. On the contrary, this church group is strong (76%) in its contention that Christians should be advocates of American-Soviet negotiations to eliminate nuclear weapons. They are also clearly opposed (87%) to the notion that Christians should insist that as a country we avoid communist nations and have nothing to do with them.

Church

The United Church of Christ is a strong supporter of church unity (84%), and an even stronger advocate of open communion (94%). Almost all the respondents (95%) want new converts to Christ to be allowed to choose their own church. Slightly over one-fourth (27%) say that it is the resurrection of Christ that gives meaning to their Christian beliefs.

Evangelical Covenant Church

Suffering and Crisis

The members of the Evangelical Covenant Church canvassed in this study accept suffering as a part of life that tests the depth of their faith but does not determine it. For the most part (77%) they do not feel that the presence of evil in the world is incompatible with the notion of a loving God. Very few (23%) see illness, calamity, and other forms of suffering and crisis as a result of sin. Most (93%) do not expect less suffering in life simply because they have attempted to lead faithful religious lives, but many (46%) do believe that suffering reminds us of our dependence on God.

Relationships

Most (60%) accept divorce as a necessary provision to alleviate insurmountable human problems. Only 5% of the Evangelical Covenant population surveyed said that artificial methods of birth control and family planning are immoral, with 22% of the sample believing abortion "always wrong or sinful." Extramarital sex is unacceptable to most Evangelical Covenant members (92%), as is premarital sex, though to a somewhat lesser degree (84%). Most (78%) of the group considered homosexuality totally immoral. Less than half (45%) of the group feel that every pupil should have a course in sex education in school.

Those Minnesota members of the Evangelical Covenant Church substantially agreed (89%) that racial discrimination is anti-Christian, but far fewer (53%) felt that helping to improve the status of minority peoples was part of the mission of the church. Furthermore, though they are concerted (95%) in their understanding that men and women are created equal in God's sight, a considerable number of them (40%) are generally unsympathetic toward the women's movement. At the same time, almost half of the group (49%) feel that women should have an equal place with men in the ministry of the church.

Personal Spiritual Development

Almost all Evangelical Covenant members (91%) believe that God plays an active part in guiding their lives and helping them to make decisions. The same percentage consider the Bible the authoritative Word of God, and even more (93%) consider the reading of Scripture important for the development of their spiritual lives. A small majority (57%) believe that the Bible contains no errors and that it is a verbal report of the message of God; 43% do not make that affirmation. Less than a third (28%) say they accept all of the teachings of the church as essential to their faith. The remainder (72%) make a distinction between the teachings of the church and the quality of their faith lives, believing that there is no reason why they cannot reject some church teaching and continue to have a deep Christian faith. Slightly over a third (35%) say that their church is "the true church" of Christ.

Control of Life

In matters of providence and free will, a large percentage of these Evangelical Covenant Christians (89%) believe that God intervenes in the daily circumstances of people's lives, and almost as many (83%) believe that God also intervenes in the affairs of society. Predestination, or the role of God in individual salvation, is an issue that divides the group. Over one-fourth (28%) believe that some people are simply predestined by God to be saved; somewhat more (39%) think that is not so.

Death

Most Evangelical Covenant members (67%) say that when people who are close to them die, they do not feel inclined to despair, because they believe that they will meet again. Nevertheless, there is little consensus in the group about whether they should hear more in church about life here (33%) or life hereafter (20%), though the trend is to want guidance in circumstances now. These Christians strongly oppose both mercy killing (79%) and suicide (94%).

Sin, Guilt, and Compassion

A majority of Evangelical Covenant members (61%) did not agree that human nature is absolutely and completely evil, totally depraved and with no good in it. A few (12%) believe instead that humans are inherently good and strive toward the good. Most (83%) feel that Christians must believe all people are sinful; 11% do not. In the same manner, most consider themselves sinful (75%), while a few (9%) say they know they fall short and make many mistakes but do not consider those situations culpable. For a slight majority (58%) an innate tendency to sin is responsible for the evil that people do.

Social Issues

Among the Evangelical Covenant respondents, 41% favor the position that taking leadership in social justice issues such as racism, sexism, and economic concerns is a mission of the church. Consequently, about as many (34%) believe that true Christianity requires that the poor and oppressed be liberated, with another 27% leaning in that direction. Fewer, however, (27%) believe that Christianity requires a far-reaching change in American society and its economic system or that it is necessary for Americans to develop simpler life-styles (37%).

Foreign Policy and War

A minority of the Evangelical Covenant members who participated in the Faith and Ferment study (38%) felt that churches should express themselves on matters of government and foreign policy. A number (29%) say that they do not find the teaching of Scripture or the church clear and consistent on the relationship of Christianity to war, while 24% find consistency there. The remainder of the group is largely unsure what faith demands in these situations. That there is so little coalescence around any single response serves to confirm the confusion. Nevertheless, a majority of these respondents (55%) feel that no church should ever give unqualified support to any war. That the U.S. must be number one in the military force it possesses is given limited (37%) clear support. On the other hand, 60% of the Evangelical Covenant Minnesotans in this study favor negotiations between the U.S. and the

U.S.S.R. to eventually outlaw nuclear weapons, and 78% support relationships with communist nations, which seems to indicate that these Christians do not see the avoidance of communism as an essential of the faith.

Church

Respondents from the Evangelical Covenant Church endorse the concept of church unity (62%). They are committed to the practice of open communion (78%) and strongly (88%) believe that new converts to Christ should be given the opportunity to choose their own church. A strong majority (71%) feels that if Christ had not risen from the dead, Christian teaching would have very little value for them.

So, there they are, the mainstream Christian churches of Minnesota. Standing alone, they seem obviously unclear about some things but disarmingly certain about others. In some areas there are signs of struggle: many say, for instance, that the church should exert an influence on foreign policy, but say that its teaching and Scriptures are unclear on the subject. They say they believe that God created women equal to men, but many say that equality cannot be permitted in the church itself. They say that most sexual behavior is acceptable, but claim that there should be sex education in the schools. Are those things signs of internal inconsistency, or part of the mystery called faith? And who is to say?

2

Concerning the Sample

ROBERT FULTON AND GREG OWEN

This is a study of Christian church members in Minnesota, both lay and clergy. The purpose of the study was to elicit their responses to a variety of questions dealing with moral, ethical, and religious issues. In order to solicit their cooperation, it was necessary to involve clergy in the process of respondent identification and selection. This was done not only for the purpose of facilitating the selection and insuring the participation of church members in the study, but also of comparing clergy and lay responses.

In order to obtain a random sample of active church members in Minnesota, a two-stage sampling design was employed. The first stage utilized the seven geographical regions identical to those employed in the reporting of state vital statistics. The seven regions are as follows: Northeast, Northwest, Central, West Central, Southwest, South Central, Southeastern, and Metro (which contains the Twin Cities of Minneapolis and St. Paul). Within each region two adjacent counties were selected at random to serve as sampling domains for the study. In this manner 14 counties were selected. They were St. Louis and Lake, Polk and Red Lake, Morrison and Stearns, Otter Tail and Grant, Yellow Medicine and Lyon, Nicollet and Blue Earth, Olmsted and Fillmore, Hennepin and Anoka. Once the counties had been identified, all current regional phone directories with listings in the selected counties were obtained for the purpose of enumerating each Christian church within the sampling domain. Churches were then selected at random from the phone lists. This was done in such a way as to ensure representation from each of the regions proportional to the population of each region.

In all, 210 churches were selected. A letter was composed that described the study, solicited the clergy's cooperation, assured the anonymity of respondents, and instructed the pastor as to the manner in which subjects were to be selected. As an encouragement to participate in the study a donation of $25 was offered to each church.

Subject selection of church members is a particularly difficult task, especially when one wishes to sample a wide variety of churches. This difficulty is increased when the questions are both personal and sensitive and require a substantial contribution of the respondent's time. The clergy, moreover, served as gatekeepers for the survey. Participation by the members of a congregation depended ultimately on whether the pastor could or would cooperate. Each pastor was asked to select 10 members of his or her congregation from the membership list. In addition, the pastors were asked to complete the questionnaire themselves.

As it turned out, the initial solicitation did not elicit a sufficient number of positive replies for us to feel confident about the representativeness or size of the sample. We therefore mailed out an additional solicitation to the 210 alternate churches that had been chosen from the telephone directories in anticipation of such a contingency. These alternate churches were selected from a different set of 14 counties chosen in the manner described previously. The alternate counties included: Koochiching and Itasca, Roseau and Lake of the Woods, Cass and Crow Wing, Clay and Becker, Meeker and Renville, Le Sueur and Waseca, Wabasha and Winona, Ramsey and Scott.

In all 420 pastors received a request to participate in the survey. Of these, 188 returned a postcard confirming their willingness to distribute questionnaires. Of this number 148 returned at least one questionnaire, while five returned all 11. In order to enhance the degree of participation in the study, a follow-up letter was sent to each minister who agreed to participate, and if the letter elicited no response, a telephone call was made. Ninety-eight pastors ultimately participated in the study together with 919 lay persons. Altogether 1017 lay and clergy

church persons throughout the state of Minnesota participated in the
study. The response rate falls between 49.2% and 60.9%.*

In addition to advising the subject that the survey was both scientific and anonymous, the instructions accompanying the questionnaire
indicated that the questionnaire would take approximately three hours
to complete. The respondent was encouraged to complete all of the
answers and, if necessary, to do this over several sittings. The subject
was informed that he or she could retain the questionnaire for two
weeks, if necessary. A printed, self-addressed envelope was provided
with the questionnaire. The effectiveness of the instructions and the
time provided for the completion of the questionnaire contributed to
the wealth and completeness of the information that was collected.
This is even more notable when we consider the fact that in addition
to questions dealing with religious beliefs and ideas, opinions and attitudes were also solicited on issues such as abortion, euthanasia, extramarital sex, and homosexuality. As the survey protocol involved 243
questions, we are appreciative of the clergy and church members who
participated in the study.

An examination of denominational affiliation and church size of
sampled churches shows a reasonable approximation to overall membership characteristics within the state. The social characteristics of
the participants in the study suggest that while the average income
approximates the statewide average, the median level of formal education reported is 14 years or 1.5 years greater than the statewide
median of 12.5 years.

All in all, the social characteristics of the sample provide reasonable

---

* The total sample size used in computing the response rate includes the
total number of questionnaires mailed to churches (2068) divided by the
total number of returns (1017). The resulting response rate of 49.2% is likely
to be an underestimate. The total sample-size figure may well include questionnaires that were never received by potential respondents. It should be
noted that of the 188 churches whose ministers agreed to participate in the
study, 40 are not represented by a single questionnaire. If we were to assume
that the ministers, for whatever reason, failed to distribute the questionnaires
to members of their parishes/congregations, then the maximum number of
questionnaires upon which a return rate could be based would be 1668
(allowing for the 40 questionnaires that the ministers would have received).
This means that maximally, the response rate for the study would be 60.9%.
The response rate falls between 49.2% and 60.9%. This return rate is not too
far out of line with what could reasonably be expected, given the nature of
the questionnaire and the circumstances under which it was distributed.

assurance that the participants in the study are broadly typical of Christian communicants in Minnesota. We fully recognize that rigorous scientific precision is not possible in view of the subject matter and the limits imposed by the nature of the sampling design followed in the study. The data presented, however, provide a reliable base upon which to achieve the stated aim of Faith and Ferment: "to produce hypotheses of weight concerning the dimensions, the problems and promise of the present situation."

Methodology of the Anthropological Probe

LUTHER P. GERLACH
AND BETTY RADCLIFFE

Research Models

We felt that combining the approaches of social drama (James Peacock, 1968; Victor Turner, 1969) and trouble case investigation (E. Adamson Hoebel, 1954) would help us in our study of Christian life in Minnesota. Thus, we selected for study cases of conflict which seemed to focus on problem areas in the social, political, technological, and religious aspects of our system, and to analyze how churches and church related groups related to or chose not to relate to these problem areas. In part this project built on and overlapped with our research since 1965 on social movements and citizen mobilization, chiefly as these movements and mobilizations have appeared in the U.S. and West Germany. We had studied in succession the movements of Neo-Pentecostalism (charismatic renewal), black power, ecology, anti-Vietnam War, and the energy concerns movements. (The latter is our term for a number of interrelated movements which include protest of nuclear energy facilities and uranium mining; fossil fuel development, use and transport, including mining, particularly surface mining, of coal; and power line and plant construction. This category also includes attempts to develop and promote solar based energy alternatives.) Indeed, social movements have become our main unit of study, and we have developed techniques to examine them.

We have not found it possible to study movements using in-depth studies of the small communities involved, although we do strive to learn as much as possible about the community context in which significant movement events and activities have taken place. Participants in movements are characteristically dispersed rather then geographically concentrated. Thus we have found it most useful to examine movements according to factors of social organization, recruitment, commitment, opposition, and ideology (Gerlach and Hine, 1970), and to combine in-depth interviews and observations, occasionally also using questionnaires. In these previous studies, we were often observing events in which movements interacted with the affected institutions, or more generally with what we have called "established orders." We came to see these events as ritual dramas which were often enhanced and carried far and wide by media coverage. We also found that people in these events came to see that these dramatic encounters helped to dramatize their concerns for issues. People in movements and in the established orders challenged by protest movements were like participants, taking opposite sides in a big debate about these issues. We came to call these polemic encounters "social debates," a term encompassing drama and trouble case approaches.

Social Debates Studied in This Project

When we began our research for the Faith and Ferment project, we were just completing our study of a movement of farmers and other rural people in Minnesota (with some comparative study in other states) who were protesting the construction of high voltage transmission lines across their land. We had also conducted a comparative study of protest against the construction of nuclear plants and nuclear reprocessing and storage facilities in Lower Saxony, West Germany. People and groups in these protest movements in turn shared ideology, purpose, and organizational affiliation with people and groups who were calling for the development of solar energy resources as alternatives to these conventional fossil and nuclear based energy systems.

We did enough comparative spot inquiries to determine that this action by these various protest groups and reactions by established energy industries and government were specific instances or cases in a larger class of events generating a big social debate about our global energy future. We also learned how this debate spun off to become a symbolic focus for more general debate about what scale of technology (large or small) and what level of political decision making (centralized or decentralized) would be best for our society. Further, it contributed to debate about whether economies should or could grow or whether they would be constrained by resource limits. We had found that these movements also became the focus for debates about the extent to which Christian beliefs call upon people to be stewards or to be masters or "subduers" of the earth. We found that churches and church leaders entered this debate about our energy future in many different ways: as mediators, as shapers or leaders of it, and as active participants taking sides in the polemic, while others entered it to actively say that the issue was not a church matter. We decided to build on these interconnected energy concerns cases in Minnesota by focusing on these church roles in this debate, and thus to begin to contribute to the study of Minnesota churches in social issues.

Similarly, we were also studying, for some other purposes, other cases in which protest movements had been interacting with established orders in social debates involving churches. One was the protest of the manner in which a number of multinational food or drug corporations were marketing infant formula in the Third World. Protesters claimed that the corporations were not acting responsibly because their marketing methods led women in the Third World to give up breast feeding in favor of commercial infant formula, which they could not afford, and which brought about malnutrition and infectious disease in their children. The groups involved in this dramatic protest for what they considered to be corporate responsibility were chiefly based in churches and church-related organizations. . . .

As we pursued the role of the Christian faith and church in these cases, we were continually searching and evaluating for study other cases reflecting conflict or social debate in which churches were playing key roles. . . . We identified several cases where churches or church affiliated ecumenical groups were fostering or acting as catalysts for projects to maintain or rebuild community vitality and/or harmony; to improve the quality, effectiveness, and coverage of certain social services or medical care; and for projects to work for greater understanding and more equitable treatment of differing religious, ethnic, or economic groups in the communities or neighborhoods in which these churches or groups were located. Corporate responsibility was an issue in some of these cases.

Our observations of events which Minnesota churches and church-based groups were actively concerned about, involved in, or playing leading roles in suggested that they defined or expressed issues in these cases in significantly more secular and materialist terms than in sacred or spiritual ones. We also observed an emphasis on the tactical use of church role in these cases, for example, in bestowing legitimacy and the suggestion of power in numbers. Thus, in our interviews of the parties involved, we sought to probe the sacred or spiritual motivations or bases of their actions and concerns.

As we began to conduct our Faith and Ferment study, essentially by building on our earlier study of these ongoing movements and social debates, we realized that even though we were adding cases in which churches were involved in what could be described as "social justice," social outreach, or service programs, or in which churches were playing particularly significant infrastructural roles in their communities or neighborhoods, we were still not identifying cases which would tell us about the full range of sociopolitical opinion and action among Minnesota churches and church members.

As we were exploring ways to approach the study of the more politically conservative and/or religiously fundamentalist side, we recognized that rather specific social debates such as those about pornography, abortion, public school curriculum (especially regarding sex education and the teaching of evolution and world cultures), and the Equal Rights Amendment were all the concerns of a new social movement which was rapidly growing and generating new debates in Minnesota, and indeed, across the country. It was a movement some observers were calling the "New Christian Right," or the "Moral Majority," or "fundamentalism." We found these terms inadequate and misleading. The people in the movement also agreed upon no specific term which could be used to identify all their various groups, activities, and concerns. Thus, because there seemed to be no better term already established in the literature or among the movement participants themselves, we coined the term Conservative Christian Activism, or CCA, as a working term in our research and later in our analysis and report writing. We found that while movement participants were initially reluctant to agree that this term was the label which would best encompass their particular group and concern, they reluctantly agreed that it was better than any other single term they could think of.

Our approach to the study of involvement of Minnesota churches and church members in social dramas or debates led us to focus a good deal of our research and analysis to understanding the CCA movement. One reason for this was that the CCA subsumed the majority of the social debates or social concerns posed by the more conservative side. Perhaps even more importantly, it became apparent it was in many issues a counter or countering force to more liberal social debates and concerns. Thus, the two together comprise a megasocial debate. The contrast between these two sides then served as a way of better understanding not only what each was, and what each stood for, but what each was not. This then became a way of understanding other churches and church members, not really aligned with either side, to ask them questions, and to define their positions, and then to see how they ranged along a continuum of belief and action. Referring to this contrast in interviews also seemed to provide a good way for people in a range of positions to overtly express their Christian beliefs and principles.

In general, then, we focused on the way the CCA movement participants were challenging what they identified as secular-humanistic and evolutionary teaching in order to influence the cultural level of concepts and values, and the way they were fighting specific courses of instruction in schools as well as promoting legislation dealing with abortion, sexual behavior, and family structure. We also examined how churches and church members identified as more liberal played active roles in quite different social issues and how they responded to this conservative mobilization and began to develop a countermovement. On the left and the right, the involvement of church as institution and as religious belief and practice affected the action and interaction with other forces and each other and contributed to changing social, political, economic, technological, and religious subsystems of the sociocultural system or way of life in Minnesota.

Techniques

Within this conceptual framework, what techniques did we use in collecting our information? We did this by using the characteristic social-cultural anthropological technique of observing events and interviewing people from across the range of groups participating in these events and these social debates. We tended to concentrate on people we regarded as key sources of information, representative of bodies of information within this range. When we were just exploring an issue and an involved group, our interviews were quite open-ended, and we encouraged the interviewee to take us where he or she thought appropriate. Thus, we began with ideas and facts which accorded with the interviewee's priorities, interests, and categories. As we learned more, however, we developed hypotheses and formulated specific sets of questions to ask, although we still tried to couch these according to the terminology and categories of the interviewees. These beginning interviews then generated information which led us to new sources of information about the kinds of issues we were examining and sometimes led us to new issues. We were also often led to new issues or especially contacts through various media or newsletter accounts.

Our interviews generally proceeded in stages, the first of which we used to explain who we were, or what our objectives were, and then to gain an overview of their concerns. From this, we were then able to move to in-depth, face-to-face interviews, and finally from the open-ended or unstructured type to increasingly specific structured interviews, using items which we were also asking others in other settings. The interviewees characteristically called our attention to important subject matter which we would probably not have considered if we had followed a tight, formalized interview schedule. Interviewees also called our attention to literature which they considered to be important. They displayed evidence supporting their positions in the form of school materials, news articles, newsletters, and books. They not only gave us other names or sources of information, but urged us to speak with many of these people or to attend specific events so that we could improve our knowledge of this subject. After we followed these leads and evaluated the data they produced, we were able to return to ask more specific questions. In time, at least with some of the individuals, we were able to follow up on some subjects and seek clarification on some points through phone interviews. This was particularly useful as we analyzed and wrote up our findings.

When we completed our draft report, we sent copies of relevant chapters to those who contributed to these chapters. We asked them to check these chapters for accuracy of data and how we were using the information we obtained. In this way we asked our sources of information to call our attention to what they regarded as inaccuracies, or misinterpretations, so that we could, if need be, make necessary changes. Through this we also wanted to increase our sensitivities to the concerns of our sources.

In some of our research, particularly in the energy, resource use, and social or corporate responsibility issues, we built upon research and contacts developed in previous studies. We returned to these previously established contacts with new questions about church life and church involvement as this related to their concerns. The subject of the CCA opened a new field of study, but some of it also overlapped with previous research Gerlach and Hine had conducted and reported on concerning the charismatic renewal movement. Once Gerlach and Radcliffe learned about the CCA through our more general observations and then increasingly structured interviews, we found it useful to apply to this new examination of the CCA, our well-developed model of movement structure and function which we have reported on in other publications. This model—with its categories of organization, recruitment, opposition, commitment, and ideology—provided a framework not only for posing specifically structured questions to our new sources of information in the CCA or regarding it, but also for later analysis.

Research Team Composition, Identification, and Ethics

The anthropological research team consisted of Luther Gerlach and Betty Radcliffe over the length of the program, and for a relatively short period, Amanda Martin. Gerlach was assisted in the majority of his interviews by his wife, who contributed as an unpaid assistant on the project, attending meetings and church gatherings either with the principal investigator, or alone, and joined Gerlach in conducting some interviews. We found that some women in the CCA were grateful that this was done, clearly preferring to discuss some subjects, such as sex education and sexual deviancy, with a woman present.

We recorded data in the field by taking extensive notes and, on occasion, taking tape recordings, and at times filming events with a 35-mm slide camera. We always asked permission to do such tape recording or filming, and on occasion we even asked permission to take notes.

To those whom we interviewed or observed, we always identified ourselves as researchers in anthropology, and sought to explain our project and describe its other participants and purposes. We found that while some sources did show concern about our aims and about possible consequences of our study, our frank discussion about this led to acceptance and to frank responses to our questions in almost all cases. In our explanations, we emphasized that we sought to take an objective view and to present an objective—that is, essentially non-judgmental—analysis of the subject, and that we did not at any time consider the purpose of our research to look for maladies or to find out who was right or wrong. Rather, as we had done in our previous studies of other social movements, we sought to understand how they work, and what their aims and concerns are. Since the people we were working with were primarily taking positions—and this way, indeed, why we were learning about them—some found it difficult to accept that we would, in fact, remain nonjudgmental, even if we were at the outset. There was some tendency to believe that once they laid out their views and their evidence we would come to share their views, since both liberal and conservative sides tend to anchor their belief system in absolutes, with the conservatives being very obvious about this.

4

Personnel of the Study

DESIGN GROUP

Robert Fulton, Professor, Department of Sociology, University of Minnesota

Greg Owen, Department of Sociology, University of Minnesota

Luther P. Gerlach, Professor, Department of Anthropology, University of Minnesota

Betty Radcliffe, Department of Anthropology, University of Minnesota

Paul E. Meehl, Regent Professor, Department of Psychology, University of Minnesota

Joan D. Chittister, O.S.B., Mt. St. Benedict Priory, Erie, Pennsylvania

Robert S. Bilheimer, Institute for Ecumenical and Cultural Research, Collegeville, Minnesota

During its early work, the Design Group benefited from the encouragement and participation of the late Donald W. Hastings, M.D., University of Minnesota.

STAFF

Robert S. Bilheimer, Project Director

Joan D. Chittister, O.S.B., Research Coordinator

Dolores Schuh, C.H.M., Assistant for Administrative and Editorial Services

James P. Shannon, Consultant to the Project Director

Mr. Fulton, Mr. Owen, Mr. Gerlach, and Ms. Radcliffe, acting in a consultative capacity, directed their aspects of the study. Margaret Brudos organized and conducted the personal interviews. Stephanie Campbell, O.S.B., prepared the abstract of the transcripts of the interviews. Mr. Meehl served as consultant.

BOARD OF DIRECTORS
OF THE
INSTITUTE FOR ECUMENICAL AND CULTURAL RESEARCH

J. Elmo Agrimson

Colman J. Barry, O.S.B.

Robert McAfee Brown

Peter M. Butler

Joan Chittister, O.S.B.

Calvin W. Didier

Charles M. Grace

Donald R. Grangaard

Richard Green

Louis H. Gunnemann

James A. Halls

Terrance Hanold

Thomas Hoyt Jr.

Ronald M. Hubbs

Hella Mears Hueg

Harold LeVander

Kilian McDonnell, O.S.B.

Mary Bigelow McMillan

Dean C. McNeal

Elizabeth Musser

Larry M. O'Shaughnessy

Laverne Phillips

H. C. Piper Jr.

Jack B. Rogers

Gordon Shepard

Clifford C. Sommer

John F. Stone

Thomas F. Stransky, C.S.P.

Jerome P. Theisen, O.S.B.

Hilary Thimmesh, O.S.B.

Carl A. Volz

Douglas Wallace

Cynthia C. Wedel

Paul M. Youngdahl

SUBCOMMITTEE ON FAITH AND FERMENT

Jerome P. Theisen, O.S.B.

Hella Mears Hueg

Larry M. O'Shaughnessy

Carl A. Volz

INDEX

Note: *Denominational differences and demographic distinctions are found at the end of each chapter in Part 1. For statistical differences regarding men-women, clergy-laity, urban-rural, age and education, see* Demographic distinctions.

Abortion, 30, 39, 40, 156, 211, 277
Acquavivia, S. S., 172
Affirmative action programs, 32
Afterlife; see *Life after death*
Ahlstrom, Sydney E., 283
Aim of Faith and Ferment, 11
American Indian, 31, 33, 40, 245, 282
Argyle, Michael, 172
Aries, Philippe, 197, 206
Armaments; see *Nuclear weapons*
Arminianism, 248
Asians, and discrimination, 32, 246
Authority in the home, 27

Baptism, 139, 152, 156
Baptists, 26, 30, 38, 39, 44, 45, 47, 56, 66, 80, 96, 107, 118, 128, 135, 152, 156, 157, 158, 159, 160, 172, 203, 211, 248, 259, 324-327
Beecher, Henry Ward, 205
Beecher, Lyman, 205
Bellah, Robert N., 218
Berger, Peter, 183
Bible, 74-76, 80, 81, 112, 160, 239, 254, 274
Bible, on war, 112, 120
Birth control, 29, 30, 39, 40, 156, 177, 209-210
Black power, 31, 77, 81, 252

Blacks, 31ff., 40, 160, 212, 245-246
Boas, George, 180, 181
Bonhoeffer, Dietrich, 247
Book of Concord, 223
Bossy, John, 179, 223
Bushnell, Horace, 175, 212

Callois, Roger, 169, 170
Calvinism, 195, 248
Cash, Johnny, 268, 269
Catholics; see *Roman Catholics*
Change, attitude toward, 183
Changing relationships, 25-41, 311-312, 314-315, 317, 319-320, 322, 324-325, 327-328, 330-331
Chittister, Joan, 168, 170-171, 187, 189, 204, 205, 206, 214, 215, 216, 222, 228, 229, 230, 241, 248, 252, 255, 279
Christian conscience, 92, 93, 97, 112-113
Christian conservatism, 147
Christianity and politics, 103
Christianity, continuity of, 234-237
Christian responsibility for life, 62, 63
Church, 78, 79, 80, 137ff., 217-224, 261-262, 314, 316-317, 319, 321, 324, 327, 330, 333

Church, and ecology, 127-128
Church, and economic justice, 106, 108
Church, and foreign policy, 111, 117-118
Church attendance, 79, 80, 81, 140, 151, 219, 222, 274, 297
Church, function of, 140-142, 157
Church, historical development, 219-222
Church in social issues, role of, 105, 108, 157, 299, 305-306
Church laws, obedience to, 93-94, 97, 157
Church membership, 147
Church, mission of the, 100, 107, 143-146, 149, 153, 157, 251, 274, 276, 280, 298, 313
Communication with spirits, 53, 58
Communism, 113, 116, 314
Community, 77-78
Compassion, 83-97, 313, 316, 318, 320, 323, 326, 329, 332
Congregationalists, 172
Conscience and law, 92-94, 160, 230, 274
Conservation and technology, 124-126; see *Ecology*
Conservative Christian activists, 30, 46, 86, 105, 144, 270, 341-342
Control of life, 60-69, 195-197, 312, 315, 318,

320, 322-323, 325, 328, 331
Covenant Church; see Evangelical Covenant Church
Creationism, 144
Cremation, 51, 58, 198, 274

Death, 49-59, 197-198, 312, 315, 320, 323, 326, 329, 331-332
Death penalty, 101, 107, 156
Death, right to, 50
Death, rituals of, 50-51
de Grazia, Sebastian, 185
Delumeau, Jean, 179, 217, 223
Demographic distinctions, 40, 47, 57, 67, 80, 96, 107, 119, 128, 135, 153
Denominational differences, 39, 46, 55, 65, 80, 96, 107, 118, 128, 135, 152; see Appendix 1
Depravity, 85, 90, 227-229
Determinism, 61, 64-65, 195, 196
Development and deviation, difference between, 226-231
Discipline of children, 27, 206
Dispensationalism, 221
Divorce, 28-29, 182, 207-209
Documentation of Faith and Ferment, 14-16
Douglas, Mary, 217
Dupre, Louis, 218

Eastern Orthodox, 12, 172
Ecology, 122-129
Economic aid to poor countries, 114, 119, 120, 276

Economic concerns, 102, 103, 104, 200-201, 207, 253, 275
Economic conservatives, 184
Economic justice, 106, 108, 114
Ecumenical development, 231-233, 275
Ecumenical movement, 9-10
Ecumenism, 149, 231, 275, 282, 301
Education, theological, of laity, 294
Electronic church, 151-152, 200
Elliott, Elizabeth, 205
Environmental concerns; see Ecology
Episcopal Church, 39, 45, 56, 57, 66, 71, 80, 152, 160, 172, 181, 220, 232, 259, 292, 319-321
Equal Rights Amendment, 36, 144
Eucharist, 151, 152, 215
Euthanasia, 30, 50, 101, 107, 156; see Mercy killing
Evangelical Covenant Church, 26, 38, 45, 55, 56, 66, 80, 152, 172, 259, 330-333
Evangelization, 133, 149, 158, 196
Evil, 43, 44, 45, 48, 68, 86-88, 158-159, 244-250, 273, 276, 297, 298

Faith and Ferment respondents as theologians, 167-168
Family planning, 29-30, 39
Family relationships, 29-30, 237-238
Fidelity in the family, 28-30, 237-238
Financial support of church; see Tithing

Finney, Charles Grandison, 178, 199
Foreign policy, 110-121, 255, 275, 276, 313-314, 316, 318-319, 321, 323-324, 326-327, 329-330, 332-333
Free will, 61, 62, 64, 87
Fundamentalism, 193, 221, 262, 341
Funerals, 51, 56, 57, 58, 59, 198

Genovese, Eugene, 197
German Evangelicals, 172
Gladden, Washington, 212
Global consciousness, 126
God and evil, relationship of, 43-44, 244-250
God as person, 73-74
God, presence of, 62, 67, 68, 72, 73, 77
Gossett, Thomas F., 212
Gothard, Bill, 205
Greven, Philip, 206
Groethuysen, Bernard, 179, 223
Guilt, 83, 89-90, 96, 198, 199, 313, 316, 318, 320, 323, 326, 329, 332
Guilty feelings, 83, 89, 198, 199

Hardon, John, 178
Hays, Edward, 288
Heaven, 94, 95, 96, 157, 160, 199
Heirarchicalism, 25, 205
Hell, 95, 97, 178, 199
Hispanics, 246
Hobsbawm, E. J., 184, 190
Holy Communion, 150, 152; see Eucharist
Holy Spirit, 73, 74, 250
Homosexuality, 38, 40
Huizinga, Johan, 169
Humanae Vitae, 177, 183, 210
Human nature, 84-85, 90

Incarnational gospel, 143, 144, 145
Infallibility, papal, 223
Interdisciplinary collaboration of Faith and Ferment, 13-14
Intervention of God in human life, 61-62, 66, 67, 68, 240

Jesus Christ as Son of God, 44, 73, 161, 216, 218, 274, 301
John Paul II, Pope, 215, 224

Kelsey, Morton, 285
Küng, Hans, 184

Latin Americans, 31, 40
Latter Day Saints, 172
LaVerdiere, Eugene, 285-286
Law and order, 241-242
Lewis, Sinclair, 278
Liberation, 170, 184
Liberation movements, 77, 252
Life after death, 52-53, 55, 56, 57, 58, 161, 240-241, 274
Luckmann, Thomas, 218
Lutherans, 26, 30, 39, 46-47, 55, 56, 66, 80, 96, 118, 152, 159, 172, 181, 186-187, 211, 223, 232, 259, 293, 314-317

Mainline Christianity, 181
Marriage, indissolubility of, 28-29, 206-207
Marriage vows, 28-29, 207
Mary, Mother of God, 73, 216
McCormick, Richard, 211
Mead, Sidney, 186
Menninger, Karl, 273

Mercy killing, 50, 56, 156; see Euthanasia
Methodists, 39, 44, 47, 55, 56, 66, 71, 107, 152, 157, 160, 161, 172, 180, 232, 248, 259, 292, 321-324
Methodologies of Faith and Ferment, 12-13
Military supremacy of U.S.A., 116, 118, 119, 120, 158, 276
Ministry to the suffering, 46-48
Minnesota, characteristics of, 174-175
Miracles, 61
Mission of the church; see Church, mission of the
Mitford, Jessica, 197
Moltmann, Jürgen, 247-248
Moral motivation, 90, 92, 95, 96
Morgan, Edmund, 206
Motivation, 92-96

Natural resources, protection of, 122-124
Natural resources, use of, 123-124, 126, 128
Neill, Stephen, 218
Newby, I. A., 213
Newman, John, 180, 183, 209
"New Religious Right," 46, 147, 260, 341
Niebuhr, H. Richard, 216
Niebuhr, Reinhold, 203, 227
Nuclear weapons, 116, 120, 255

Obedience, 27, 134, 206
Obedience to law, 92-94, 157
Occupation and Christian faith, 131, 135, 242
Open Communion, 150, 152, 232, 258, 275, 301
Open marriage, 29, 238

Ordination of women, 35, 37, 39, 40, 214, 215, 259
Organ transplants, 56
Orthopraxis, 287

Pannenberg, Wolfhart, 225
Parenting, 27-28
Parker, Theodore, 212
Parochial education, 152, 271
Paul VI, Pope, 209, 224
Peguy, Charles, 184
Personal relationship to God, 71-73
Personal spiritual development, 70-82, 312, 315, 317-318, 320, 322, 325, 328, 331
Pieper, Josef, 169, 170
Pluralism, 27, 193, 194, 303-304
Political process, participation in, 103, 107
Pollution, 126-128
Poor and oppressed, 100, 107, 108, 254
Prayer, 71-72, 77, 80, 238-239, 288, 297
Prayer, frequency of, 26, 71, 239, 269, 274, 296
Presbyterians, 39, 46, 56, 65, 66, 96, 107, 119, 128, 135, 152, 161, 172, 181, 232, 259, 317-319
Predestination, 53, 158, 301
Proselytism, 149, 150, 152, 153, 157, 232, 275, 299, 301
Protestants, 29, 39, 96, 156, 196, 210, 220, 230, 249
Protestant social gospel, 212
Psalms, 198, 203
Psychological therapy, 89
Public affairs, and mission of church, 146

Public schools, and sex education, 27, 40
Punishment, 43, 47, 94, 95, 97, 200
Purpose of Faith and Ferment, 22-23

Racial justice, 31-32
Racial prejudice and the church, 33
Racism, 31ff., 102, 161, 212-214
Radio, religious programs on, 151-152
Random sample of sociological survey, 335-337
Reimers, David, 213
Relationship with God, 26, 28, 44
Research models, 338-339
Resources, proper use of, 123, 124
Responsibility for life, personal, 62-63, 65, 66
Resurrection, 54, 56, 57, 58, 59, 73, 161. 216, 224-226, 268, 274, 276, 281, 285, 292, 302
Revelation, 160
Roman Catholics, 26, 29, 30, 39, 40, 45, 47, 55, 56, 57, 65, 74, 80, 96, 107, 119, 128, 135, 140, 152, 156, 157, 159, 160, 161, 172, 177, 179, 181, 203, 208, 210, 220, 223, 226, 232, 249, 259, 269, 286, 300, 311-314
Rubenstein, Richard, 249

Saints, prayer to, 73, 216
Salvation, 53-54, 63, 68, 139, 158, 195, 300
Sample of sociological survey, 334-337
Satan, 85, 86, 87, 96, 229, 298
Schechter, Solomon, 236
Schillebeeckx, Edward, 184, 287

Schoenherr, Richard, 286
Scott, Anne Firor, 190
Scriptures; see Bible
Secular humanism, 30, 143, 306
Security, personal, 99
Sex education, 27-28, 40, 192-195
Sex, extramarital, 28-29, 38, 238
Sexism, 34-38, 102, 214-215, 270
Sexism, reverse, 37
Sex, premarital, 38, 40, 238
Sexual ethics, 38-39, 41, 98
Sin, 77, 84, 85-88, 90-93, 159, 229, 273, 297, 298, 313, 316, 318, 320, 323, 326, 329, 332
Smith, H. Shelton, 196, 213, 229
Social behavior, 176-181, 189-201
Social issues and the church, 105-107, 108, 251-253, 276, 282, 313, 316, 318, 320-321, 323, 326, 329, 332
Social justice, 33, 98-109
Spalding, James, 212
Strong, Josiah, 212
Suffering, 43-48, 158, 159, 189, 191, 203-204, 247-250, 259, 311, 314, 317, 319, 321-322, 324, 327, 330
Suicide, 50, 55, 56, 59

Techniques of anthropological study, 342-344
Technology, 53, 104, 124
Television, religious programs on, 79, 151-152
Theology, defined, 167
Theophane the Recluse, 288
Tillich, Paul, 230, 231
Tithing, 151

Tradition, 184
Trinity, 73, 81
"True church of Christ," 79, 150, 153, 157, 232
Tucker, Henry Holcombe, 213

United Church of Christ, 39, 56, 65, 66, 71, 80, 96, 107, 135, 152, 157, 160, 161, 259, 327-330

Vatican Council II, 218, 222, 226, 267
Vitz, Paul, 203
Vocation and ministry, 131-133, 135
Vuilleumier, Marion Rawson, 175

War, 110-113, 115-118, 156, 158, 254-255, 275, 276, 313-314, 316, 318-319, 321, 323-324, 326-327, 329-330, 332-333
Waugh, Evelyn, 197
Weber, Max, 184
Whitehead, Alfred North, 218, 250
Women in ministry, 34-35, 37, 39, 40, 102, 107, 161, 215, 275, 276, 292
Women in society, 36, 102, 157, 161, 275, 276
Women, role of, 34-38, 190-191
Women's movement, 35-36, 40, 77, 81, 191-192, 215, 252, 292
Word of God; see Bible
Work of faith, 133, 136
Worship, 26, 140, 142, 151, 200, 219

Yinger, J. Milton, 182, 210